Addicted to Pain

My Life, Your Story: From a Broken Girl to a Healing Woman

Brandy Grillo

SayThat Publishing

ADDICTED TO PAIN

My Life, Your Story: From a Broken Girl to a Healing Woman

Album of My Life

1. Dedication   1

2. Intro   3

3. Side A   5
   Seeds Of Destruction

4. Chapter 1   9
   Picture In A Broken Frame

5. Chapter 2   23
   When The Hero Becomes The Monster

6. Chapter 3   45
   No Safe Place

7. Chapter 4   69
   Grave of Lust

8. Chapter 5   79
   A Mother Too Soon

9. Chapter 6   99
   The Lie That Followed Me

10. Chapter 7   111
    Circle of Friends

11. Chapter 8   119
    The Night I Lost Myself

12. Chapter 9   131
    Fast Money Slow Death

13. Chapter 10   145
    I Became What I Judged

14. Chapter 11   161
    New Norm

15. Chapter 12   175
    Addicted to the Hope of Him

16. Chapter 13   191
    Life Be Lifeing

17. Chapter 14   205
    Guns, Roses, & Money

18. Chapter 15   215
    Lines Crossed

19. Chapter 16   231
    The Chimichurri Incident

20. Chapter 17   251
    The Making of a Double Life

21. Chapter 18   263
    When Hope Left

22. Chapter 19   275
    The Final Goodbye

23. Chapter 20   287
    Dancing for Survival

24. Chapter 21   293
    Second Chances in the Small Things

25. Chapter 22   301
    When the Mirror Finally Spoke

26. Chapter 23   311
    My Son, My Mirror

27. Chapter 24   319
    A Night to Remember

28. Chapter 25   335
    When God Interrupted My Destruction

29. Chapter 26   341
    The Father I Couldn't Save

30. Chapter 27   357
    The Gift of Presence

31. Side B   373
    The Gardens

32. Chapter 28   375
    When the Past Meets the Promise

33. Chapter 29   389
    My Name Is Shame

34. Chapter 30   395
    The Long Road to Understanding

35. Chapter 31   401
    The Beauty of Becoming

36. Chapter 32   407
    My Son Walked Into the Water

37. Chapter 33   419
    This Time, I Choose Life

38. Chapter 34   423
    Addicted...

39. THE END   431

40. Resources: 433

41. About The Author   439

42. Connect   441

Dedication

To the fearful child. To the broken teen. To the addicted young adult.
This is for you.
There is a woman inside of you. A fervent woman of God. She will be
saved. She will be healed. She will be loved.
Just hold on.
She will emerge from the mud, rise from the depths, and transform
her struggles into something sacred.
Like the lotus that blooms from the mire.
I see you. I am you.

Intro

This journey has been long... and it's still unfolding.

I was born into fear and raised in a state of survival. For most of my life, I viewed everything through a lens shaped by trauma and the world's definition of strength. I didn't know there was another way to live, or that there was a spiritual reality underneath everything I could see.

What you're about to read is not polished or glamorous. It's real. Raw. Sometimes uncomfortable. But there is beauty buried in the pain, and glory in the places that look like ruin.

This is not a story about a destination. It is about the journey, the digging, the wrestling, the failing, the rising.

The memories in these pages are drawn from my lived experiences. Some are still tender. Some I revisited through tears while writing. To protect the privacy of others, I've changed names and focused the spotlight on my own heart. What you read here may not be *someone else's* version of the story, but it is *mine*. And it is honest.

In these chapters, you will see two landscapes:

SIDE A: The Seeds of Destruction, everything that was planted in me before I even knew how to protect myself: fear, shame, lust, addiction, abandonment, anger. These seeds grew into patterns that defined my life for years. They became the way I coped... and ultimately, the way I died inside.

SIDE B: The Garden, the place where God began to replant me. Where truth replaced lies. Where healing replaced hiding. Where identity replaced insecurity. The Garden is where I finally came to life.

I invite you into both places, the grave and the garden. Into the trauma. Into the breaking. Into the rebuilding.

Come not with judgment, but with empathy. Because we all have graves. We all have gardens.

We all carry wounds we've tried to bury... and we all need a Savior who can resurrect what we thought was dead.

By the time you finish this book, you'll meet two versions of me, two different women: One soul transformed by grace...and carried, every step, by Love.

That, dear reader *and friend*, is the glory of God.

Side A

Seeds Of Destruction

BRANDY GRILLO

Before we begin this journey together, I need to define what I mean by *destruction*. Google defines a grave as *"a place where a broken or discarded object lies."* I wasn't lying in a grave physically. But spiritually, mentally, and emotionally, that's exactly where I lived for many years.

Buried beneath shame, guilt, anger, addiction, and generational patterns, my true self was trapped under layers of dirt I didn't know how to shake off. That's what I call **Seeds of Destruction**, the hidden things planted in us early that eventually grow into graves.

Those seeds shaped how I responded to life. They shaped how I saw myself. And they grew into a reality where pain felt normal.

The facts of what I'm about to share are not easy. They are raw. Some still trigger me, even now. But I believe there is power in telling the truth.

The seeds of destruction turned me into a slave to lust and anger. I numbed myself with substances, sex, violence, self-hatred, anything that would silence the screaming inside me.

You might ask: *Why would anyone stay in a grave? Why not climb out? Why live in a place that slowly kills you?*

Those are good questions. And as we walk this journey together, I'll answer them. Maybe I'll even answer questions you haven't thought to ask yet.

Because when you grow up with certain seeds planted, when destruction is all you've ever known, you don't recognize it as destruction. You think it's normal. You internalize the dysfunction of your family, the culture you were raised in, and the lies the world told you about who you are. You stop *living*. You start *surviving*.

The Oxford Dictionary defines fear as *"an unpleasant emotion caused by the belief that someone or something is dangerous, likely to cause pain, or a threat."*

I was raised in an atmosphere saturated with fear.

And studies in psychology confirm what I lived firsthand: Fear wounds the heart. It creates anxiety, distrust, and insecurity. It teaches a child that even the people meant to protect them... might harm them.

One of those people was my father.

And that's where the story truly begins.

Chapter 1

Picture In A Broken Frame

A frame is meant to hold something precious: a memory, a moment, a life. It is designed to protect and display beauty. But what happens when the frame itself is cracked? When the structure holding everything together is already broken before the picture is even placed inside?

This is where my story begins, inside a frame that looked beautiful from the outside, but underneath had cracks running through its very foundation. Cracks that stretched back generations.

My father was born in the summer of 1951 on the west side of Tampa. He grew up with two biological brothers, although whispers floated through the family that one might not be his father's son, and a third brother who joined their family through adoption.

His mother, Alvalee, was Irish: tall, red-haired, and blue-eyed. My dad used to tell me how her long strides could catch up to him in an instant whenever he misbehaved, and with a swift hand, she would discipline him using a "switch." For those unfamiliar, a switch is a thin, flexible branch, an object that many children of that era learned to fear.

His father, Sergio, was Hispanic: dark-haired, brown-eyed, and temperamental. The man was a storm, known for smashing doors off their hinges in fits of anger. Yet, he could also charm a room, dance through life as a "viejo chulo," an old flirt, and ultimately, a cheater. It was Sergio's infidelities that would shatter their marriage.

They met when they were only teenagers. Sergio had several sisters, and he brought young Alvalee from Alabama to his family's home in Tampa, a household where no one spoke English. Isolated in a foreign tongue, she learned Spanish the hard way, alongside cooking Bistec de Palomilla, arroz con frijoles negros, and Caldo gallego, mastering cultural cuisines.

But the language was the least of the challenges. Sergio's family history carried shadows darker than dialect. Mental health struggles ran through the bloodline. Stories of desperation, like a sister who set herself on fire over a boy, were whispered around the family. Trauma was woven into the very fabric of their lives.

In search of their own footing, my grandparents eventually moved into a small house built in the 1930s on the west side of Tampa. It was a modest two-bedroom, one-bath home sitting on a 5,000-square-foot lot. Two long, brick-red steps led up to a small porch that matched the simple brown and cream-colored exterior. Inside, a small living room welcomed you, with two large windows letting in warm sunlight, one facing the front yard and the other overlooking the carport. A simple archway connected the living room to the kitchen and dining area, where brown wooden cabinets lined the walls, and the linoleum floor had yellowed over time with age.

Laundry was scrubbed by hand and hung out on clotheslines in the backyard, where mango and tangerine trees stood tall.

The bedrooms were spacious, but the closets were barely big enough to hold the dreams stuffed inside them. The bathroom, with its small window facing the backyard, let in slivers of light. You had to pass through one bedroom to reach the bathroom, a reminder that privacy was a luxury, not a given.

Massive oak trees towered beside the house, standing guard over the carport. A nearby alleyway offered a shortcut to the next block, a secret path used by generations of barefoot children running through the Florida heat.

I know this house so intimately because eventually, it would become one of the first places I called home.

I remember the stories my father used to tell about being the youngest of his brothers, growing up in that little house in West Tampa, and how often they called him the runt of the family. His older brothers constantly picked on him because of his size. He hated it. He would share how they pinned him to the ground and tickled him until he cried, and even then, they wouldn't stop until it hurt. It left him not just feeling physically weak, but small as a person. While his father Sergio and his brothers loved to spend their time hunting and killing animals, my father found no joy in it. Instead, he spent his days fishing and playing baseball. Baseball was his passion. It was his dream to play in the major leagues. He would spend hours playing with the neighborhood kids, a few of whom would go on to make a career out of the sport. But not my father.

He would often recount the story of how he lost his batter's eye, a tragic fall from a tree during childhood. A sharp root struck his head with such force that it temporarily blinded him in both eyes. Though his sight eventually returned in one eye, his depth perception was never the same. "After that," he'd say, "my swing just wasn't right." Baseball, his dream, his escape, was stolen in an instant.

Some part of him never forgave the world for that. He never forgave *God*, either.

He wasn't an atheist; he believed in *something*, but he didn't believe in a loving God. Not the God I learned about in school. He thought of Jesus not as the Son of God, but merely a prophet. He believed in purgatory, in karma, in the idea that no one truly got away with anything. But he didn't believe in grace. He didn't believe in redemption. And he definitely didn't believe in one true living God who loved him.

To my father, life was just something you had to get through, a cycle you didn't ask for. You lived, then you died. God was who He was, and he, as a man, was who he had become. He didn't expect kindness from the world, and certainly not from God. That's how he made sense of all the things he'd lost, his eye, his dreams, his peace. It was easier to resent a distant God than to sit with the pain he never dared to unpack.

After the accident, the anger that had always lingered just beneath the surface began to harden into something more permanent. He became defiant, refusing to be told what to do, when to do it, or how it should be done. Everything had to be done *his* way, and only his way. It was a stubborn pride that pushed people away and cost him more than he ever gained.

His family carried its own legacy of pain. His oldest brother, a heavy drinker, died of a massive heart attack in his fifties, alone on his boat after making love to his wife. It was the kind of death that made people whisper, then laugh uncomfortably, as if to cover the sadness in the room.

His second-oldest brother, just five years his senior, had a more complicated relationship with him. They had fought growing up, but had also been close, playing sports, sharing secrets, and getting into trouble together. But as they got older, their bond was tested by darker choices. They both got involved in drug trafficking, connected to a network with ties to Colombia. At some point, the business fractured, loyalties were broken, and the consequences were devastating. My uncle was arrested and held on a million-dollar bond, his name plastered across Hillsborough County headlines. By then, he and my father weren't even speaking.

No one talks much about why. The family has its stories, each version shaped by loyalty, bitterness, or silence. But whatever the truth is, it left a permanent crack in the family. The kind of crack that never fully closes, just gets passed down.

In his early twenties, my father joined the Marine Corps, but he couldn't make a career out of it. He went AWOL, running toward a beach bum life rather than following orders. He never looked back. Eventually, he joined the Union and learned a trade, becoming a plumber.

My mother was born in 1954 at MacDill Air Force Base in Tampa, Florida. She had one sister, a year and a half older. Because of financial struggles, my mother moved constantly and rarely stayed in the same school for more than a year, making it difficult for her to form lasting friendships. She was embarrassed about her parents' divorce, something far less common in her generation than it is today. Her father was rarely present, so it was her mother, working long hours as a waitress, who raised the two girls alone after the divorce when my mother was only eight years old. With her sister marrying at seventeen, much of my mother's teenage years were spent alone, clinging to the small things she loved to get by.

While her sister was outgoing and social, my mother was shy and kept to herself. She had few close friends in middle and high school, but she found joy in the weekly dances and trips to the drive-in movies around West Tampa. In high school, she worked retail jobs and helped at warehouses. More than anything, her dream was simple but deeply rooted: she wanted to be a mother, to have a big family gathered in a beautiful home filled with warmth and love.

She married her first husband at nineteen, but their lives drifted apart, and after five years and no children, they divorced.

At twenty-seven, my mother met my father. He was thirty. They first crossed paths at a local sports center, an oyster bar that was popular at the time. She said he was handsome, charming, and funny. He showered her with compliments, painted her dreams of a big home filled with children and a life filled with laughter. She was living with a friend at the time, but when their lease ended, she moved into her own apartment at River Gardens in West Tampa. My father, who was still living with his mother, started spending more time with her. They went to the movies, ate out, and loved to go dancing at a place called Casaba, located inside a Holiday Inn with live bands on the weekends.

After a few months of dating, my father moved in with my mother. At first, everything felt like a fresh start. But it didn't take long before she began to see another side of him, one that emerged when he drank hard liquor. He became someone else entirely. The man she loved would disappear, replaced by someone verbally abusive, sometimes even physically aggressive. He would mush her face, pin her down, yell at her until his rage simmered. Then, as if it wiped everything clean, he'd apologize. Blame the alcohol. Swear he didn't mean it.

Despite her better judgment, she stayed. She was in love. And she wanted to believe in the future he painted with his promises. That love would be enough to change him.

They stayed in that apartment until tragedy struck. My father's aunt, Cookie, was murdered, caught up in a robbery in Ybor City. Her body was found stuffed into the back of her own car, which had been set on fire. The story spread like wildfire. Whispers turned into accusations. Family members, even detectives, tried to tie it back to my father and uncle's past connections with the Colombians.

Fear crept in. Cookie had been at Abuela's house the night she disappeared. She was the last one to see her alive. Out of concern for Abuela's safety, my parents packed up and moved back to my father's childhood home in West Tampa. They stayed there for a few years, trying to outrun the shadows of violence and suspicion.

Eventually, they found a small duplex owned by one of my father's friends. It was quiet. Tucked away. A place where they could try to start over again. And it was there, in that little duplex, that my mother became pregnant with me.

During her pregnancy, my father gave up hard liquor, though the beer stayed, every day like clockwork. Still, despite the rough edges of their relationship, there were soft moments too. There was still love.

Maybe not the perfect kind, but the kind that builds traditions and laughter and memories that hold.

He called her Sugarbritches.

Not "sweetheart" or "honey" like in the movies. It didn't make sense to anyone else, unless you heard the way his voice softened when he said it. Like he meant it more than any name in the world.

Come Halloween, he'd build whatever wild idea she had. Pumpkin arches, wooden ghosts with glowing eyes, fake tombstones with rhyming names that made the neighbors stop and stare. She'd sketch something on a napkin or the back of an envelope, and a few days later, it would be alive in our yard. He did the same for Christmas, even though he didn't care much for the holiday. But she did, and that was enough.

When I was younger, they'd leave me at abuela's house and go out dancing. I'd watch my mother put on her lipstick and heels, my father waiting by the door with that same crooked grin he always had when she caught his eye.

He loved to grill. Had a smoker too. He'd marinate the steaks while she made the sides, and together they'd turn dinner into something sacred. The air always smelled like fire and woodsmoke when he grilled, meat searing on hot grates, thick enough to taste before a single bite. He stood at the old black grill like it was a throne, beer in one hand, long-handled tongs in the other, squinting into the smoke like a man with a mission. He liked it when she stayed close, not hovering, just near enough to pass the foil or whisper some quiet joke he'd answer with a grunt and a half-smile.

Sometimes she'd bring out a bowl of her herb butter and tease, "You finish them, right now," and he'd grumble like he didn't need the reminder, but he always used it.

The sizzle when the steaks hit the grates was instant. He'd nod to himself, flip them once, never more than once, and press the surface lightly with his tongs. "You feel that? That's medium-rare," he'd say to no one in particular. Maybe to her. Maybe just to remind himself he was still good at something.

Summers meant beach days. He loved the water. She loved the sun. Their rhythm never clashed. While she disappeared into a paperback under the shade of her wide-brimmed sunhat, he was in the pool with me, making waves.

She didn't mind. She'd kiss him on the forehead, hand me my goggles, and stretch out on her towel like the world had nothing else to ask of her.

And then he'd look at me, eyes squinting, arms open, and say, "Come on, kid. Let's make some waves."

He'd toss me into the deep end again and again, letting me scream and splash while he laughed loud enough to turn heads. He taught me how to dive, how to float, how to trust the water. His love was kinetic: loud, alive, full of motion.

Sometimes, he'd climb out, still dripping wet, and drop onto the lounger beside her just to shake like a dog and soak her pages.

"You're getting my book wet!" she'd squeal, swatting at him with the paperback.

He'd just grin, towel off, and dive back in.

Some of my earliest memories of my father are from when I was no older than four. Back then, he was my hero. Anytime he grabbed his keys, I would run to the door, barefoot and eager, chasing after whatever adventure he was heading toward.

"Daddy, are you leaving? Can I come with you, please?"

He looked up from patting his pockets, eyes scanning the table for his keys. When he saw me, he smiled the way only he could.

"Hey baby... yeah, I'm just tryna find my keys," he mumbled, still searching.

"Are we going to see Wella?"

He paused, then gave me a knowing smirk.

"You readin' my mind again, huh? Go let your mama know you ridin' with me."

I didn't even budge. I just yelled from where I stood, clinging to his leg.

"Mom! I'm leaving with Dad!"

He laughed and scooped me up with one arm, grabbing a cold beer from the counter with the other.

"Alright, you ready?" he asked as we headed for the door. "You think we can beat those big trucks this time?"

"Yes!" I squealed. "We can if we go real fast!"

He kissed my cheek, his beard scratchy against my face, and I giggled. At that moment, nothing else existed. Just me and my dad.

I remember riding shotgun, my little legs swinging, a big grin on my face as we pulled out of the driveway. We were headed to Abuela's house, and that always felt like a celebration. On the way there, he'd challenge me to spot a semi-truck, and once I did, we were off. We were racing.

When traffic got heavy on the interstate, he'd slide off the exit and take the back roads, darting through streets only he seemed to know.

I'd watch the truck disappear behind us, and when it finally came back into view in the rearview mirror, I'd smile to myself, convinced we had won.

Those drives weren't just fun, they were everything. They made me feel special, chosen. Seen. And in those moments, with the wind in my hair and my dad in the driver's seat, I believed the world was a safe place.

When we arrived at Abuela's house, I never wanted to leave. My father would run his errands while I stayed behind, soaking up every moment with her until he returned to pick me up.

Some of my most cherished memories with my father took place at McFarlane Park, just a short walk from Abuela's house. The park was a little world of its own, lush grass, towering oak trees draped in Spanish moss, and winding paths that invited you to explore. At the top of a small hill stood a white gazebo, quiet and elegant, like something out of a fairy tale. But my favorite spot wasn't the gazebo. It was the hill itself.

My father would help me push my little bike to the top, and I'd come barreling down like a rocket. The wind would whip through my curls, the handlebars shaking wildly beneath my grip, my heart racing as I screamed with delight. For a few seconds, I felt like I was flying. After a while, his back would start to ache, but I wouldn't let that stop me. I'd drag the bike up myself, determined to do it again, and he'd stand at the bottom cheering like I was in the Olympics.

"You got this! Keep going! Woohoo!" he'd yell, fists in the air, eyes sparkling with pride.

In those moments, I felt unstoppable. I felt loved.

Another memory that still glows in my chest is the nights we went crabbing together. Just me and my daddy. He'd teach me how to read the clouds, how to watch the water. "We need low tide, baby girl," he'd say, squinting at the sky like it was an old friend sharing secrets.

We'd head out late, 10, sometimes 11 at night, toward Courtney Campbell or Cypress Beach. I'd be dressed in old clothes and worn-out sneakers, the kind Mama wouldn't mind getting wet and muddy. We packed a metal tub we called a *tina* (tee-nah), tied it around one of our waists with rope, and waded into the water side by side. Our lanterns would cast long shadows across the shoreline, and we'd whisper to each other like we were on some secret mission.

"Move slow, Brandy. Let your eyes adjust. They'll be shining under the light. Watch for the flicker," he'd say.

And there they were, dozens of blue crabs crawling across the sand, fish darting in and out of the shallows. I'd squeal every time I caught one.

"Daddy, look! I got one!"

"That's my girl! Scoop it in! Don't let him pinch you now!"

We dumped them into the tina, the clang of shell on metal echoing into the night. Sometimes we wouldn't get home until two or three in the morning. I was never allowed to stay out that late otherwise, and it made me feel grown, trusted, seen. Like I was part of something ancient, something sacred.

"We eatin' good tomorrow," he'd laugh, dragging the tina back up the sand, crabs still clattering inside.

The next day always had its own rhythm. My dad would be outside with a hose and a bucket, scrubbing the crabs while my mom started cooking. They moved like a team: wordless, practiced. She'd be in the kitchen preparing *cangrejos enchilados*, a rich red Cuban-style crab stew that filled the house with the scent of garlic, peppers, and love. She made a big pot of spaghetti noodles to go with it, tossed together a salad, and always had warm, soft Cuban bread ready.

"You cleaned 'em good this time," she'd tease him from the kitchen window.

"I always do," he'd call back, tossing her a wink.

Those meals were more than food. They were celebration.... Of tradition. Of family. Of hard work and soft moments.

My father's joy wasn't limited to food or fatherhood; it stretched into baseball, too. His heart belonged to the Yankees. He'd watch games for hours, yelling at the TV like they could hear him. He talked often about Lou Piniella, his childhood friend who made it to the majors. There was pride in his voice, but also something quieter, more haunting.

After those stories, he would sometimes go quiet. He'd rock his feet, stare at the screen, lost in thoughts only he could see. I'd call out, "Daddy!" just to bring him back. He'd smile and nod, murmuring, "Now watch this pitcher, baby. He's about to throw a fastball."

As I got older, I understood those silences better. They weren't just about baseball. They were about dreams deferred, first a career lost to a fall from a tree, then a military path that didn't pan out. Now he was a plumber with a wife, a child, and a quiet ache that lived just under the surface. And when regret began to overflow, it turned to something sharper.

At that age, I didn't have the words for it, but I could feel it, his anger turning into aggression. It never hit me directly, but it changed the air. My mother carried the brunt of it. Her light dimmed under the weight of his frustration, and our home, once filled with laughter and crab boil steam, began to darken around the edges.

Looking back now, I see both sides of my father, the cheerleader at the bottom of the hill, and the man lost in his own what-ifs. I remember both, and I love them both. But I also understand now that the same hands that pushed me forward were the ones battling to hold themselves together.

Chapter 2

When The Hero Becomes The Monster

G rowing up as an only child in Tampa, Florida, during the vibrant 1980s was like living in a Technicolor dream. The world
was bold, loud in the best way. Neon outfits, jelly bracelets, oversized
sweaters, scrunchies stacked on our wrists and in our hair, everything
shouted for attention, and we loved it.

I have old photos that make me laugh out loud. I'll hold one up and
think, *What on earth was I wearing?* But that was the beauty of the
'80s, it didn't ask for permission. It just *was*.

The soundtrack of my childhood played through a mix of Michael Jackson, Prince, Whitney Houston, and, especially, Madonna. There was something about her, her rebelliousness, her style, her raw honesty, that fascinated me, even as a little girl. She pushed boundaries, and in some small way, she gave me permission to do the same.

Two of my favorite movies were *Back to the Future* and *E.T.* I was mesmerized by the idea of time travel, and Michael J. Fox had a kind of charisma that made even the impossible feel possible. *E.T.*, on the other hand, made me believe that maybe, just maybe, aliens could be friends. That scene with the bike soaring across the moonlit sky still gives me chills.

At home, my parents watched *Cheers* and *The Cosby Show*, their laughter mingling with the clinking of dishes and the low hum of the TV. Meanwhile, my world revolved around Pac-Man, Donkey Kong, and *Super Mario Bros.* Classics that cemented their place in the hearts of every child thanks to the Super Nintendo. But nothing had my heart the way the *Teenage Mutant Ninja Turtles* did. My room was a shrine: posters on the walls, toys neatly lined up, and bedsheets that turned my dreams into turtle-powered adventures. Every Saturday morning, I'd be glued to the TV, rewinding my favorite episodes on VHS until I could quote every line.

But of all my childhood memories, the sweetest were those slow Saturday mornings with my father. We'd stretch out on the couch, legs tangled under a shared blanket, munching on Fudgesicles while cartoons danced across the screen. The cold chocolate would melt down our fingers, and we'd laugh without a care in the world.

Even back then, I wondered, *Who enjoyed those cartoons more, me or him?*

Now, I know the answer.

It was him.

His laughter filled our living room like music. He especially loved Yosemite Sam and Foghorn Leghorn, shouting their lines with wild energy and perfect timing. He didn't just quote them, he *became* them. With booming voices, outstretched arms, and animated expressions, he brought those characters to life. His storytelling was electric. You didn't just listen, you *experienced* it.

He could walk into a room and have every eye on him in seconds. His voice, his presence, his way with words, they held a kind of magic. He didn't need a spotlight. He *was* the spotlight.

Looking back, I realize now what he gave me was more than just laughter and Fudgesicles. He gave me a legacy: a love for joy, for imagination, for connection. He taught me the power of story. Of voice. Of presence.

In those moments, he wasn't just my dad. He was a maestro, conducting something bigger than either of us could see at the time, a symphony of memories, notes of joy that still echo in the quiet spaces of my soul.

He was my hero.

He dreamed bigger dreams for me than he had ever dreamed for himself. He would sit me down and talk about the life he wanted me to have, a life free from financial struggles, a life where I didn't rush into adulthood but took the time to experience the world. He wanted me to travel, to see beyond Tampa, to learn about different cultures and people, to love history the way he did. He encouraged me not to chase after straight A's to make others proud, but to focus on finishing school, finding a passion, and making a meaningful life for myself.

He gave me the gift of space, to be a kid, to ride bikes, play outside, and go on little adventures around town without the heavy burden of expectations weighing me down. His love was big, and his desire to protect my innocence was even bigger.

Even though school wasn't always my favorite place, my father's deep love for history sparked something inside me. I was fascinated by the idea that centuries of life had come and gone before I was even born. It made the world feel so much bigger, more mysterious, and full of possibility.

I dreamed of going to college, building a career, and traveling the globe, walking through castles, climbing mountains, standing in ancient ruins, and experiencing all the world has to offer firsthand.

Those dreams were born in a small living room in Tampa, between bites of Fudgesicles, the roar of cartoon laughter, and the quiet, steady love of the man who, at one time, was my entire world.

Although I didn't have a specific vision for my life growing up, I knew deep down I wanted a life different from the one unfolding around me. My father's aggression towards my mother was no longer something that I could pretend wasn't real. I no longer just felt it, I saw it. Whenever he would raise his voice at my mom, yelling, shouting, and calling her nasty names, I would hide in my closet, curl into a ball, rock myself back and forth, biting my nails until they hurt for comfort. My mother, despite all this, would still find time to read to me at night. I remember the *Nancy Drew* mysteries she introduced me to. Those books were more than just stories; they were my escape. They opened up a world where courage won, where wrongs were made right, and where I could imagine a life far beyond the fear and dysfunction I was living in.

ADDICTED TO PAIN

From an early age, I discovered that performing, whether through singing, dancing, or acting, gave me a voice when I felt invisible at home. My mother, in her own way, tried to support me. She would set up a video camera and record me, giving me a few precious moments where I could just be a kid.

Music also became my safe place. In a home where anger, tension, and silent resentment filled the walls, music drowned out the noise. I would sit for hours, recording songs off the radio onto cassette tapes, desperate to capture a piece of something beautiful. Each song became part of a soundtrack that spoke the words I couldn't say out loud.

My love for writing truly took root through journaling. A private world where I could confess my fears, my anger, my heartbreaks without judgment. When I got my first computer, I discovered the notes section, and that's where my first book was born. A fiction story, pieced together in chapters during late nights when I couldn't sleep. That manuscript is long gone, but those hours spent writing, often with DMX or Tupac playing in the background, were some of the first times I felt like I had power over my story, if only on paper.

When my father would raise his voice, sometimes, I would turn up the music as loud as I could just to drown out the sound of the anger swirling around me.

Even with these moments of terror, I longed for more family, someone else who could share the weight of what I was carrying. I imagined that if I had an older brother or sister, they would protect me. Maybe they could shield me from the brunt of my father's rage, or even protect my mother.

Growing up as an only child meant I had no built-in playmates, no brothers or sisters to fight or laugh with. So I clung to the cousins I did have. On my mother's side, my Tía had two boys, and I became especially close to Cayden. On my father's side, time at my Abuela's house brought comfort through my cousin and her daughter, Bella. Those relationships were bright little sparks in an otherwise lonely childhood, temporary flickers of connection that always seemed to fade too quickly.

Even at six years old, I remember asking my mom, "Why don't I have a brother or sister?" She never really had an answer that made sense to me. It was hard to imagine anyone choosing to raise a child alone. To my young mind, being alone wasn't freedom. It was confusion. And it made me feel like something was missing, like I was missing.

Still, there were perks to being the only one. My parents, especially my mom, spoiled me when they could. Material things came more easily for them than emotional comfort. One year, my dad built me a two-story Barbie dream house out of real wood, cut, sanded, and painted with his own hands. It was beautiful, intricate, the kind of gift that makes other kids jealous. But even as I squealed with delight, a part of me wanted something else. I wanted *him*. The version of my dad who used to race trucks with me while we drove on the interstate, who pushed me up hills at McFarlane Park, who made me feel seen and safe.

My mom showed love the way she knew how: with a shopping bag. If we walked through a toy aisle, she couldn't help but grab a new Barbie outfit or game, even if I hadn't asked. As a kid, it felt magical. But in hindsight, I know what I really needed was for her to sit with me. To hold me. To help me make sense of the yelling in the other room or the silence that followed it. Instead, I got glittery shoes and brand-new dolls to distract me from the ache.

Looking back now, I don't think they were trying to buy my love. I think they were trying to offer the only version of love they'd ever known, one built around survival. They didn't grow up with much, and maybe they thought that giving me more than they had would be enough. Maybe they hoped it would fill the holes inside me that they couldn't reach.

But all it taught me was to equate love with things. If someone didn't give me what I wanted, I felt rejected. If there wasn't a gift, I assumed there wasn't love.

My parents lived paycheck to paycheck. We weren't poor, but we were definitely on the stretch-it-till-it-screams side of middle class. My dad wore plain clothes, no jewelry, no brands. My mom was the queen of layaway; Christmas shopping started in July. Birthdays, too. She'd find treasures in clearance aisles, flea markets, yard sales, thrift stores, Big Lots, and Dollar General. She could take a $15 Barbie and, with enough searching, find it for $10. She didn't hang out with friends. My dad didn't party at clubs; he drank at home or with his buddies at theirs. No lavish vacations, just local beaches, group trips, carpooling to save on gas.

Everything in our house had a story. The couch had been someone else's. The dishes mismatched. The furniture came from warehouse closeouts or secondhand stores. But they made it work. And because I was their only child, whatever was left over from my older cousins was passed down to me, especially their toys.

There was a time I had bunk beds, just because. A trampoline, even though we barely had a yard. A TV with a built-in VCR. Barbies in bins, Jeeps and dollhouses, and a Nintendo system. My room looked like a toy aisle had exploded. Their bank account looked like a dried-up desert from spending what very little they had. But no matter how many presents showed up, I still felt alone, sitting on a plastic throne in a kingdom of things.

Christmas, though, that was different.

My mom had this magical ability to transform our little house into something straight out of a holiday movie. Lights twinkled, music played, the scent of cinnamon and pine filled the air. The tree glittered like it had been dipped in sugar, and the presents? They seemed endless. I was certain Santa had us on a VIP list.

We didn't have much, but Christmas made it feel like we had everything. My mom would press record on the camcorder as I tore through wrapping paper, each squeal captured like it was gold. For those few hours, we were a perfect family. We laughed, we hugged, we felt close.

That's why Christmas became my favorite day of the year. Because for one day, the arguing stopped. The sadness took a break. And under that mountain of wrapping paper, it was easy to believe we were okay. That we were whole.

But eventually, the lights came down, the camera turned off, and the silence returned.

And I was still just a little girl in a big room, surrounded by stuff, longing for someone to notice what I really wanted... couldn't be bought.

Christmas was always a time of tradition for us, gathering gifts, piling into the car, and visiting relatives across the city. We always started with my mother's side of the family before making our way to my father's. I remember Sonia's home in West Tampa, where Christmas exploded in every corner of the house. It was the first place I ever saw a white Christmas tree, its branches glittering like snow under the soft glow of string lights. Beneath it sat mountains of wrapped presents, each one labeled for someone in what felt like a crowd of a hundred. Music poured from the speakers, the scent of arroz con gandules and pernil filled the air, and the rooms pulsed with laughter and conversation, stories leaping between generations like sparks from a fire. It should have felt magical. And in a way, it did.

But even surrounded by family, I often felt like I didn't belong. My cousins, people I was told were part of me, felt more like strangers. They patted my head, told me how much I'd grown, and smiled politely for pictures. But their words didn't land, not really. Their joy felt like something I was supposed to feel, not something I actually did. I smiled because that's what kids do. But deep down, I felt like a guest in a life that wasn't mine.

And sometimes, the joy evaporated the moment we stepped outside.

That night, something shifted in my father. I felt it before he said a word, sensed it in the way he slammed the car door, loud and final. The echo of Sonia's laughter still floated behind us, but the warmth I'd carried from the party vanished in an instant. My heart began to race.

Even as a child, I knew how to read the signs. I knew what kind of night it would be by the tightness in his jaw, the silence in his stare. Still, I didn't say anything. I didn't want him to get in trouble. I didn't want anyone to see the monster.

That's how manipulation works. It teaches you to protect the one who's hurting you.

All I wanted that Christmas was for my parents to love each other. Just once. To be together without the fighting, without the fear. I thought maybe, just maybe, the magic of the holiday would be enough.

But it wasn't.

I sat in the back seat, directly behind my mother. My father climbed into the driver's seat. And without warning, the screaming began.

"You fucking bitch! What the hell is wrong with you?" His voice cracked the air like a whip. He reached over, grabbed her by the hair, and yanked her head back violently.

"You're hurting me," my mother cried, her voice breaking.

"You are a fucking moron! You see this, Brandy?" he snarled, twisting around so his rage could find me, too. "Your mother doesn't give a damn about me, she only cares about her fucking self!"

I didn't know what she had said or done to set him off. Later, I'd learn it rarely took anything. The smallest things, an eye roll, a misplaced word, could ignite him. That's the danger of living with a live wire. You never know what will spark the flame.

Until that night, I had only heard their fights through the walls. I had pressed pillows to my ears, wishing the yelling, hitting, and crying away. But this time, I saw it. I saw the monster.

He grabbed her again, her hair, her neck. His hands clamped down like a vice. Her face flushed red. Her eyes welled up with tears. And I froze.

I didn't move. I didn't speak. I couldn't. My body locked into silence while my mind screamed. I sat there, crying without sound, praying that if I stayed still enough, he would stop. Eventually, he did. But not before he spat a few more knives in her direction, words so sharp they could've shredded skin. If pain were visible, she would've been bleeding out on the seat in front of me.

That night marked a shift in my understanding of the world. The monster didn't just live inside our house. He came with us now. He was in the car. He was in public. He was inescapable.

I realized then, maybe for the first time, that no one was coming. No neighbor. No family member. No hero. I didn't know who could save us. I just knew it wasn't going to be me.

In the framed picture of my childhood, everything looked perfect, so perfect it sparked envy in other kids from the neighborhood. I had everything anyone could dream of, at least on the surface. But beneath the gloss and glamour of this seemingly perfect life, the reality was far from idyllic. The toys and gadgets that filled my room were a poor substitute for the peace and safety I desperately needed but never had when the monster was home. Fear was my constant companion, casting shadows over every joyful moment.

In those moments of terror, no amount of material wealth could soothe or undo the pain that went unspoken. I can't recall a single time my father apologized for his drunken rants that kept us up all night or for the ways he hurt my mother and me. My mother, trapped in denial, never acknowledged our reality. She made excuses for his rage, pretending we weren't living in a home haunted by domestic violence. Her silence became its own kind of betrayal, and I was left to piece together my confusion and fear on my own.

I witnessed verbal, emotional, and physical abuse, often daily. These experiences distorted my understanding of love. I began to associate affection with violence. That dissonance, between what others saw and what I lived, left me emotionally unanchored.

A home is supposed to be a place of love, safety, vulnerability, and trust. A sanctuary. Mine was none of those things.

Some of the best times of my life were spent at my abuela Alvalee's house, my father's mother. Her home was my definition of *home*. I felt so safe there that my mom often had to beg me to leave. There was nothing extravagant about her home, and it wasn't filled with expensive toys. What it was filled with was something far more valuable: love.

Her affection was a balm to my soul. At abuela's, there were no distractions. No yelling. No fighting. Just peace. The kind of peace that made it okay to breathe, to let your shoulders drop, to forget the world and just be a child.

I could sit on the floor and watch TV. I could play freely, giggle loudly, make a mess, and would not worry that any of that would lead to my parents' next imminent argument. Her home was like another world. A gentle getaway from the storms that constantly swirled around me at home.

"My darling, I love you so much," she said one morning as I lay across her lap while she rocked us in her old wooden chair.

"I love you too," I whispered, snuggling in closer, letting her voice wrap around me like a blanket.

"What TV show do you wanna watch?" she asked, brushing the hair from my forehead.

"Ummm... Nickelodeon."

She chuckled, a soft sound that made my chest warm. "Honey, that's a network."

"What's a network?" I asked, genuinely curious.

"My baby," she said with a smile, "it's a place where all your shows get to play and you get to watch. Now I gotta get that oatmeal started for you. Do you mind sitting on the couch for a minute?"

"Yes," I said quickly, hopping down and making my way to the couch.

She grabbed the remote and turned on the TV. "Now don't sit too close to the screen, ya hear me?"

"Okay. Love you!" I called out.

"Love you too, baby," she called back from the kitchen.

Abuela's house was warm in a way that didn't come from heaters. It came from her. From the way she spoke, the way she moved, the way she cared.

I'd sometimes sleep in her bed, other times on the pull-out couch in the living room, the blue one with red and white stitching that always amazed me because it transformed into a bed like magic. The TV sat in the corner, right near the big window that faced the front yard and porch. Sunlight would stream through the curtains in the morning, and I'd sit with my oatmeal watching *Chip and Dale Rescue Rangers*, *Duck Tales*, *The Smurfs*, *David the Gnome*, and *Adventures of the Gummi Bears*, each show its own little world that helped me escape mine.

Her house was never just a house. It was a haven. A place where I didn't have to try so hard to be okay.

She never raised her voice or laid a hand on me, unlike how my father remembered her from his childhood. She lived with Papa Charles, her brother-in-law, who also adored me. He'd take me outside to play or let me watch Disney movies in his air-conditioned room.

One of my favorite memories with Abuela was going to work with her at Krispy Kreme on Kennedy Avenue. The smell alone, warm sugar, fresh dough, a hint of coffee, felt like magic. I got to stand behind the counter with her, dipping donuts into tubs of chocolate or vanilla icing. At first, I'd sneak a taste here and there, licking icing off my fingers before I realized how obvious I was being.

"Brandy, don't be licking those donuts, ya hear me?" Abuela called over her shoulder, trying to sound stern, though the corners of her mouth tugged into a smile.

"I'm trying not to," I said through a giggle, eyeing the hot glaze dripping down a fresh batch. "They're just so delicious and tempting."

She turned around and walked over, wiping her hands on her apron with mock seriousness. "Darlin', let me see those fingers, look at you, no self-control," she teased, gently taking my hands in hers. "Here. Let me give you some gloves before you get us both in trouble." Then she reached behind the side tray and pulled out a few slightly misshapen donuts. "And these," she added, handing them to me, "these are for your temptations."

I clutched them like treasure. "Wella, you're the best."

She looked at me with eyes full of warmth and said something I will never forget. "No, my baby, you're the sweetest joy I've got."

I didn't just feel loved in those moments. I felt seen. Valued. Like I mattered.

Her house, just like her heart, was always open. She rarely locked her doors. Her two close friends, Dotty and Clementina, came by often, always with something to talk about. Clementina's son lived in the little blue house across the street, and she'd stop in for coffee, chatting for hours in Spanish. Sometimes she'd take us out to eat at Morrison's, a buffet-style restaurant with food I wasn't crazy about, but that always felt like a treat because of the company.

Being with Abuela made everything better. She gave me something no one else really could back then, stability wrapped in sweetness, and a love I never had to question.

The kitchen was her kingdom. Her oatmeal in the mornings, palomilla steaks for lunch with black beans and rice, and the house salad lightly dressed with Italian seasoning, it was all divine. And her lemon cake, topped with icing that melted in your mouth like cotton candy, was legendary. I loved helping her cook, even if my version of "helping" meant licking the bowl.

Her favorite place in the house was her rocking chair near the front door. She smoked tobacco, a habit she'd had since the age of nine. The house felt enormous to me as a child, not because of its size, but because of how much love it held.

Back in my home, we didn't talk through our problems; we dodged them, buried them, or let them explode without resolution. Our family dynamics weren't just strained, they were broken. I grew up watching my parents argue dysfunctionally far more often than I ever saw them resolve anything with mutual respect. Conflict wasn't something we handled; it was something we endured.

My father had little to no patience. You could see it clearly during even the most mundane moments, like our family car rides. He preferred back roads, while my mother felt safer sticking to the main roads. This difference in preference would often set him off. He'd snap at her from the passenger seat, barking orders or mocking her expressions when she got upset. She rarely responded directly to his

37

jabs, just kept driving the way she always had, which only enraged him more. Some drives ended with my father getting out of the car at a red light and walking the rest of the way, no matter how many times my mother circled the block to get him back in.

There were also stretches when we only had one car, and my mother needed it for work. Even routine inconveniences, traffic, forgotten errands, or my father asking her for money she didn't have, could ignite a full-blown screaming match. I remember pulling into my mom's job one day, just for him to keep yelling at her outside the building. He didn't care who was around. He cursed her out in public, called her names I won't repeat. I shrank into myself, humiliated and afraid as strangers looked on with a mix of confusion and pity. It was like watching someone unravel right in front of you, and being powerless to stop it.

Dinner in our house could turn into a battlefield with no warning.

One moment, we were sitting down to eat like a family. Next, it was a war of words.

I remember one night clearly, the smell of baked chicken still lingers in my memory. We were all at the table when my father took a bite, chewed for a moment, and then spoke with that familiar edge in his voice.

"Did you even add any seasoning to this chicken?"

My mother didn't even look up. "Yes, I did, Samuel," she said flatly, her tone already laced with exhaustion.

He scoffed and shook his head. "Tastes like dirt. No salt, no pepper. This is a classic dish, Lynn. How the hell do you mess it up?"

"If you don't like it, then don't eat it," she snapped, slamming her fork down.

"Fuck you! I won't then. Always trying to tell me what to do and feedin' me garbage." He pushed his chair back and stood abruptly, the force rattling the table.

I just sat there, still chewing the same piece of chicken I had started a minute ago, now soggy and flavorless in my mouth. I couldn't swallow. I couldn't move. I hated when this happened.

"It's okay, Mom," I whispered, trying to calm her with my eyes. "Just let it go. Don't get him mad, please."

But he wasn't done.

"There she goes with the lizard look," he sneered, glancing at her with a beer already in hand. "She must be pissed now, Brandy." He disappeared into the living room, cracking open the can before the TV even flickered on.

Mom didn't say another word. She just sat there in silence, staring at her plate.

Discipline in our house wasn't any better. My parents didn't believe in spanking, but they could never agree on anything else either. My mom tried to create structure, grounding me when I messed up, having hard conversations, and explaining consequences. She wanted to raise me with a sense of accountability.

But my father? He'd blow it all up.

If she grounded me, he'd let me go outside anyway. If she told me no, I learned to ask him instead. Half the time, he'd say yes just to piss her off. I figured that out early, how to play them against each other. I didn't realize then the damage I was feeding into.

My mother felt undermined, disrespected. But she also knew better than to push too hard. His temper was a switch, fast and unforgiving.

So we all learned to tiptoe. Dinner wasn't just dinner. It was a minefield. And most nights, I ate in silence, pretending not to flinch.

Whenever I was allowed to spend the night at a friend's house, it felt like stepping into another world, one I never wanted to leave. I'd beg my mother to let me stay just a little longer, silently wishing she could step inside these peaceful homes and understand why I clung so tightly to them. Their parents didn't fight like mine did. Their homes felt safe. No yelling, no tension riding the air like a storm about to break. In those houses, fear didn't live in the corners. Anxiety didn't wrap around me like a second skin. Deep down, I knew that this, what they had, was what I needed in my own home.

At school, we learned about bullying, how calling people names and making fun of them wasn't okay. But I didn't need a classroom definition. I witnessed it every day in my own home. My father bullied my mother with his words. He didn't shove her on a playground or steal her lunch money, but the way he tore her down wasn't any less harmful. He picked at her expressions, her tone, her looks, calling her names like "lizard lips," turning her insecurities into jokes, trying to get me to laugh with him. Sometimes he shouted insults that made my heart ache, calling her "stupid," "dumb," or worse. As a child, I didn't have the language to label it. But I could feel the wrongness in my bones.

It was very different from what I saw at my friends' homes, especially Milani's. We met in elementary school, both attending the same private school. Her mother was a single mom, strict but consistent. They lived just a few blocks from my Abuela's house in West Tampa. Milani wasn't allowed to spend the night at my place. At first, I didn't understand why.

As we got older, by middle school, we became inseparable. We'd hang out at the skating rink every weekend, laughing until our sides hurt. But no matter how close we had gotten, she still couldn't come to my house.

My dad could be unpredictable. Explosive. I hated that. I hated how his behavior stole pieces of my childhood, sleepovers, birthday parties, just the chance to feel like a normal kid.

My mom tried to advocate for me. She brought it up to him more than once. But he brushed her off, like he always did when the topic didn't center around him.

My parents were opposites in almost every way. My mother was quiet, gentle, and reserved. She didn't socialize much beyond her sister and our grandmother. She held herself together in public, careful with her words, always trying not to ruffle feathers. My father, on the other hand, was bold and loud, a classic extrovert who loved attention. He was charismatic when he wanted to be and careless when it came to consequences. He had a high tolerance for alcohol and a low regard for rules. He wasn't drinking hard liquor anymore; he drank beer, often while driving, like it was soda, and treated traffic laws like suggestions. His defiance made him seem fearless, but it was really just recklessness.

He brought that same recklessness to work. As a plumber, he had no problem walking off the job if a boss rubbed him the wrong way. He didn't care that we needed the money, that the bills had to be paid. He believed in doing things his way or not at all. When trouble found him, he never owned it. It was always someone else's fault. My mother was, again, the opposite: cautious, law-abiding, always trying to keep the peace. She was a social drinker who couldn't hold much alcohol

41

and who cared deeply about what people thought of her. Where he pushed the world away with arrogance, she tried to quietly disappear.

My mother loved shopping and gift-giving. It was her language of love, especially on birthdays and holidays. As an only child, I often found myself on the receiving end of her generosity, which could border on excessive. She went above and beyond, yet never seemed fully satisfied with her offerings. Even after giving a thoughtful gift, she'd anxiously ask, "Do you like it?" followed by, "I could've done better." Joy would flicker in her eyes only briefly before self-doubt crept in.

On weekends, she and my Tia would shop for hours, sometimes without buying a single thing. They'd window-shop across Tampa, stopping in nearly every store, only to circle back and purchase the first item they saw. It drove me crazy. But rarely were those shopping bags filled with anything for my mother. Most of the time, her cart was packed with items for the house, for me, for my father, for my cousins, never for herself.

My father, on the other hand, was the complete opposite. Simplicity defined him. His wardrobe consisted of shorts, t-shirts, and sandals, the only things he'd ever ask my mother to buy. He didn't care for shopping, didn't care about brand names, and certainly didn't care what anyone thought of how he looked. His shirts were often stained with grease or dirt from working under houses, fixing plumbing, or tinkering with the car. He wiped his hands on his clothes when napkins weren't around and carried himself not like a professional tradesman but like someone just getting the job done.

Despite their differences, both found comfort in the predictability of routine. Yet, they lived by entirely different rulebooks. My mother operated with reason and logic, always aware of how her actions might affect others. She overthought things, stressed about details, and tried to maintain a sense of order. My father was driven by emotion and impulse. He did what he wanted, when he wanted, consequences be damned.

And that contrast created a friction that never let up.

Each day, fear quietly took up space in our home, growing louder in my mind. Some days it came in the sound of my father's voice, raised in anger. Other days, it came in the sound of his heavy footsteps approaching my mother. My heart would race, palms sweat, knees tremble. The shift in atmosphere was sudden, like the air had been pulled out of the room. A threat loomed constantly, emotional or physical, and I learned to read the danger before it arrived.

The monster within my father didn't sleep. It grew louder and stronger, feeding off the silence and submission around it. It demanded to be worshipped like a king, his temper the sword, his words the whip. When challenged, he responded with violence. And when life tested him, anger was the only tool he reached for. That was who my father became.

Yet, as strange as it may seem, the love my parents gave me was a different version altogether. They adored me. I was the apple of their eyes. They never raised a hand to me or yelled at me the way they did at each other. They were proud of me. They took pictures, recorded videos, and rarely said "no." They gave me everything they had to give, hoping it would build a better life for me.

But the love they gave each other was tainted, heavy with blame and resentment. My father saw my mother as both his burden and his enemy. My mother, in return, had lost respect for the man she once loved. She'd defend him to others, but at home, she could barely stand him. She made excuses for his behavior while quietly despising the hold he had over her. It was as if she felt obligated to love him, trapped in a relationship that demanded all of her and gave nothing in return.

I rarely saw affection between them. No holding hands. No "I love you." No shared bed, no date nights, no real signs of a marriage built on anything but routine. Their love was not a bond, it was a battlefield. And year after year, their dysfunction became more visible, more grotesque. It eroded the very foundation of our home, leaving behind the broken pieces of what could've been a family.

Chapter 3

No Safe Place

The unresolved emotions that swirled within my father became the nocturnal demons that haunted our nights. These demons would transform the man I once called my hero into a shadowy figure, a monster cloaked in rage.

With each haunting note of Ed Sheeran's *"Make It Rain,"* my soul trembles, and memories rush in with an intensity that defies time. As a child, I was adrift in emotions I couldn't name. As an adult, the weight of those memories is almost unbearable.

We lived in a red brick home on Hamilton Street, tucked at the end of the road next to a quiet pond, home to ducks and, alarmingly, water moccasin snakes. The house had a driveway and a carport. Its layout was simple yet functional: a spacious living room, a short hallway leading to a small bathroom on the left, my bedroom with bunk beds, and my parents' bedroom tucked away in the back. The kitchen and dining area were connected in an open-concept layout before it became a trend. White walls, linoleum floors, and sliding glass doors led to a backyard that felt like my small slice of paradise. My father built our first deck there beside the inexpensive above-ground pool, and though I wasn't supposed to, I loved leaping from the deck into the water, feeling free, if only for a moment. My parents kept a modest garden on the side, a space they tended to together, sometimes in harmony, other times in silence.

That house carried both joy and darkness. I made forts in the dining room and danced to old-school hits from the '60s and '70s, The Beach Boys, The Temptations, Bee Gees, The Jackson Five, along with my era's favorites like New Kids on the Block. It felt like a home. But it was also where trauma took root. Where the air sometimes grew so tense it shattered more than silence. Where police showed up during the worst fights. Where rumors whispered through the walls that my father was using cocaine.

I don't recall much of the décor, but the living room left a lasting impression. A brown glass coffee table sat atop a Western Star rug in earthy tones: brown, beige, white. One night, I was jolted awake by piercing screams. My mother wasn't in bed. I followed the sounds, trembling. The moment I stepped into the living room, it looked like someone had spilled red paint all over the rug. The glass table was shattered. Slivers glinted in the dim light as I tiptoed barefoot around the fragments, tears streaming down my cheeks.

My heart pounded as I followed the sound of my father's voice into the kitchen. He stood over the sink, hand soaked in blood, cursing violently. My mother, small and quiet, hovered beside him, whispering in panic, tending to his wounds while ignoring her own. She told me to stay back, not to get cut. But I was already cut, invisible wounds etched beneath my skin. That night carved itself into my memory like glass, jagged, sharp, unforgettable.

He blamed her, of course. Didn't check to see if she was okay. Didn't apologize. His rage was hers to shoulder. He said it was her fault. That she made him angry enough to punch through glass. I never saw the start of that argument, but I saw enough to know it wasn't just about a fight. It was about control, anger, and the slow disintegration of a home from the inside out.

The next morning, the sun rose like any other day. We put on our clothes. My parents got ready for work. I got ready for school. We walked out the front door and into the world as if nothing had happened. The picture was intact again, framed just right for outsiders to see. But inside, the frame was broken.

Dysfunction was normal.

The cycle of trauma repeats itself like a relentless echo, haunting each generation unless someone decides to break the silence. As children, we're still learning, shaping our understanding of love, fear, safety, and self-worth. Our environments, especially in our most formative years, become the blueprint for how we interpret the world and our place in it. From our parents, we learn not just how to survive, but what it means to be human, for better or worse.

My father had the ability to shift from calm to belligerent in an instant. One minute, he could be the life of the party; the next, he became a stranger, dark and volatile. His signature phrase, "I'm not going to argue with you," always came moments before a storm. Once those words were spoken, all bets were off. His impatience, his refusal to listen, his explosive temper, all wrapped in profanity and threats, became part of our everyday reality. As a child, it was disorienting. I couldn't always tell who was right or wrong, who was the aggressor, and who was the victim. The lines were constantly blurred, painted over with fear.

My mother's family saw what was happening long before she could admit it out loud. Her sister. My aunt. My grandmother. They all told her to leave him. Urged her to get out. But like so many women trapped in the web of abuse, she stayed. I won't pretend to speak for her, not completely. But I saw it. I saw what it did to her.

She was always tired. Not the kind of tiredness you fix with sleep. This was something deeper. Worn down. Hollowed out.

Fear was everywhere. Not just in moments of yelling or broken furniture, but in the quiet, too. It settled into the walls like smoke after a fire. It followed us from room to room, always lingering.

But even more dangerous than fear was the victim mindset. It didn't show up all at once. It crept in slowly, like fog rolling over a familiar road. It told us we had no way out. That we were lucky he hadn't hit my mom that day. That his apologies meant something. That this, somehow, was love.

I remember one visit to my grandmother's house, just me, her, and my mom sitting around the kitchen table.

"Lynn, you need to leave Samuel," my grandmother said gently, but with an edge of firmness in her voice.

My mother didn't meet her eyes. She just sighed and changed the subject. "When's your next doctor's appointment?"

But my grandmother wouldn't let it go.

"I'm serious. Do you even see how this is affecting you? And Brandy? That man is a maniac. Did you know he called my phone five times the other night, yelling, cussing, acting like a damn fool? And I still don't even know what he wanted."

"Samuel doesn't mean any harm," my mother said softly, folding and unfolding the corner of a napkin. "Brandy loves her dad. He just... has these moments."

Her mother's voice rose, sharp with disbelief. "The hell he does! You can't keep letting that man treat you this way, Lynn. It's not right. It's not safe. And now he's blowing up *my* phone, like I'm supposed to do something? You better stop waiting for someone to come save you."

My mother stood up, grabbed her purse. "Alright, Mama. I gotta go. It was good seeing you."

My grandmother just stared at her as she left, her eyes full of that worried silence that always meant she'd said too much, or not enough.

Being a victim doesn't just bruise your body. It rewires your mind. You start lowering the bar so low that survival becomes the win.

I wasn't praying for peace or freedom. I was praying he'd get drunk enough to pass out early. I was hoping the yelling would be short. I was scared the police would come, scared they *wouldn't*. And when they did, I lied, because the alternative was worse.

I hoped my mother wouldn't say the wrong thing. I hoped I wouldn't. I hoped the walls wouldn't shake and that tomorrow, we could pretend again.

That's what survival looked like:

It turned hope into something meager, *not* a grand vision for something better, but into merely a *wish* for less damage, hurt, and pain.

My mother's fear played out in her behaviors, too. She hoped for change and that he would be different, maybe even believed his apologies. But I think she also hoped that if nothing else, time would take care of the problem, that maybe one day he'd just... be gone. The shame she carried silenced her. She hid the truth behind forced smiles, behind well-kept appearances, behind holiday photos and quiet nods. Everyone knew. But still, she hid.

There were no signs that my father's demons were fading. If anything, they grew stronger with each passing year. And my mother, whether out of fear or simply not knowing how to start over, chose to stay. Denial was her armor. Silence was her strategy. She buried her pain, her needs, and her identity, while trying to care for mine...and even his.

The darkness of nighttime cast a long shadow over my childhood, disrupting sleep and enveloping our home in my mother's suffering. Fear of the unknown lurked in every corner, gripping my heart with anxiety. The night itself gave license to the disorder within our walls. Even now, I remain hyper-aware of every faint nighttime sound, echoes of the terror that once gripped me.

I slept beside my mother until I was thirteen, believing my small body could somehow shield her. Night after night, we'd lie there tense and silent, waiting to see if the hallway stayed quiet or if the doorknob turned.

Because in our house, the monster didn't hide under my bed. He slept in the room next to mine.

***

A low creak, just enough to snap me awake. The door eased open, and my father's silhouette filled the frame.

"Samuel, what are you doing?" my mother whispered, voice already shaking.

"Where's the money I gave you?" he asked, stepping inside.

"I used it for her bills," she said, nodding toward me. "What do you need money for?"

He slipped his hand into her purse.

"Hey, please, don't do that. I don't have any cash, Samuel."

"Shut the hell up, bitch. Ye,s you do. You're hiding it."

"You're going to wake Brandy," she begged, barely above a breath. "Please... just leave us alone."

"Oh, now you care about waking her up?" He laughed, cold and low. "You weren't worried about her when you started hiding my money."

"I don't have your fuck..."

It was all he needed.

Before the final syllable left her mouth, he lunged. The mattress dipped; his weight crushed her voice and the air in my lungs. He ripped off the covers, rummaging, accusing, cursing.

Some nights, he dragged her down the hallway by her hair, their shadows jerking across the walls. Some nights, he wrapped a hand around her throat until her pleas turned to rasps.

And every night, I lay frozen, tears sliding into my ears, praying he'd stop, praying he'd leave. But I could do nothing.

When sunrise finally slipped through the curtains, a different man emerged. The loving father appeared, smiling for neighbors, tipping his hat, cracking jokes, and the world adored him.

Only we knew the truth: nighttime wasn't just for nightmares; nighttime *was* the nightmare. And the monster lived right down the hall.

***

In middle school, I never packed a lunch. I didn't have to. My father brought me fast food every single day: McDonald's, Taco Bell, Wendy's. My classmates were in awe.

"Wow, you're so lucky, Brandy. I wish my dad brought me lunch. This cafeteria food *sucks*," one of them said as we walked toward the lunch area.

Another chimed in behind me. "What'd he bring you this time?"

"I think Taco Bell," I answered, glancing toward the curb where I saw his car already parked.

He rolled down the window, grinning as he waved at my teacher. She nodded, giving me the signal that I could go meet him.

"Hey, baby, how was your day?" he asked, handing me the food. "Man, your teacher is a hot one," he added with a chuckle, nodding toward her.

"I got your favorite, three regular tacos with cinnamon twists. Here you go."

"Thanks, Daddy," I said, trying to mask the discomfort that stirred in me every time he made comments like that. "I'm doing okay. Just hungry and ready to go home."

"School'll do that to you. If I had your teacher, I'd be paying attention too," he teased, winking.

I forced a smile and stepped back toward the school building. "I'll see you later."

"Love you," he called out.

"Love you too," I said, hurrying back toward my teacher, who was waiting with a gentle, watchful eye.

That was my father. In public, he was charismatic, generous, the cool dad. The one who brought extra food so I could share with my friends. The one who waved and smiled. But behind the charm was a very different reality.

At home, police visits became part of our rhythm. Domestic violence calls. Doors slammed, voices raised, furniture broken. I don't remember how many times they came, I just remember the fear. I remember being pulled aside, asked questions I didn't want to answer.

I lied. Every time.

To protect him. To keep the image intact. Because even with everything, his rage, his cruelty, I didn't want to lose him.

I wanted to believe in the man he could be.

And for a few minutes each day, holding a warm paper bag full of tacos, I could.

But over time, it became harder to pretend.

There was one day, I don't even remember what started the fight, but I remember how it ended. My father was shouting, pacing the kitchen like a lion in a cage. My mother stood her ground, her voice quiet but firm, the way you speak when you're trying to protect a child from escalation.

I was that child.

But I was also no longer a child. I was old enough to know what domestic violence was. Old enough to know that normal families didn't have to hide in bathrooms or memorize the sound of footsteps that were a sign of an impending argument or all-out violence. And yet, too young to do anything but freeze.

He slammed his fist on the table. I flinched.

Mom turned to me, eyes wide, not in fear, but in a silent plea: *Please don't react.*

The doorbell rang.

It was my best friend's mom, here to pick me up for a sleepover. I wiped my face, grabbed my bag, and ran to the door like nothing was wrong.

"Oh, hey, Mrs. Porter," I said, voice light. "Let me grab my jacket real quick."

Behind me, my father stepped into the hallway, suddenly calm.

"How you doing, ma'am?" he asked her with that same smooth smile. "Brandy's been looking forward to this all week."

He walked me to the car, opened the door like a gentleman, and kissed me on the forehead.

"Be good," he said. "I'll see you tomorrow."

Mrs. Porter looked at me as we pulled away. "Your dad is so sweet," she said. "You're lucky to have a father who cares that much."

I didn't answer. I just looked out the window, heart pounding, stomach in knots. Because I couldn't hold it anymore. The performance. The pretending. The duality. I didn't know how to tell her that I had just left a war zone.

That my backpack didn't just carry pajamas and a toothbrush, it carried secrets. It carried shame. It carried the weight of knowing that love and fear could exist in the same house, in the same man.

And the scariest part? I didn't know which version of him would be waiting when I got back.

Once, he took me without permission and drove me to my abuela's house in West Tampa. My mother, terrified, called the police. They came, and I was returned. But by the next day, he was home again, angry, but present. My abuela blamed my mom for involving the cops. She wanted everything to stay quiet, hidden.

No matter the abuse and fear, she prioritized my relationship with him. She made excuses for his absence, never telling me why he was arrested and in jail. However, when my father was incarcerated, she didn't let her pride stop her from taking me to see him.

I still remember the first time I saw him behind bars, at the old Morgan Street Jail in downtown Tampa. I was only six. The brown and white building, with its cold walls and stricter silence, felt like a world apart from everything I knew. But for us, jail became a routine. At eight, he was at Orient Road. Then, work release. By ten, he was in Pensacola for drug charges. He missed my birthday that year.

And still, I remember the excitement of picking him up, the drive north. I thought hail was snow, anything to make that day magical. Anything to believe that things would be different this time.

Despite the challenges, there were moments of unexpected beauty. Even though he wasn't home for my birthday one year, my father managed to have a fellow inmate draw a brown teddy bear with a blue ribbon on a card and sent it to me with a handwritten birthday message. That small gesture, so simple, yet so sincere, meant the world to me. To this day, it remains one of the most cherished gifts I've ever received.

Through it all, my mother remained my anchor. She sacrificed her own happiness for mine, constantly putting herself last. Even as she endured my father's degradation, she maintained a facade of normalcy for my sake. Her emotional reactions were like quiet cries for help, reminding me of the pain she carried, but she never let go of her love for me.

Collect calls from jail became a regular occurrence. Each one carried a price, literally and emotionally. The bills climbed high, and the calls usually ended in arguments. My mother bore the brunt of it, paying to be insulted, berated, and blamed. She was already carrying the weight of a one-income household, and now she was financially and emotionally burdened by a man who wasn't even present.

His repeated incarcerations brought a strange duality into our home. Yes, I missed him. But his absence often brought an unfamiliar peace. The fear didn't leave, it only changed form. Fear of bills going unpaid. Fear of our secrets being discovered. Fear that staying would destroy us, but that leaving might, too. And a lingering fear that my mother simply wouldn't be enough to hold us together.

Witnessing the way my father degraded her left an imprint on my heart. I asked questions, but my mother always brushed them aside or minimized the truth. This created a wall between us, an emotional distance that hindered our closeness. Her love never wavered, but her energy, what she had left, was so often spent surviving, not connecting.

It was a slow, insidious brainwashing. My father's words weren't just cruel, they were calculated. He painted my mother as weak, incapable, and undeserving of respect. And the more I heard it, the more that narrative tried to root itself in my mind. Only later did I see her choices for what they were, acts of strength disguised as survival.

She carried physical wounds that she tried to hide, never filing charges, never seeking justice, just enduring, always enduring. In that environment, a dangerous belief took root: that women were meant to be silent, submissive, small. That belief was a seed planted by my father's voice and watered by fear. And it would take years to uproot it from my soul.

As I grew older, his demons grew more malevolent. Our home became a house of horrors, a place where tension was constant and peace was a stranger. My mother tried to leave multiple times, but financial chains always dragged us back. We'd pack up our lives, carrying hope in garbage bags, finding refuge in motels or at my Tia's house.

Living at my Tia's house brought an unexpected kind of discomfort. I missed the small luxuries of our old life, the cable TV, my own room, my neighborhood friends just a few doors down. I didn't understand the full scope of what we had escaped. All I could see was what I had lost, not the danger we'd left behind.

Instead of gratitude, I responded with frustration. I complained constantly, threw tantrums, and lashed out at my mother. I blamed her for everything, for taking me away from my space, for the boredom that consumed my days, for taking me away from everything familiar. What I couldn't see then was that she wasn't just trying to survive, she was actively trying to rescue us. She had walked away from my dad, risking everything, and I, unknowingly, became part of the pressure driving her back toward it.

"I am bored!" I whined, throwing myself on the bed, staring up at the ceiling in the spare room my mother was in.

"Brandy, what do you want to do?" Mom looked up from reading her book.

"I want to hear music, Mom."

"We can see about going to the store later, okay?" Mom already had a boom box on layaway at K-Mart without my knowledge.

"Okay, what do I do until then?" I sat up and looked at her.

"I don't know, Brandy, what else can we do to make you not feel bored?"

"Can I go see my friends?"

"I can't just drop you off in the neighborhood."

"Why not? I'm bored. I have no music. No friends. This sucks, Mom," my whining got more intense.

"Brandy, how about we go to the library and get some books, and then go to the store and see a boom box? Would that make you happy?"

"Yes! Let's go!"

My father only fed the fire. According to my mother, I began seeing him again even before she did. She allowed it, hoping that easing my restlessness might give us both the space we needed. But instead of clarity, I returned from those visits more confused, filled with his words, his rewritten stories, his manipulations.

Whenever I spoke to him, he wove fantasies meant to win me back. "I cleaned the pool just for you," he'd say. "Your friends stopped by asking where you were. It's not the same without you." He crafted a vision of a carefree life, a house filled with laughter, fun, and all the freedom I had grown used to. In that version, my mother was the one keeping me from happiness. Not him. Not the violence. Not the addiction.

And I believed it.

I didn't realize he was twisting my longing for comfort into a weapon against her. My loyalty wavered. My complaints got louder. The more my mother tried to create boundaries, the more I pushed against them. I began to equate love with what could be given, what could be bought. I wanted things, not lessons. I craved ease, not healing.

If I wanted something, I got it. If I didn't like something, I threw a fit. If I needed money, I just opened my hand. My father rarely told me no, and until we left him, my mother didn't either. But that began to change at Tia's house.

Now there were rules. I couldn't go outside as freely as I did at our house or Abuela's. I couldn't blast my music at night, my room shared a wall with my mother and Tia. I couldn't tie up the phone line for hours with my friends because my Tia might be expecting a call. I couldn't stay up late like I used to.

And I hated it.

My Tia, who saw through my father's ways, urged my mother not to go back to him. But between my complaining and her own exhaustion, my mother eventually caved. We returned to the very life we had tried to escape.

What I couldn't yet see was that the man I missed so much was falling apart. The father who once placed cash in my mother's hands now demanded it back within hours. At first, it was occasional. Then it became routine. He began rifling through her purse, searching for what he believed was his. His addiction had begun its quiet conquest, stripping away the man he used to be, piece by piece, dollar by dollar.

I watched the same cycle unfold with my abuela. I saw him beg her for money, manipulate her, and, when she said no, rummage through her belongings anyway. The desperation in his eyes was unmistakable. It was no longer about us. It was about the addiction.

Every time he took something, it wasn't just money. He was stealing from the version of himself I once believed in. He was taking away the last shreds of stability I'd clung to. Each dollar spent was another piece of the man who used to be my hero, lost forever.

Through it all, my mother stood firm. Her version of love was painful, hard, impatient, and unreciprocated. She gave herself completely to a man who shattered her repeatedly. Somewhere deep inside, she must have believed that real love meant sacrifice. That maybe, if she gave enough, endured enough, he would change. But the price she paid for that hope was everything.

As an adult, I see my mother in a completely different light. She is, without question, one of the strongest women I've ever known. The life she ended up living was not the one she had envisioned when she dreamed of being a wife and mother. Yet, through it all, she carried more than her fair share, and then some.

Her strength wasn't loud or boastful; it lived in the little things, in the rituals she created to bring beauty and normalcy into our home. Holidays were her canvas. Christmas transformed our house into a winter wonderland, and Halloween into a haunted mansion complete with cobwebs and spooky figures. On Valentine's Day, hearts and soft pinks filled the rooms, and Easter brought cotton-tailed bunnies and pastel decorations. Even St. Patrick's Day didn't go unnoticed. The only holiday that wasn't overdecorated was the Fourth of July, we were usually out at the beach or attending an event, but she still made it special in her own way.

She had a true gift for finding beauty in the mundane. Shopping with her meant bargain hunting at its finest. She could spend an entire day searching for the perfect item at just the right price, and she almost always found it. An avid reader, she built a personal library of novels and fiction that she read cover to cover with a passion only true book lovers understand.

And her cooking? Unmatched. If she tasted something once at a restaurant, she could recreate it perfectly at home. She cooked as if feeding a family of ten, even though it was just the two of us. No one ever left our home hungry. It was her love language, nurturing through nourishment.

Her creativity flowed effortlessly. She could sew clothes, design Halloween costumes from scratch, refurbish old furniture, plan events, and craft decorations with flair and precision. From lollipops made of candy canes to diaper baskets and homemade jewelry, her hands created magic out of everyday things. School projects? Masterpieces. Volcanoes that erupted, clothes hanger Christmas trees, you name it, she did it.

I often urged her to sell her creations, to share her talents with the world. But she never wanted to monetize her gifts. "This is just for family," she'd say with a smile. Her generosity, especially toward her sister's children, knew no bounds. Even when I was well into my thirties, she still made me an Easter basket, as if I were still her little girl.

And through all of this, she never once publicly shared her pain. She tucked it away, hidden beneath the surface, behind smiles and holiday ribbons. She carried on, working hard, raising me, and loving my father despite his brokenness. Some people define strength as leaving. And maybe that's true in some cases. But I believe there is also great strength in staying, in surviving, in choosing to show up and build joy in the middle of brokenness.

She didn't just hold our family together...she became its heart.

In the depths of my mind, a belief quietly took root: that loving oneself came last, and that love itself was a tool for manipulation. This wasn't a sudden revelation, but rather the slow unraveling of self-worth, thread by thread, woven through years of watching my parents' turbulent relationship. Over time, I adopted a victim mentality, believing I was powerless, that life just happened to me, not for me.

Even so, something stirred within me, a spiritual yearning that began in the halls of my private school. It was there, not at home, that I first encountered the awe-inspiring concept of God. I learned of His mercy, the power of prayer, and the sacrifice of His son. Those early lessons planted seeds of wonder and hope. But outside the structured safety of school walls, the connection frayed. Without reinforcement at home, the God I learned about remained distant, like a lighthouse I could see but not reach.

The dysfunction that brewed in my childhood home created a storm of emotions I didn't yet know how to name. Beneath my anger at my parents was a deep craving, for love, for protection, for their approval. I longed to be close to them, even as fear pushed me away. This internal contradiction, wanting to be near, yet needing to run, created a chasm I didn't know how to cross.

ADDICTED TO PAIN

As adolescence approached, that tug-of-war intensified. What the
world saw as rebellion was really a war within, between good and bad,
love and fear, peace and war. In an attempt to escape the tension, I
leaned into socializing. My outgoing nature made it easy to connect
with others, but those connections became less about joy and more
about avoidance. Parties, laughter, friendships, they became my armor, my distractions, my way of drowning out the noise inside.

But avoidance doesn't equal healing. The more I chased distractions, the deeper my pain rooted itself. I was running, but I wasn't free.

The weight of it all began to wear me down. I was tired of being
scared. Tired of the tight chest, the racing heart, the pit in my stomach.
I wanted someone to fight for me, to help carry the burden. I needed
an advocate. I needed rest. I needed to know this wasn't all life had to
offer.

Much of my frustration was directed at my mother. I resented what
I saw as her weakness. Why hadn't she left? Why were we always broke?
Why didn't she rescue us? At the same time, my once-close bond with
my father faded, replaced by fear. He became a stranger, someone I no
longer recognized, someone I no longer trusted.

I asked questions I couldn't answer: Why was our house full of
yelling, not love? Why did my childhood feel like a never-ending struggle? Why would a loving God let this happen to me?

The anger festered, fed by comparison. Friends with big families, celebrities with perfect lives, they had what I didn't, and I grew
ashamed of what I did have. To cope, I turned to weed, chasing a
calm that never lasted. It dulled the pain but deepened the fog. I was
losing parts of myself, drifting farther from the person I used to be,
the version untouched by trauma, still full of hope.

Caught between two broken parents, my perception shifted. My mother's quiet strength was eclipsed by my father's loud, destructive voice. Her pain was invisible, his rage unforgettable. And so, I stopped seeing clearly. I drowned myself in hip-hop, friends, anything that could take me away from what I didn't want to face.

More than anything, I wanted to be someone else.

Despite the turmoil between my parents, I never doubted that they loved me. My mother never laid a hand on me, and my father, who once swatted me on the behind when I was a toddler, used to laugh when telling the story of how I looked up at him, teary-eyed, and said, "You gave me a booboo." He swore he never touched me again after that. He often spoke of his own upbringing, vowing not to repeat the same mistakes with me.

I didn't know much about my mother's childhood, she kept that part of her life locked away, but my father's stories always painted him as the one who was a victim, but was a victor by not allowing anyone to control him or claim ownership over him. Yet, the unspoken expectation was clear: I was supposed to take his side. When things went wrong between them, he'd lean on me to validate his frustrations with her, to mirror his disappointment. I didn't realize at the time how heavy that burden would become.

Caught in the crossfire of their brokenness, I couldn't save my mother. I tried. But I couldn't stop her pain, and I couldn't stop the monster my father had become. I was exhausted, tired of crying alone in my room, tired of the shouting matches, tired of pacing the floor, wondering which parent I was supposed to love more. It was a cruel choice for a child to have to make.

The Monster had fully eclipsed the man I once called my hero. He wasn't just angry anymore; he was paranoid, arguing over things that existed only in his mind. The consequences, however, were very real. He stopped paying bills, spent money on his addictions, and kept finding new ways to get in trouble with the law. I missed my father deeply, not the man he had become, but the man I believed he used to be.

I believed in God, but I was no longer convinced that God knew my father. I certainly couldn't find God inside my home. He existed in the chapel at school, in the Bible stories I learned in class, but not in our living room. And soon, even that small thread of spiritual refuge would be taken from me. I had attended private school from kindergarten through eighth grade, but now, as high school approached, the financial strain became too much. The tuition payments were a weight my parents could no longer carry.

When they broke the news that I would be transferring to public school, I put on a brave face. If I'm honest, I was a little excited, no more uniforms, no more rigid routines. WHOOP WHOOP, right? It felt like a fresh start, an escape into something unknown. But I had no idea what was waiting for me.

Middle school ended quietly, and with it, my private school years came to a close. High school was supposed to be a new chapter. And it was.

But not in the way I had hoped.

***

As I entered high school, the strain between my parents only deepened. Their arguments, once frequent, now felt relentless, louder, longer, and more damaging. Despite the chaos at home, I found a small pocket of peace in our new neighborhood near Lowry Park Zoo. Our backyard bordered the edge of the zoo, and I could occasionally glimpse behind the scenes, zookeepers tending to animals or hear the distant sounds of exotic creatures. It gave me a strange comfort, a distraction from the turmoil inside our home.

Before moving into the Clifton Street house, my parents had talked about buying a home, there had even been serious discussions about a property on Hamilton Street. But somehow, my mother and her side of the family were blamed when that deal fell through. Clifton became the fallback, another rental, another temporary fix. This would be the last house we ever lived in together as a family.

As I grew older, the signs of my father's addiction became harder to ignore, even if I didn't fully understand them. I never saw him use drugs directly, but his behavior started to change in disturbing ways. He'd spend long stretches locked in the bathroom, and when he came out, the air carried a sharp, chemical odor I would later recognize as freebase cocaine. His personality warped, more agitation, paranoia, and outbursts. He talked to himself more often, pacing around the house, muttering things that made no sense.

It was like watching someone be consumed from the inside out, his mind overtaken by something dark and volatile. He wasn't just unpredictable; he was becoming unrecognizable.

The men he brought around didn't help. They loitered in our yard, drinking, talking loudly, laughing like life was carefree. But their presence only added to the instability. My mother often said these were the men who introduced him to crack. And as his drug use deepened, so did the violence.

I remember the accusations, outlandish, paranoid, cruel. He accused my mother of cheating with one of his friends. Of secretly moving a 50-gallon aquarium. Of chopping down kitchen cabinets in the middle of the night. None of it made sense, but he believed it all, and that belief made him dangerous.

His outbursts became savage. He would chase my mother through the house like a predator hunting prey. He would pin her down, wrap his hands around her throat, spit on her, and scream insults meant to break her spirit. It was like he wanted to erase her completely, to strip her of dignity, of womanhood, of humanity.

Chapter 4

Grave of Lust

Lust is often linked to sinful desires, cravings that prioritize pleasure over principle. In a broader sense, it reflects any intense longing that leads one to chase gratification at the expense of moral clarity. The Bible warns of lust's many forms, not only physical desire, but the hunger for control, validation, or escape from pain. In every context, it cautions us against letting desire rule over discernment.

In the depths of my being, the flames of others' hatred and my own self-loathing forged a low self-worth that warped my identity. My moral compass faltered. I no longer walked in truth; I drifted toward a fractured reflection of myself that felt more real than the girl I used to be.

The wounds of my childhood had been left unhealed. And in that vulnerable soil, promiscuity took root. It sprouted as a vine of false comfort, cloaking me in the illusion that lust was love, that desire meant devotion. I didn't yet understand that I was searching for safety, for wholeness, in the arms of people who couldn't give it.

By fifteen, I was desperate to feel something other than fear or sadness. That's when I met Mateo. We lived near Lowry Park Zoo, and our meeting felt like a cosmic twist of fate, timed perfectly, even divinely. He became my calm in the storm. Within a few months, he had moved into my room, offering me a sense of security I had never experienced at home.

Mateo was tall, handsome, and Puerto Rican. He played baseball, dressed like a "pretty boy" with crisp polos and fresh sneakers, and had a natural charisma that drew people in. He was goofy, sweet, and romantic, the kind of guy who gave you red roses just because. He saw me, not just the tomboy I sometimes presented, but the girl beneath who was afraid to be fully seen. He made me feel beautiful.We were all at the park near Lowry Park Zoo, me and the neighborhood kids, when Mateo appeared out of nowhere.

"Hey, it's Brandy, right?"

"Yes, that's me," I said shyly. My thoughts spiraled, *Why is he talking to me? I'm not pretty enough.*

"I'm Mateo. Nice to meet you." He sat down right next to me.

"Aren't you Cutia's cousin?" I asked, trying to keep my voice steady.

"Yeah, I am. Our families aren't blood, but we all grew up together. My mom's over at their house right now, and I heard everyone was down here, so I came by to hang out... and then I saw you."

I didn't know what else to say. I was too nervous. There was a pause, awkward, but electric.

"Well, do you wanna hang out later? We could get some ice cream or something?"

"Umm... yeah. But how would we get there?"

"I've got a car. I can pick you up."

"Really? You want to pick me up and hang out with me?" My cheeks burned, I was blushing so hard I could feel it in my ears.

"Yeah, why not? Do you have a boyfriend or sutin'?"

"Nah... no, no. Me? Have a boyfriend? No." I laughed nervously. "But okay, I'll see you later then?"

"For sure."

From that day on, we spent nearly every day together. Watching TV in my room. Hanging out at GameTime and the Malibu Grand Prix arcade. Driving to the beach or catching a movie. He had a car before I did, so our freedom expanded fast.

Being with him was like living in a teenage dream, something I never thought I'd have. I had been used to surviving, not smiling. But Mateo changed that.

We went to my first homecoming dance together. We dressed up. We danced. We laughed like kids who didn't carry the weight of the world at home. We took photos at Star Image, dined out at restaurants, and even made a trip to Universal Studios for Halloween Horror Nights, our first big trip as a couple. He was my first love and, for a time, my closest friend. At that point in my life, Mateo wasn't just a boyfriend. He was my escape. My better half.

Yet, even in my relationship with Mateo, the ache for companionship wasn't satisfied. I longed to be surrounded by people, friends who might silence the negative voices in my mind and help me forget the haunting scenes at home. I didn't understand what true friendship meant back then. I just wanted someone, anyone, who could share the weight of my pain, even if we never spoke about it. I let people in without hesitation, out of desperation.

My circle of friends came from all walks of life. Some lived in homes just as broken as mine. Others were survivors of abuse, neglect, and the harshness of street life. We were a ragtag group, all wrestling with trauma in our own way. Despite our differences, we bonded through shared pain, as if unspoken suffering was the glue that held us together.

My mother tried to place boundaries on who could come over and when, but that only pushed me further toward those friendships. Rejection, in any form, felt unbearable, so I became agreeable to a fault. I conformed, mimicked, and followed, just to be included. I didn't see how I was slowly molding myself to fit into their worlds, instead of shaping my own.

In my naivety, I confused closeness with connection. I mistook proximity for loyalty. And while some friends did bring fleeting light into my darkness, each one eventually faded, leaving me once again in the shadows I was trying to escape.

My friends became my first form of safety, their approval, my first measure of self-worth. I trusted easily, almost blindly, assuming their love for me was pure, assuming they had my best interest at heart. I believed they liked me, valued me, understood me... but most of them didn't. Not truly.

During these days, I made a series of misguided decisions, none more damaging than choosing the wrong friendships. I was easily influenced. My sense of identity grew smaller as the voices around me grew louder. I became a version of myself I didn't recognize, lost, reactive, and unsure.

What I didn't yet understand was this: your voice is the echo of your inner truth. And inside, I was scared. I was broken, searching outwardly for healing, for affirmation, for belonging. I looked at my friends and envied their confidence, their freedom, their ability to seem okay. I let them become my saviors, not realizing they were drowning too.

My dreams slowly faded. The girl I once imagined becoming got quieter and more distant. High school marked a major turning point. I had too much freedom and not enough direction. I skipped school, sought thrills, chased attention, and got caught in the current of poor choices. My parents never physically caught me in the act, but my report cards told the truth. My grades dropped, not because I lacked intelligence, but because I had started to value street smarts over academics. I wanted to be accepted more than I wanted to succeed.

In high school, I didn't know where I fit in. Not racially. Not socially. Not even in my own skin.

I wasn't Spanish enough for the Latinas. I wasn't white enough for the white girls. And though I longed to connect more deeply with Black culture, the music, the style, the power, I always felt like I was lingering on the edge, looking in. I didn't belong anywhere. And after a while, I stopped trying to.

The bullying wasn't always loud. Sometimes it came in sideways glances or in whispers that quieted when I walked by. Other times it was blunt and biting, comments about how I dressed, how I talked, how I wasn't "this enough" or "that enough." Each one chipped away at my sense of self until all I wanted was to disappear.

And so I did. I hid in plain sight.

Baggy pants. Oversized tees with Tupac, Master P, and the Bad Boy Records crew splashed across my chest. Sterling silver chains. Fresh sneakers that matched every outfit. My clothes became a shield. If I looked hard enough, maybe no one would see how soft I actually was.

I wasn't trying to be sexy. I didn't want that kind of attention. Honestly, I didn't think I was pretty enough for it. Tight clothes? Midriffs? Mini skirts? That wasn't me.

Not because I judged it, but because I didn't think I could pull it off. That kind of beauty felt like it belonged to other girls. The ones who knew how to be wanted. The ones whose skin fit them like a promise.

Mine felt like a question I didn't know how to answer. Outside of Mateo's compliments, I hid behind attitude. Behind humor. Behind music.

Always, the music.

When the ache got too big to hold, I slipped on my headphones. When I didn't have the words, the lyrics spoke for me. Music wasn't just noise, it was my escape, my sanctuary, my teacher. It wrapped itself around my teenage mind and gave shape to feelings I hadn't learned how to name.

The R&B I clung to taught me that love was mostly about sex. That desire looked like silk sheets and candlelight, slow kisses and breathy moans. That being wanted meant being touched. Being claimed.

The rap told a different story, grit, hustle, survival, seduction, power. Nas. DMX. Jay Z. Eminem. Tupac. No Limit. The Hot Boyz.

I memorized verses like scripture. Their metaphors. Their bravado. Their pain, dressed up as power. I was mesmerized. I started writing too, just little rhymes in my notebook. Punchlines, flows, anything that helped me take what I was feeling and spit it back out in a way that felt controlled. Honest. Safe.

But there was a shadow in it. Those lyrics I worshipped also carried a message I didn't fully understand at the time.

The women in the songs weren't loved. They were used. Wanted, yes, but only for what they gave. Their curves. Their sex. Their ability to please. They weren't seen.

And I... I wasn't them. I wasn't sexy. I wasn't exotic. I wasn't wanted. And I didn't know how to be. So I stopped trying.

I started moving through high school like a ghost with a loud mouth. Visible but not really seen. Loud but not really heard. I was finding a voice, but it was built on pain. I was building an identity, but it was shaped more by rejection than by truth.

At the time, I didn't have the language for any of this. But looking back? That was the start of my disappearance. That was the start of me surviving instead of living.

My curiosity about sex grew.

It never came dressed as romance or intimacy, only as images half-lit in the glow of late-night TV and glossy magazine pages I shouldn't have been touching. I'd watch the women in music videos, hips swaying, hair glistening, and think *that must be power.* I'd find my father's hidden porn magazines, flip through them in secret, and wonder if beauty could really make people pay attention, if flesh alone could unlock the kind of belonging I'd never felt.

Sex, the way it arrived in my world, was impersonal. Detached. Dirty. It was bodies, not souls; pleasure, not purpose. People did it to feel good, to feel seen, to feel anything at all. And deep down, that's all

I really wanted, to feel something other than the ache of being the girl who never quite fit anywhere.

Mateo and I had been orbiting each other for months when the question slipped between us. We were in my room, the door cracked just enough to stay out of trouble, legs tangled at the foot of the bed, nerves buzzing louder than the box fan in the window.

"Are you sure you're ready? This is...a big one, B," he said, eyes locked onto mine as if an honest answer could save us from ourselves.

"Is it?" I tried for confidence I didn't own. "You're my first love. I don't want to miss doing this with you."

He exhaled and looked everywhere but my face. "Listen, I ain't never, you know..." He gestured vaguely, cheeks darkening.

"Done what?"

"You know." Another gesture...awkward, earnest.

"Oh, sex? You've never had sex before?" I said it too loudly; he shushed me, glancing at the hallway. "But I thought you told me you did...with your ex?"

"Nah, I was frontin'," he confessed.

I felt a surge of relief and panic all at once. "So...how do we do this? I've never either."

We laughed, not because it was funny, but because fear didn't give us any better lines.

When it finally happened, it was clumsy and quiet, a tangle of limbs and shallow breaths. We crossed a line we could never uncross, believing it would stitch us closer together. Instead, when I rose from that bed, I felt as if something important had slipped out of me and left the door wide open.

I lost my virginity that night, but I lost something I didn't even know I was supposed to guard: a sense that my body was mine first, that desire could wait for self-worth to catch up. In its place sprang lust, confusion, a hunger that pleasure never managed to satisfy.

No one had taught me that innocence was worth cherishing, or that *yes* should come from fullness, not emptiness. I thought sex might be a cure for loneliness, that giving my body might earn me the love I ached for.

I was wrong.

Chapter 5

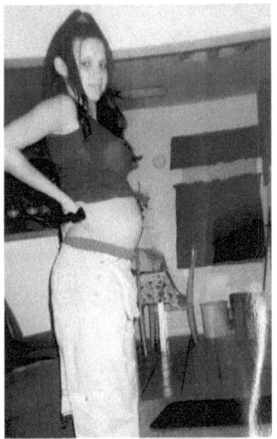

A Mother Too Soon

Soon after losing my virginity, Mateo's cousin Arturo, got out of prison. He was affiliated with the Latin Kings and quickly pulled Mateo deep into that world. I watched helplessly as the boy I once loved disappeared into something unrecognizable. The sweet, funny boyfriend who once surprised me with red roses was replaced by a hardened stranger. His clothes changed, his language hardened, and something inside him turned distant and cold.

Soon, rumors began swirling, Mateo was with other girls, and Mateo was denying we had ever been together. Hearing whispers in hallways and on the streets felt like cuts, each one deeper than the last. The emotional wounds were fresh and raw, and just like that, my first love vanished into the streets.

As Mateo sank deeper into that world, I found myself spending more time with his stepbrother, Asael. He wasn't in the gang. He was around, accessible, easy. Always ready with a joke or quiet company when I needed it most.

I was tired of chasing after people who were pulling away, desperate for someone, anyone, to see me, choose me, and stay. Without realizing it, I started slipping into the patterns I had watched my mother endure my entire childhood. I silenced my voice. I tolerated behaviors that made my stomach turn. Attention began to feel like love, and dysfunction became the closest thing I knew to connection.

Mateo was drifting further, disappearing for days at a time. Every missed call, every ignored text, every whispered rumor chipped away at my heart. And Asael was there, more and more, filling in the spaces Mateo left behind.

One afternoon, Asael and his friend Carter pulled up to my house, music blaring from the boom box they were carrying.

"Wassup, Brandy?" Asael called, walking up the driveway with that easy, lopsided grin of his.

"Hey! Not much," I called back. "I'm just about to hop in the pool. Y'all bring swim clothes?"

"Nah," Asael smirked. "But I got basketball shorts."

"Same here," Carter chimed in.

I smiled, suddenly reckless. "Last one in's a loser!"

We raced to the backyard, Mama calling from the porch, "Y'all better rinse your feet first!"

But it was too late. We hit the cold water laughing, splashing, the chill stealing my breath and replacing it with a rush of freedom.

"Damn, this water cold," Asael said, swimming close.

"Yeah, but it feels perfect," I told him, smiling. "Can you do a handstand?"

"Nah. Show me."

I dove down and flipped upside down, holding myself under for a second before surfacing. Asael was right there, grinning mischievously, flicking water into my face. I splashed him back. Before long, it turned into an all-out war of laughter and splashing.

Then something changed. He moved closer, teasingly tickling my sides.

"Stop! I'm mad ticklish!" I squealed, squirming away.

"Oh, I know," he teased, coming closer again.

Without thinking, he grabbed me around the waist, effortlessly lifting me. My legs wrapped instinctively around him, my laughter trailing off into silence. Our faces were inches apart, breathing quick and unsteady.

My heart was wild, racing not from play but from the intensity of this sudden intimacy. We stared into each other's eyes, caught off-guard by how easily the line between us had blurred.

Then clarity struck like lightning. He wasn't mine. He had never been.

"Hey, y'all tryna smoke or what?" Carter shouted from the edge of the pool.

We pulled apart instantly, pretending like nothing had changed, like that moment hadn't just rearranged the ground beneath us.

But I knew better.

In that brief blur of comfort, attention, and misplaced longing, I'd crossed a line I couldn't uncross. Something had fractured inside me, something permanent.

Asael and I began with innocent flirting. Just like that carefree afternoon in the pool. It felt playful and harmless at first. But soon that casual energy shifted into something deeper, a subtle pull neither of us openly acknowledged.

We'd spend hours watching movies in my room, often waiting for Carter to show up. I would curl up next to Asael, my head resting comfortably against his chest, listening to the steady rhythm of his heartbeat. In those quiet moments, his hands began to move, slowly and hesitantly slipping beneath my blouse. Each time, I gently pushed them away, murmuring that he should stop, but never with real conviction. The truth was complicated. The truth was that part of me wanted this closeness, wanted the attention, wanted the intimacy, even if another part of me quietly knew it wasn't right.

Over time, these secret touches grew more frequent, each gentle push-and-pull drawing us closer together. We were dancing on a line I knew was dangerous, but I couldn't bring myself to fully step away. It felt good to feel wanted again, to feel seen, even in such a fragile, uncertain way.

In those stolen moments, Asael became my refuge. He made me feel less alone, less invisible. And even though I knew this closeness blurred boundaries, for a while, I chose not to see clearly. I chose to ignore the voice inside warning me that this was something I might regret.

ADDICTED TO PAIN

Sometimes I'd sleep over at Carter's house, spending time with his sister Sa'Niyah while Asael and Carter hung out in the next room. Those nights felt easy and carefree. We'd stay up late playing board games, smoking weed, creating silly dances to our favorite songs, and watching movies until we fell asleep. For a little while, I felt like I could let go and simply be a teenager.

One night, Carter brought out a tattoo kit, though calling it a "kit" was generous. It wasn't professional equipment; it was just some tattoo ink, a small needle, and a makeshift handle he'd rigged together from a piece of wood. The others dared each other to get tattoos, laughing nervously at the idea. At first, I hesitated, unsure if I wanted to join in. But then Asael quietly offered to do mine himself, and I felt a rush of warmth. Of everyone there, I trusted only him.

We chose a spot carefully, below my belly button, nestled discreetly into the curve of my waist, hidden safely where my parents wouldn't discover it. He painstakingly etched a small Chinese symbol meaning "destiny," carefully pressing ink into my skin one gentle prick at a time. The process took hours, but I didn't mind. There was something comforting about it, the quiet hum of music playing softly in the background, the occasional glance between us, his careful attention as he marked my body with something that felt like a secret shared only between us.

I lay there, the slight sting of each prick accentuating the bond forming between us. In that simple, reckless moment, I felt connected, protected, and strangely hopeful. Like maybe, somehow, this mark truly represented destiny, whatever that would come to mean.

Most weekends ended the same way: a movie still flickering on the screen, the smell of weed fading into quiet, and a tangle of blankets spread across Carter's living room floor. Somewhere in the middle of those late-night lulls, Asael and I always drifted toward each other, first shoulder to shoulder, then hip to hip, until sharing a blanket felt inevitable.

What started as whispered jokes turned into hesitant kisses. Soft at first, almost shy, they soon lingered long enough for curiosity to take over. His fingers traced the edge of my T-shirt, slipping just underneath, testing how far I would let him go. I nudged him away, then pulled him back; neither of us, sure how to say yes or no with words, so we let our bodies choose for us.

We explored each other, his mouth on my chest, his hand sliding beneath my waistband, both of us learning as we went. He tried to go down on me once, tentative and unsure. I guided him, equally unsure. Sometimes his fingers found the spot that made my breath catch; other times we just fumbled and laughed. Mostly, we pressed our hips together, clothed and impatient, dry-humping like we were chasing a feeling we couldn't quite name.

Those nights were messy and innocent and confusing all at once, two teenagers searching for comfort in each other's skin, not yet brave enough for sex, but hungry for everything that led up to it.

Then came the night when everything felt like it was leading to sex. The tension between us was thick, electric, we were curled up under the same blanket again, breathing in sync, the room dark and quiet except for the low hum of the TV. His hands moved more deliberately this time, his mouth lingered longer, and I felt myself inching toward a line I wasn't ready to cross.

He was close. I was close. Everything in the air said this was the m oment.But something in me, something deeper than fear, whispered,

Not yet. It wasn't about shame. It wasn't even about him. It was about me, finally hearing my own voice through all the noise.

I pulled away. "I can't," I said softly, my hand on his chest. "Not tonight." He paused, searching my face, then nodded. "Okay," he said, his voice low. "It's cool."

That time, I listened to myself. And for the first time in a long time, I didn't feel guilty for choosing me.

Soon after, I found out I was pregnant.

I had just gotten my period for the first time at fifteen, later than all my friends. For so long, I'd felt out of place, waiting for that rite of passage while everyone around me carried pads in their backpacks and whispered about cramps between classes. When it finally came, I was actually excited. I felt like I was catching up. Like maybe now, I was becoming a woman too.

But then it disappeared.

And for a while, I convinced myself it was nothing. I'd heard of girls having irregular cycles, especially early on. So I waited. One week passed. Then two. And still, nothing.

Then came the nausea. It started in the mornings, sudden and violent. I'd barely open my eyes before I was running to the bathroom, throwing up whatever was (or wasn't) in my stomach. I figured it was something I ate. Maybe the school lunch. Maybe food poisoning. I tried Pepto. Ginger tea. The meds my mother kept in the cabinet for stomach bugs. But nothing worked.

By the third week, a different kind of worry started to settle in my gut. I called Mateo.

"Mateo... listen. We need to talk."

His voice came through the phone, casual, unbothered. "What is it, Brandy?"

I hesitated, my breath already shaking. "I'm scared. I don't know what's happening to me."

He sighed. "Can you be more specific? I'm not sure I understand."

I tried to explain, the words tumbling out in a rush. "I haven't had my period. It's late. I've been feeling sick every day, like really sick. This just isn't like me."

There was a pause on the line. "Hello? Are you there?" I asked, my voice rising.

"Yeah... I'm here," he said finally. "You think maybe you just ate something bad? Aren't you on birth control?"

I nodded, even though he couldn't see me. "Yeah... I mean, I take them. When I remember to."

I didn't realize how much that mattered. That you had to take them the *same time every day*, without missing a single dose. But I was fifteen. It was explained, but I didn't realize how important that particular step was to avoid pregnancy.

"When you remember to?" He sounded irritated now. "Brandy, I don't think that's how they work."

"I didn't mean for this to happen!" I cried. "My mom just thinks I've got a stomach bug. I haven't told anyone."

He was quiet again. Then, carefully: "Brandy... do you not get it?"

I froze. "You think I could be... pregnant?" I whispered. The word felt huge in my mouth. Like it didn't belong to me. Like I was borrowing it from someone else's story.

"Look, I don't know," he said. "But we need to get a test. Just to be sure."

I pressed my face into my hands, sobbing. "I didn't do this on purpose. I don't even understand how this could happen."

He didn't say much after that. "I'll come by later. We'll go to the store. Just... don't tell anyone yet, okay? Not until we figure this out."

That night, I sat in my room staring at the ceiling, my world already shifting. The test confirmed what I, deep down, already knew.

I was pregnant.

The news hit me like a tidal wave, fast, overwhelming, and impossible to outrun. I was a sophomore in high school. Still a child. But suddenly, I was preparing to bring another life into the world. I felt the fear lodge itself deep in my body. Not just fear of the future, but of my father. Of what he would say. What he would *do*.

And Mateo? By then, we were already slipping apart.

We barely saw each other anymore. And when we did, it was strained, like we were performing a version of something we had already lost. The intimacy was gone. The honesty had evaporated. And neither of us said what we both felt: that we had crossed lines with other people, and whatever we had... wasn't whole anymore.

The trust was broken. The distance was undeniable. And now, I was carrying a baby.

Alone.

One night, I was at Carter's house. We were all in his sister Sa'Niyah's room watching a scary movie. I was curled up next to Sa'Niyah, Asael's head resting on my leg, Carter on the other side of me. It felt like just another chill night, until it wasn't.

Arturo, Mateo's cousin, the one who had just gotten out of prison, showed up out of nowhere. And he wasn't alone. Mateo and a few others from the gang were with him. When Arturo opened the bedroom door, it was like someone had dropped a match into gasoline.

"Yo, what the fuck is going on in here?"

We all jumped like roaches when the light comes on.

"Baby, you scared me," Sa'Niyah said, trying to defuse him.

He didn't even look at her. "Nah, what I wanna know is why Asael and Brandy all cuddled up? Does Mateo know y'all chill like this?"

Panic hit me hard. My mind started spinning, what did he know? What had he seen?

"Baby, we all just cuddled up, stop trippin'. Brandy and Asael? Seriously?" Sa'Niyah laughed nervously.

Then he shouted, "Mateo!"

I could hear music outside, a full-blown party forming. Asael walked up to dap Arturo like nothing was wrong, but Arturo pulled him into a playful headlock and dragged him toward the living room. It didn't feel playful anymore.

I peeked out the window. "There are a lot of people out there," I said to Sa'Niyah, my voice shaky. "I'm nervous."

"Why, girl? Mateo's here."

"Yeah... but I don't know if he'll be happy to see me. All we do is fight now." A tear slipped down my cheek. I wiped it fast.

The house morphed into that dreamlike chaos. I heard voices rising outside. Then Carter burst into the room, his face pale.

"Yo, Mateo's heated. He's about to fight Asael!"

I froze. Couldn't move. Conflict always did that to me, froze me solid.

"What? Oh shit," Sa'Niyah gasped, then both she and Carter ran out. I stayed, pacing like a trapped animal. The fear felt too familiar, like when my parents fight.

Time passed. I don't know how much. Then Sa'Niyah came back in, looking ghostly.

"Brandy, this is bad. Mateo's accusing you and Asael of being together. Some of the Queens are outside, saying they wanna jump you. Girl, what the fuck is going on?"

"I don't know... I can't fight. Who's saying that? Where's Asael? Where's Mateo?" I was inching toward the living room, trying to figure out how to disappear.

"My brother's with Asael. Arturo's holding Mateo back. But you can't go out there. They're gonna jump you."

"Mateo won't let that happen. Right?"

She stared at me. "At this point? Mateo's ready to fight his own blood. No disrespect, but who *are* you to him?"

I didn't know anymore.

"I can't get jumped. My mom will kill me if I show up with a black eye."

The night spiraled and ended just as quickly. Neighbors came out threatening to call the cops, and the crowd scattered. Asael left with Mateo and Arturo. I didn't see him again after that. Sa'Niyah and Carter waited an hour before walking me home, once they were sure everyone was gone.

And then it was just me. Pregnant. Alone. And terrified.

The pain was layered. It wasn't just the chaos at home. Or Mateo pulling away. Or the weight of a growing belly I hadn't planned for. It was all of it, stacked, tangled, and suffocating.

I felt invisible. Unworthy. Like I didn't matter unless I was being used, blamed, or broken open.

Home was spiraling. My father's rage was relentless. My mother, already shattered over the pregnancy, carried her disappointment like a ghost. She didn't yell. She didn't cry. She just *deflated*, like all the air had gone out of her.

And my father? He didn't ask. Didn't notice. Didn't care.

He didn't see that the little girl who once begged to ride with him to abuela's was now a terrified teenage girl carrying life inside her, with no idea how to protect it.

***

Then came the night we left for good.

Unlike all the other times, he was home, and he was angry. My mother's bruises were harder to hide. A jammed finger. Dark marks on her arms. Her spirit was breaking in front of me, and mine was unraveling with it. We had promised ourselves we'd leave. And this time, we meant it. This time, we wouldn't come back. But leaving him was never simple.

That night lives in my bones.

The screaming started again. I picked up the phone and called the only person I could think of: Mateo. I didn't know if he'd answer. We weren't even on good terms. But I didn't care. I needed help.

"Hello?"

"Mateo..." I was whispering, crying. "I need you to come. Now."

"Where are you? Why are you whispering? Are you okay?"

"No... I'm at home. In my room."

"Is it your dad again?"

"Yes. He's hurting her. It's bad, Mateo. Hold on, " I muffled the phone, climbed off the bed, and crept toward the door to listen for the yelling. "I gotta go, he's coming. Please hurry." I hung up.

Seconds later, the door burst open, and he dragged my mother in by her hair. Her face was red and swollen. Her body was limp from the beatings. "Brandy, your mother did this! This is her fucking fault!" he shouted.

"Stop! Leave her alone!" I screamed, clutching my head.

He dropped her. She crawled to me and I pulled her onto my bed, wrapping my arms around her shaking frame.

"You're taking this bitch's side now? You too?" he yelled. "Has she been filling your head with lies? Did she tell you she stole the Hamilton Street house from me? That she talks shit behind my back?"

"Stop yelling and hurting her!" I shouted, my voice shaking.

He stormed toward us.

And with the last bit of strength she had, my mother threw herself in front of me.

"Samuel, you will NOT touch my daughter!"

He turned to me then, his rage now locked on me. And in that moment, for the first time, I felt a new kind of fear. Not for her. For myself.

But she stood her ground. Bloody, trembling, broken, and said the words I'll never forget:

"No. You will not touch her."

He raised his hand again, furious. "Who the fuck do you think you are, bitch?" Then he shoved her face with an open palm. And that's when the back door swung open. Mateo stepped into the room.

Everything shifted.

The Monster, so loud seconds ago, hesitated. His rage bent into something else. Something pitiful. Like a man trying to lie to himself in front of a witness.

"Hey, what's going on here?" Mateo said, his voice calm but firm.

My father seized the moment to rant to an audience. "Brandy, your mother did this! She's trying to turn my daughter against me! Take my house!"

"You're an addict, Samuel," my mother said, tears rolling down her cheeks. "You're destroying this family."

He lunged again. Mateo stepped between them. "Go to hell, bitch!" my father spat at her.

"Samuel," Mateo said, steady, "let's talk away from them. You don't want cops showing up."

"Fuck the cops! Let them come! Everyone blames me! I'm a disabled man! I take meds, and now I'm an addict?"

"I get it, Pops," Mateo said softly, guiding him backward toward the hallway.

"She nags all the time! I help pay the bills, and when I ask for twenty dollars, she acts like I'm begging! She's turning Brandy against me!"

I whispered to my mother, "You need to go to the hospital." But he overheard.

"You two-faced bitch, you're not going anywhere to spread more lies!"

"Leave me alone! Let go of me!" she shouted.

Mateo stepped in again. I ran to grab whatever I could, clothes, school books, anything. My hands were trembling. My heart wouldn't slow down.

Eventually, somehow, my father let us go.

We had a small window of time. That was all.

We stuffed bags. Ran. Didn't look back.

As we backed out of the driveway, I glanced at the house. The man in the doorway... he wasn't my father anymore.

And as I looked down at my growing belly, something new moved inside me.

Not just the baby. Not just fear.

Hope.

For the first time, I believed, really believed, that maybe something better was waiting for us on the other side.

That night was the last time he ever laid hands on my mother. And it was the first time we ever truly saved ourselves.

***

Life after my father was not the freedom I had imagined. It was messy. Loud. Heavy. The kind of freedom that still carried bruises. My mother and I had escaped him physically, but the emotional wreckage lingered like fog, thick and hard to see through. I wore my pain like armor. Anger hardened me. Trust felt impossible.

And then, as if things weren't already unraveling, here I was, pregnant. A teenager. Still a child. And now carrying one.

I had barely begun to understand how to care for myself, let alone raise another human being. Our home was no longer the one we had shared with him; it was smaller, older, chipped around the edges, and suffocating in its new reality. The furniture came from yard sales and warehouse clearances. Every wall whispered struggle. It was survival, and survival didn't make room for beauty.

Money was tight. Tighter than it had ever been. We no longer had the small privileges we'd once taken for granted, brand-name snacks or small vacations to the beach. My mother, who had already sacrificed so much, handed over her entire tax refund so I could buy a car. That car was supposed to give us some hope. Instead, I wrecked hers. She had to replace it with a clunky lemon of a stick shift that rattled so loudly you could hear her coming from two blocks away. It had no air conditioning, broken windows, and a sound like metal gasping for breath.

She never complained. But I could feel her frustration in the silence between us.

We shopped at Dollar Tree. Always. The cart was usually half-full, loaded with off-brand versions of things I used to love. I remember stopping in front of a shelf lined with bright orange bags of Goldfish crackers, real Goldfish, not the knockoff ones shaped like blobs.

"Ma," I asked, trying to sound casual, "can we just get the real ones this time? They're two for five."

She glanced at the shelf, then at the cart. "We can't," she said gently. "Not today."

I sighed. "But the off-brand ones taste stale. They're not even shaped like fish."

She rubbed her temples. "Look, I know. But we're not shopping for favorites right now. We're shopping for what we can afford."

That answer, the one I'd heard before, made something sharp rise in my throat.

"You always say that. Why can't we just get the good stuff one time? I'm tired of eating 'whales.'"

She turned to face me, her voice lower but firm. "Because 'one time' adds up. You think I don't want to give you everything you're used to? I do. I hate this too. But this is what it is right now."

"It's not fair," I muttered. "I didn't ask for any of this."

She paused, biting back whatever was sitting on the edge of her tongue. "Neither did I. But I'm doing what I can. I can't make magic out of a paycheck that's already gone before I even get it."

We stood in silence in the middle of the aisle, surrounded by cheap candy and off-brand cereal. She looked tired. Not just in her body, but in her spirit. Her eyes held years of compromise. I hadn't noticed before how heavy her shoulders looked under the weight of holding us both up.

"Pick a snack under two dollars," she said finally. "That's what we've got for treats this week."

I grabbed the box of whales and tossed it into the cart. "They're dry and weird," I muttered.

She pushed the cart forward with a tight smile, and I followed, quiet now, embarrassed, not just by our struggle but by how much I had taken for granted.

My mother was rebuilding from the ground up, one grocery trip, one bill, one breath at a time. She had left a man who broke her, only to find herself responsible for a daughter trying not to fall apart. She had every reason to give up, but she didn't. She loved me fiercely. Quietly. Practically. Her strength didn't roar, it whispered, day after day: *We will make it. Even if it's just with whales instead of Goldfish.*

She became my example of resilience, even when I didn't realize I was watching.

For me, the months that followed were marked by a strange, suspended kind of silence. I was paralyzed by the weight of what was coming, this baby, this new life, this colossal responsibility I hadn't asked for but now had to prepare for. I was still healing from everything I had already endured, but there was no pause, no grace period. My mother reminded me, gently but firmly, that whether I was ready or not, the baby *was* coming. And I had to grow up before adulthood even had a chance to take root.

The farther my belly grew, the smaller our world became. It was just me, the child inside me, and the ghost of the boy I once thought I knew.

Every phone call with Mateo turned into a fight. We weren't even talking; we were sparring. Words became weapons. The issue was never just a missed appointment or a change in plans. It was abandonment, mine, swelling with each OB-GYN visit I sat through alone, watching other couples huddle over ultrasound photos with soft smiles and linked fingers.

One afternoon, after another lonely checkup, a nurse asked if the baby's father was just parking the car. I smiled and said, "He's working," but the lie burned my throat like acid. On the drive home, I called him anyway, still hoping.

"Mateo, you missed another appointment," I said, trying to keep my voice calm.

"It was today?" he asked.

"Yes, it was today. I reminded you."

"Why you always pressin' me? It's just a doctor."

"You're the father. I didn't do this alone."

"Damn, B. I had stuff to do. I don't even got my whip right now."

"You're always disappearing. People look at me like I'm a fool for believing you'll show up."

"Why it always gotta be about your feelings? You don't even ask how I'm doin'. You just call to bitch."

"I needed you for our baby. But you're already gone."

He paused, then muttered, "Maybe I ain't meant to be in this. You always knew who I was."

"No," I said quietly. "You changed. You used to be kind. Smart. Now you're chasing street games."

"You don't get it. You never did."

"You'd rather run with your crew than be a father. That's the truth."

"Don't act like you perfect."

"I never said I was. But at least I'm still me. You? I don't even recognize you anymore. And I hate that I still care."

"Then stop. I don't need you to care."

Click.

The arguments always ended the same way. A sharp goodbye. A silence that screamed. A heaviness I carried to bed.

The love that once floated us down Tampa streets in his mother-of-pearl E70 Corolla had hardened into something jagged. He stopped respecting me. I stopped recognizing myself. And I couldn't tell if I wanted him to come back or just wanted him to hurt as much as I did.

It wasn't just that he left. It was *how and when* he left. When I needed him. When I couldn't even tie my own shoes. When I was crying myself to sleep. When I was begging for any kind of stability. He chose to walk away.

I felt abandoned. Not just by a boy. But by the dream of a family. Some nights, I'd lie awake with my hand on my belly and whisper apologies to the baby inside me.

"I'm sorry your dad isn't here.""I'm scared.""I'm trying. I promise, I'm trying."

How do you grieve an ending while preparing for a beginning? How do you mourn the death of a love while carrying the life it created? I didn't have the answers.

All I had was this baby. Still growing. Still coming. Still waiting for me to be ready. So I did the only thing I could. I decided I would be. No matter what.

Chapter 6

The Lie That Followed Me

In one year, everything flipped. From first love to first heartbreak. From teen dreams to single-mother fears. From innocence to uncertainty.

My future blurred before me. But inside me, the baby kept growing, calm, patient, insistent. As if whispering, *even in the wreckage, something new is still possible.*

Fear gripped me tighter each day. I was barely more than a child, no job, no plan, no road map for raising another human being while still trying to untangle my own pain. While girls my age were picking prom dresses, gossiping about boys, and choosing colleges, I was counting down weeks of pregnancy, researching Medicaid, and wondering how to stretch a box of diapers when the money ran out.

One poor decision didn't just change *my* life. It sent ripples through the people around me: my mother, my friends, and most painfully, the child growing inside me.

The rumors started not long after. And even without social media, they spread like wildfire, through whispers at bus stops, behind lockers, in group chats I was never part of. Somehow, my business traveled across two high schools and landed squarely in the mouths of people who didn't even know me.

By the time I turned sixteen, I wasn't just a pregnant teenager. I was a scandal. The story? That my baby wasn't Mateo's... but Asael's. That lie cut me deeper than most people will ever understand.

It wasn't just gossip; it was a quiet form of violence. A way to erase everything I still held sacred. My dignity. My story. My voice.

People labeled me without blinking:*She's fast.She's dirty.A slut.*

They said these things casually, like I couldn't hear them. Like I wasn't human.

I even began to question myself. I replayed every moment with Asael. The touches. The kisses. The blurred nights. Had we gone further than I remembered? Was it possible I didn't stop it in time?

The truth was this: we went far, but we didn't have sex. We stopped short. I said no, and Asael, whatever else he was, he heard me.

But the lie was louder than the truth. And I didn't have the language or knowledge to defend myself. I didn't understand ovulation or fertility windows, sperm, pre-cum, none of it.

No one ever told me how it really worked. So when that test came back positive, I wasn't just afraid of being a teenage mom; I was ashamed to be a teenage mom.

I remember one teacher whispering to another in the hallway, thinking I couldn't hear her. "She had so much potential. Such a waste."

In school, I was a walking cautionary tale. Some looked at me with pity. Others with disgust. And then there were the ones who just stared. Stared at my belly like it was a confession. Like it was a scarlet letter.

I felt like I was on display all the time, every hallway a runway I didn't choose to walk, every glance a spotlight I couldn't escape.

The worst part? I felt invisible. Unworthy. Like I didn't matter unless I was being judged, blamed, or used. And still, somehow, I stayed with Mateo.

It wasn't love, not anymore. It was the ghost of something that used to be sweet. A thread I kept holding on to, even though it cut my hand every time I tightened my grip.

We still saw each other off and on during the pregnancy. Some days, he was tender. Other days, distant. I tried to read his silence like a language I had forgotten.

Then came Thanksgiving.

I was six months along. My belly was round, undeniable. My back hurt. My ankles were swollen. I was exhausted. When Mateo said he was coming to my Tía's house, I felt the smallest flicker of hope. Maybe this meant he wanted to be involved. Maybe, somehow, we were going to figure it out together.

He showed up with that familiar half-smile, hugging my Tía like everything was normal. I tried to believe it too. But it didn't last.

Later that night, as we sat on the porch, the air thick with silence, I finally asked, "Why did you come?"

He looked at me, confused. "What you mean? It's Thanksgiving."

"No, I mean... why now? You haven't been around."

He rubbed the back of his neck. "I'm here, ain't I?"

I swallowed hard. "Yeah, but only for today. You think that's enough?"

He stared out at the yard. "I didn't ask to be a dad right now, Brandy."

"And you think I did?" I said, louder than I meant to. "You think I wanted any of this?"

He didn't answer. Just got up, muttered something under his breath, and walked back inside.

And that was that. Another holiday, another heartbreak.

After the blowup between Mateo and me, my cousin Cayden pulled me aside behind the garage. The party noise still floated around us, music, laughter, car doors slamming, but in that moment, it all faded beneath the weight of his voice.

"You need to let that dude go," he said, staring at me like he needed me to hear it in my bones. "He's been messing with another girl, I know who she is. You deserve better, B. Get yourself tested, and please, stop giving him chances."

He didn't say it like he was trying to stir drama. He said it like someone who had watched me sink too many times and couldn't stand on the shore anymore. Someone who loved me enough to say the hard thing.

And even with the truth sitting right there in front of me, sharp and undeniable. Still clung to the idea that Mateo and I had something real. I wanted to believe the boy I loved was still somewhere inside that cold, unreachable version of him. I still wanted to believe in us.

When I confronted him, he didn't even try to explain. No denial. No apology. He just looked at me with that same blank expression he'd been wearing for months. Not anger. Not guilt. Just... nothing. And somehow, that hollow look cut deeper than any curse or confession could have.

Christmas still came.

He spent the night with me; his presence was like a ghost of what we used to be. We sat under the soft glow of the tree, opening presents we'd barely wrapped. My mother cooked a full meal like she always did, determined to keep things normal, festive, whole. I smiled for pictures. Laughed at the right moments. But something inside me had already begun to shut down.

That night was the quiet beginning of the end. We didn't fight. We didn't cry. We didn't scream or break things. We just drifted. There were so many things we didn't say. And somehow, that silence spoke louder than all the arguments we'd ever had.

Meanwhile, the pregnancy refused to let me forget what was real.

I threw up almost every day for nine months. That morning sickness didn't fade after the first trimester like the books promised. There was no glowing. Just heaving over toilets, clutching my stomach in grocery store aisles, falling asleep during classes. I was exhausted in every sense, physically, emotionally, spiritually.

I was growing a life while quietly unraveling. I was sixteen. Pregnant. Abandoned. And every kick inside my belly reminded me of what I was about to become, and what I had already lost.

But through it all, I wasn't entirely alone. My mother, despite her own heartbreak, stayed close. She didn't have all the answers, but her presence mattered. And then there were my girls, Amara and Milani, my life preservers, in a season where I felt like I was sinking. They didn't judge me. They didn't vanish when things got hard. They stayed.

They made me laugh when I thought I'd forgotten how. They helped me pick out baby clothes, brought snacks when I couldn't get out of bed, and held me together on the days I felt like I might fall apart.

Amara and I didn't start close. We met during my sophomore year at Leto High. I didn't like her at first, mostly because of the insecurity I carried around my relationship with Mateo. She wore a rainbow skirt that day, paired with a crisp white shirt and white sneakers. I passed her in the hallway between classes, dressed in my usual boyish clothes. We locked eyes for thirty seconds straight. And in that moment, it was obvious, I didn't like her, and she didn't care.

But life has a way of reshaping things. After I left Leto and transferred to a pregnancy school for my junior year, Amara ended up at the same school for her senior year. That's when everything shifted. We started talking more, finding common ground in unexpected places.

Milani had been around since elementary school, but Amara became part of my healing in a way I never saw coming. When I looked at the two of them, I didn't feel like a cautionary tale. I didn't feel like a mistake. I felt human. Seen. Loved.

And maybe that was the most important gift I received that Christmas season, proof that I could still be loved, even in pieces. Even while becoming something I never expected to be at such a young age.

A mother.

Eventually, I had to tell my father. I wasn't afraid of physical retaliation, I was afraid of the disappointment in his voice, the judgment in his eyes. So I told him the truth over the phone:

"Hello?"

"Hey, Daddy, it's me."

"Hey, baby! Man, it's so good to hear your voice."

"It's good to hear yours too... umm, I need to tell you something."

Chuckling, "Oh man, did you rob a bank or something? Are you on the run?"

"No, Daddy, nothing like that." I hesitated, then let it out. "I'm pregnant. I know you're going to be upset, and I'm sorry."

"OOH MAN... OOH wow... OOOHHH shit... OOH okay, baby. No worries, I'm going to help you, don't you worry. OOH man, I can't believe this! Is it a boy or a girl?"

"A boy."

I was completely taken aback. This was not the reaction I expected from the man who once warned, "Don't get pregnant, travel the world, meet people, don't waste your life before it even starts." I braced for judgment, but instead, he gave me grace. He was happy, excited even, and, for a moment, I felt that the hero I once adored still lived inside him.

That moment mattered to me. It showed me that despite everything, my father still loved me. But I couldn't let him all the way in. Not after everything. When my son was born, my mother and Mateo were in the hospital room with me. My father showed up unexpectedly and wanted to be in the delivery room, but I didn't allow it.

I didn't know it at the time, but healing would take far more than one phone call. It would require boundaries. It would require honesty.

And most of all, it would require time, time I hadn't yet learned how to give myself.

Mateo was in the delivery room when Amadeus was born. He signed the birth certificate without hesitation, no questions asked. That moment gave me hope. It felt like confirmation that, despite all our drama, he believed this was his son. That he was choosing to be a part of his life. Of our lives.

He stayed the first night with me, mostly because Amadeus had to be placed in an incubator to regulate his body temperature. He was so tiny, the newborn clothes we brought hung off his little frame. He couldn't stay with me in the hospital room, only the nursery. I could only visit him in moments, for feedings or brief touches. I would sit there, staring at him through the glass, marveling at this small, fragile being. A miracle. A new beginning.

But even as I held that miracle, the cracks in my heart deepened.

The very next night, Mateo left. His cousin, the same one who had pulled him into gang life, came to pick him up. Later, through a friend, I found out they had gone to a club. She said she saw Mateo there, drinking and laughing, surrounded by other women. That truth sliced through whatever illusion I had left. I had just brought a child into this world, and he was already out chasing the same reckless life that had taken him from me the first time.

And yet, he returned.

The night Amadeus and I were discharged from the hospital, Mateo showed up unexpectedly. He stayed with us for a few days, and I allowed myself to hope. He told me he'd moved out of the house where he lived with his gang friends, saying there had been issues and that he was back with his mother and stepbrother. Part of me clung to his words, hungry for stability, for a version of him that would stay this time.

I thought maybe this could be our reset. Our second chance.

But within the first month of Amadeus's life, rumors began to surface. Whispers that turned into loud truths. Word on the street was that Mateo had a new girlfriend, Zara. A known "Queen" in the Latin Kings, the female counterpart to his gang. It didn't take long before I confronted him about it.

This time, he didn't lie. He didn't dodge. He just looked at me and admitted it.

"Yes," he said. "I'm with someone else. Her name's Zara."

Just like that, our fragile reunion shattered. The dream I had of our little family, gone. My heart broke all over again, but this time, it wasn't just for me. It was for the baby sleeping beside me, too small to understand the fracture already forming in his world.

***

About six months after I gave birth to my son, Amadeus, I was sitting at my girlfriend's house getting my hair braided when she casually dropped a bomb that shattered any last hope I had for reconciliation with Mateo.

"Zara's pregnant," she said without warning. "With Mateo's baby."

The room faded around me. Everything went still.

Whatever lingering hope I had that Mateo and I might eventually find our way back to each other disappeared in an instant. A hollow silence wrapped around me, and I felt my heart cave in. It was the kind of heartbreak that didn't cause you to cry, it just left you frozen.

What followed was a spiral into a depression I didn't even recognize at the time. I carried so much shame, the belief of being unworthy, of being not enough, of being permanently broken. It wasn't just my parents I feared now. It was everyone. The judgment, the whispers, the pointed fingers, they drove me inward. I numbed myself with distractions, but my anger only grew, boiling over into bad decisions. My identity became a pile of mistakes I couldn't seem to stop making, each one cutting deeper than the last.

When Zara's pregnancy became public, my mother insisted we file for child support. She didn't know that Mateo had started voicing doubts, planted and nurtured by Zara, that Amadeus wasn't even his. And once the legal paperwork was filed, the harassment began.

Zara weaponized his uncertainty, twisting rumors and building lies that turned others against me. Threatening phone calls became common. Verbal attacks came from every angle. Arguments with Zara drained whatever strength I had left. Even though Mateo never requested a DNA test, something he was legally entitled to, something he could've done for free, he had signed the birth certificate after the delivery and after I filed the paperwork, started paying child support without protest.

Still, I knew I had to protect my son. I made the painful decision to stop visitation. He'd started coming home upset, telling me things no child should have to say, about being mistreated, about not wanting to go back. I listened. I believed him. I couldn't let him suffer just to maintain an illusion of shared parenting.

But cutting off Mateo didn't mean things changed for the better.

Zara took control of everything. She acted as if she were Amadeus's mother, stepping in as gatekeeper between Mateo and me. She made sure we had no contact, no phone calls, no in-person talks, nothing. Mateo wasn't allowed to come to my house, wasn't present at doctor's appointments, and when I dropped off my son, it wasn't even Mateo who came to the door, it was Zara.

She showed up everywhere, inserting herself into spaces that weren't hers. She even arrived at one of Amadeus's ER visits after he got RSV. Mateo wasn't allowed to come. Instead, Zara stood there, her once-dark hair now dyed the same red as mine, her clothes eerily similar to mine, gold jewelry sparkling under the hospital lights. It was like watching someone morph into a distorted version of me while trying to erase me altogether.

And she wasn't acting alone.

Her crew, gang members, friends, and Mateo's cousin, all joined the campaign of harassment. They loitered near my home on Emma Street. They robbed us multiple times. We were never home when it happened, but the violation was unmistakable. It wasn't just the loss of belongings, it was the loss of safety, of security, of peace.

Then came the visits from the Department of Children & Families. Accusations poured in, fabricated complaints.

"You're not keeping Amadeus clean.""You're not feeding him.""Your home is a mess."

Every time they showed up, my heart dropped into my stomach. There was never any proof. But the fact that someone thought me unfit, that strangers could question my love and care for my son, was soul-crushing.

Through it all, Amadeus was my anchor. The one thing that made sense. The one thing I never doubted. But even that bond was tested.

One evening, after a visit with Mateo, Amadeus came home with his beautiful black curls hacked off. His scalp was covered in scabs. The haircut was so close, so rough, that it physically hurt him. I was livid. Mateo had been there. I rushed to confront him outside of Zara's mother's house, and we had a screaming match in the street.

A few days later, DCF showed up again, this time accusing me of neglect for injuries I hadn't caused. It felt like I was on trial every day. The world had already decided I was guilty, guilty of being young, of being a mother, of making mistakes. No matter what I did, I couldn't prove my worth. I was just trying to survive the war zone that had become my life.

So what does a teenage girl do when the world becomes too much? She looks for another escape.

Chapter 7

Circle of Friends

That's when Wes came into my life, a male I could genuinely call a friend.

We met most unexpectedly: through a mutual friend who had set me up on a blind date to help me get over Mateo. We were all at AMC 24, and my friend was convinced the guy would be perfect for me. He wasn't. The date was a disaster; the guy was awkward and weird, and I never saw him again. But Wes? He left an impression.

There was something about his presence; his ambitions were a stark difference from the drama of my life. And I needed that.

Wes was talented and driven, with dreams bigger than most people dared to admit. He rapped with ease, freestyling like it was second nature. His lyrics were sharp, raw, and real. He believed in me in a way I hadn't experienced before. He'd read my journal scribbles and say, "You've got something...put it to a beat." He wanted me to find my voice in music. But while Wes could ride a rhythm effortlessly, I was still trying to find my rhythm in life. Still, he never made me feel small for it. His belief in me felt like an anchor, steady, unwavering.

Wes had two best friends who used the nicknames Knox and Benny. Together, they were less like a group of friends and more like a pack. Each had a distinct energy, yet their bond ran deep. Of the three, Wes was the most grounded, focused on his goals, and less caught up in the recklessness that defined the other two. His steadiness felt like a safe harbor compared to the unpredictable chaos that followed Knox.

The day I met Knox, I understood why Wes called him "a lot." He barged into my mother's house, needing to hide his uncle's car from the police. The energy he brought was hostile and thick, like he owned the space. I caught an attitude immediately. Who did this stranger think he was? Wes calmed me down and explained that Knox had already lived through more than most adults. At just 16, he was expelled from school, barely attending his alternative program, and lived with no curfew or restrictions. That kind of freedom had hardened him fast.

Knox stood about 6'2", Puerto Rican-Dominican, with a thick, imposing build. Scars and tattoos told stories he didn't have to say out loud. He was a contradiction: young, but war-worn. In the streets, his name held weight. He was known for throwing hands and, when necessary, pulling triggers.

Then there was Benny, the complete opposite. Lighthearted, jokey, with a pretty-boy look that didn't match the pain he kept hidden.

His Cuban heritage wasn't obvious; he could pass for white, especially when the sun turned his face tomato red. Benny wasn't confrontational. He used humor to sidestep the heaviness all around us, which made him the comic relief in their trio.

Wes, though? He was the bridge between the two. Dominican, about six feet tall, heavyset, and always thinking. While he didn't engage in the violence Knox seemed to thrive in, he wasn't without his own battles, especially with anger. He wasn't a fighter, but when provoked, there was a storm inside him. What made him different was how he handled it. He read. He studied. He fed his mind instead of his fists. Wes channeled his rage into learning, always searching for something more.

Their bond was forged in struggle. Broken homes, absent fathers, fractured families, they carried that weight together. Wes had never known his dad, raised instead by his mother and grandparents. Knox was raised by a step-grandfather, his siblings scattered across Puerto Rico, the mainland U.S., and the Dominican Republic. Benny had his mother and two sisters. But when they were together, none of that mattered. Hanging out at Knox's grandfather's house, smoking weed, cracking jokes, it was their escape. Their version of peace.

Knox had more street smarts than Wes and Benny combined, and even the glimpses I caught of his darker side were more than enough. Wes warned me about him constantly, especially when I was first getting to know him. He'd share stories of Knox and his crew hitting major licks, robberies I wanted no part of. Wes had endless tales: Knox and his older brother taking down bouncers at clubs with a single punch, reassembling firearms in seconds. By the time I met Knox, he was already a legend in our circle.

At just fifteen, Knox had survived a shootout. He took multiple bullets to the leg, requiring rods and screws to keep it together. Some bullets were never removed, silent reminders of his battles. Even at eight, he had shot himself in the hand with a gun he found lying around the house. He bore war wounds before he even became a man, and fear of gun violence never followed him.

Wes never shared all the details; street code was sacred, but he told me just enough to understand that Knox wasn't like everyone else. He wasn't just a kid from the neighborhood; he was the type of figure you'd see in a gangster film or hear about in a rap verse. Before his uncle got sentenced to multiple life terms, Knox had already been helping him run "Diesel" (slang for heroin), learning the trade in real time.

He moved through the world with intensity, always on edge, always scanning the room. His instincts were a blend of paranoia and precision. He didn't just command respect; he demanded it through intimidation. Desperation and ambition drove his every move. His world was cutthroat, taking territory, making fast money, and eliminating threats without hesitation. Planning didn't exist; he lived moment to moment, willing to win by any means necessary.

One night, I went to a birthday party, nothing major, just an acquaintance's place. I noticed a guy there who had a reputation in the streets as a "snitch." Moments later, I heard someone say Knox's name outside. He burst through the door with two other guys, guns drawn, masks on. They grabbed the boy and dragged him out. No one moved. No one said a word. Knox was known, and in our world, you didn't get in his way.

Outside of their violent side, I saw the other side of them. We hung out at parks, the AMC 24 theater, and mostly at Knox's grandfather's house. That was our hub. We'd relax, smoke weed, escape our individual storms, mine being teen motherhood, theirs being the streets. His grandfather never minded, as long as we kept it quiet.

Knox had access to cars before any of us, thanks to his uncle. We'd ride around town, joyriding, feeling invincible. But during those drives, I started to see how complicated my relationship with these boys really was. I had friend-zoned all of them, but I could feel the tension; that's not what they wanted. Knox didn't believe in being "just friends" with girls. His trust issues ran deep, and his degrading comments about women often sparked arguments between us. It was a clear reflection of how warped my own views on relationships had become.

The scars from my father's abuse and Mateo's abandonment ran deep, and I carried them into every interaction with men. I was angry. I was wounded. And I was desperate for attention, for affection, for someone to see me and stay. I had my "boyz," but what I truly longed for was an emotional anchor, someone to lean on when the weight of my world became too much.

That desperation led me into dangerous emotional territory. I was surrounded by people, yet profoundly alone.

***

I was seventeen, entering my senior year of high school, already carrying the baggage of a lifetime. I was still searching for something solid to hold onto, still hoping someone would stay and not turn away.

One particular night is burned into my memory, no matter how much I try to forget it.

It began innocently enough, at the movies with Wes and two of my girlfriends. We were laughing, enjoying ourselves, escaping the pressures of life for a couple of hours in the comfort of a dark theater. But toward the end of the film, I slipped away to the bathroom.

As I stepped back into the hallway, I spotted Umar, a known leader in the Latin Kings, the same gang Mateo had once been tangled up in, and beside him, KiKo, the father of my friend Amara's baby. They both recognized me immediately and came over. Umar started talking, then flirting. It felt casual, almost harmless, he invited me to a party he was heading to.

That invite lit up something inside me. For so long, I'd been on the outside looking in, branded by rumors and judged by my past. Now here I was, with someone like Umar giving me attention. It felt like an opportunity to flip the script. Maybe if I went, the whispers would stop. Maybe I'd finally be accepted.

Sure, the thought of being the only girl with two guys crossed my mind. But I didn't dwell on it. I just wanted to belong. They said they needed a ride, and I offered mine, my dusty '95 Toyota Tercel, without hesitation. I didn't stop to think twice.

Back inside the theater, I slid into my seat next to Wes. "I'm gonna head out," I whispered.

He turned to me, confused. "With who? Aren't you gonna finish the movie?"

I shrugged, trying to sound casual. "I'll catch the rest when it comes out on DVD."

His eyes said more than his words ever could, concern, maybe even hurt, but I didn't have time for guilt. My two girlfriends leaned in, listening now. I gave them a quick explanation: Wes would take them home. I'd fill them in later. They weren't thrilled, but we were mid-movie, and there wasn't space for an argument. As I stood up to leave, one of them followed me into the lobby.

"Wait, seriously? You're just leaving?"

"Yeah," I said, trying to brush it off. "Look, we've been hanging out all day, and this is a big deal for me. Wes is cool with taking y'all home."

She gave me a half-smile, half-sigh, then softened. "Alright. Just call me when you get there, okay?"

"Promise." I hugged her quickly, then turned toward the exit, my keys already in hand.

I walked out of that theater buzzing, excited, reckless, and naïve. I told myself this was a night to remember.

And it was. Just not in the way I imagined.

Chapter 8

The Night I Lost Myself

U mar had always been one of those guys who didn't need to talk tough, his presence did all the work. He was popular, attractive, and intimidating. People respected him out of fear. I'd seen him in fights before. He wasn't the kind of person who talked things through, he acted. And things around him always escalated fast.

"I'm glad you decided to come and drive us over this way. I know it's far from your side," Umar said, giving me a quick glance.

"Yeah, I'm glad to be invited to the party," I replied, trying to play it cool.

"Tonight is gonna be dope!" he said, clapping his hands and turning toward Kiko, who was scrolling through his phone.

"I know you Mateo baby moms and all," Umar leaned in toward me, his voice low and reassuring, "but don't worry about him showing up and causing problems, aight?"

"Cool. I did have that thought," I admitted. "Other people will be coming, right?"

"Yeah, it's a party. We finna have it all. Look, just relax, we got drinks, we got smoke, we got pills. Whatever you need, shorty."

When we pulled up to the apartment, I expected music, laughter, and people. Instead, there were just two guys inside, strangers. They nodded when we came in, already drinking, already loud.

They said more people were coming.

One of them handed me a red cup. Goldschläger. I wasn't really into hard liquor, but I took a few sips. It burned on the way down, but I laughed like it didn't.

My phone rang. I stepped into the bathroom to take the call, it was my girlfriend. Just checking in.

"Yeah, not many people here yet," I said, glancing at my reflection. "I might head out soon..." The screen went black.

Dead battery.

I remember coming back out, asking to borrow a charger. Nobody had one. I sat back down next to Umar. Kiko was in the kitchen mixing drinks. The other two were still talking, still laughing. I finished the drink.

And then everything started to blur.

My body felt heavy. My eyelids, slow. The voices around me grew louder, but also farther away. Like I was slipping underwater.

I tried to stand. Tried to say something. But my mouth didn't work the way it was supposed to. My legs didn't either.

Then someone was leading me, guiding me down a hallway. I couldn't remember who. The world spun. After that, everything broke into pieces.

I drifted in and out of consciousness. I remember the weight of him on top of me. I remember trying to scream, and my mouth not working. I remember the feeling of being paralyzed, helpless. When I finally came to, I was in a dark room, my clothes torn, my body aching.

The door opened. A shadow stood there. I screamed, cried, begged for help, but the figure just muttered cruel things and walked away. I crawled to the bathroom, collapsed, and vomited on myself. I couldn't move. I couldn't breathe. I just lay there.

The pain between my legs. The blood on my underwear. I knew.

Kiko eventually came in and tried to help. He gave me water, wiped the vomit, and whispered that I needed to leave. But another man stormed in and screamed at him to get out.

Later, a stranger, the one I didn't recognize, opened the bathroom door, started masturbating, and ejaculated on me.

When the house finally quieted, I pulled myself together, searching for my phone and keys. The party had never existed. No one else ever came. I found Kiko asleep and gently woke him. He helped me gather my things. My keys had been in Umar's pocket.

I left that apartment feeling like I had been buried alive. I had taken drugs before, but nothing had ever made me feel so weak, so lost, so destroyed. Whatever was in *that* drink had rendered me defenseless in the worst way imaginable.

In the aftermath of the assault, I felt like I was floating in a fog, utterly alone. I couldn't bring myself to tell anyone the full story. And before I even had the chance, the rumor mill kicked into overdrive.

The story that spread wasn't about a girl who'd been drugged and violated. It was about a girl who "let it happen." Who "got passed around." Who "deserved it." My past mistakes had already bruised my reputation, so when this new story hit the streets, people were more willing to believe the worst. It was easier to accept the lie than to face the ugly truth.

The shame was suffocating. It piled on top of every wound I had carried up to that point. I didn't go to the hospital, because I was underage and didn't want them to call my mother. I couldn't bear to break her heart. And I didn't go to the police, because I was scared. Scared that Zara and the gang-connected girls who already harassed me would make my life even more unbearable if word got back that I'd talked.

Wes and Knox heard about it, like everyone else. But neither of them said a word to me, not even to check if I was okay. I hadn't expected much from Knox, but I thought maybe, just maybe, he'd grown up enough to see me as more than just "the girl who tagged along." I was wrong.

But Wes? That one broke something in me.

I found out he and Knox went to a party the next week, one where Umar and his boys were laughing it up like nothing had happened. Wes said nothing. Did nothing. So I confronted him.

"Wes, I know you've heard what people are saying about me," I said, my voice trembling. "Not once have you called. Not once have you asked if I'm okay. Why?"

He looked at me like I was inconveniencing him. "Come on, B. You left us at the movies that night. I told you not to go. I heard the rumors, yeah, but I wasn't there. I don't know what happened."

"That's exactly it," I said, fighting back tears. "You didn't ask. You didn't care enough to find out?"

He shrugged. "It's not my place to pick sides over something I didn't see."

"I was assaulted, Wes," I snapped. "I was drugged. And then you go to a party with the same people who did it to me?"

He held up a hand. "These are people I've known for years. And from what I heard... it wasn't like that. People are saying you let them run a train on you. I wasn't there. I don't know what's true and what's not."

I stared at him, stunned. "You think I *let* that happen?"

"I'm saying I don't know what happened," he said, shifting on his feet. "You want me to burn bridges with people I've known my whole life, and for what? A story I wasn't there to witness?"

I shook my head, feeling like the floor had fallen out beneath me. "I didn't need you to fight anyone. I just needed you to believe me. To care. To not stand next to people who hurt me like I asked for it."

He looked at me with something between pity and frustration. "I'm sorry you went through that. I really am. But... you kind of brought this on yourself."

And there it was.

That sentence hit harder than any punch. I walked away from him that day with a new wound. Deeper than all the rest. Because that was the day I realized even the people closest to me could become complicit in my pain, not by their actions, but by their silence.

Hearing Wes say those words felt like a punch straight to the gut. It confirmed what inner voice had already been whispering to me: *You deserved this.* I replayed the choices I made, leaving the theater, going to that apartment, and a part of me couldn't help but wonder if he was right. Wes had warned me not to go. He had tried to talk me out of it. But still... I didn't need him to fight my battles. I just needed him not to stand beside the people tearing me down.

I didn't know what had gone down at that party he went to, but I knew he hadn't defended me. Maybe it was selfish to expect him to take a stand. Or maybe it was selfish of *him* not to. How could he stay neutral when someone he called a friend was being dragged through the mud, especially over something so violent, so violating? Was he ashamed of me, too?

I couldn't wrap my head around it. Friends are supposed to be there when things fall apart. But Wes didn't even call. I had to reach out *first*, after hearing what he did. This wasn't a misunderstanding. It wasn't gossip. This was a violent act against my body, and Wes's silence felt like a betrayal.

Everything around me was unraveling, and I was unraveling with it. Every choice I made seemed to drag me deeper into the mess, and I didn't know how to climb out. I didn't even try to reach out to Knox. If Wes couldn't show up for me, I knew Knox would be even colder. So I let them both go.

I wasn't asking them to pick fights for me. I just wanted them to respect me, *to respect women*. Rape isn't just a physical act; it strips you of safety, autonomy, and dignity. And now, the people I had called friends were treating my trauma like a rumor or a joke.

Maybe I was wrong about them. Maybe I was wrong about myself.

But even in all that darkness, one person remained constant, Amara. She was my one light, the one person who never turned her back on me. We had known each other since the early days of our pregnancies, but our bond had grown into something rare. Unlike the others, Amara didn't live the street life. She didn't carry herself with hard edges or put up fronts. She was honest, stable, grounded, and I looked up to her more than she knew.

Amara never judged me. She kept it real, always. And when everything else felt fake or broken, she was my anchor. What I didn't fully understand then was that she had her own storm brewing beneath the surface.

Years later, she said something to me I've never forgotten.

"It's amazing how God works," she told me one quiet afternoon. "He plants a seed in your life when you're young and lost, because He knows the future. He knew I needed my best friend. And my best friend needed me."

And she was right.

Her life hadn't been easy either. She lost her dad when she was twelve. Her mom spiraled into alcoholism, and by thirteen, Amara was so deep in pain she attempted suicide. She survived, but the numbness lingered. Like me, she got caught up with the wrong people and was searching for comfort in all the wrong places.

Still, she kept going. She had her first daughter at seventeen, her second at nineteen, and her third at twenty-one. My son was born in December. Her daughter came in February. And just like that, our kids grew up side by side, the way we did.

In a world where so much felt fake, Amara was, and still is, the realist thing I had.

When the assault became public and the story twisted into something grotesque and unrecognizable, I was terrified of losing the one stable friendship I had left. I knew Amara wouldn't judge me, not in the way others did, but I also knew she was a mother now. A woman protecting her peace. I feared she wouldn't want to associate with a girl rumored to be "letting guys run a train on her," especially if one of those guys was her baby's father.

Not long after my confrontation with Wes, Amara called me. Her voice was calm, but I could hear the concern underneath. "Hey, B," she said gently. "How are you? I heard something... and I wanted to talk to you directly."

Tears instantly welled in my eyes. The weight of everything, the rumors, the shame, the isolation, crashed down on me. "Hey, Amara... I'm hurting," I whispered. "I don't know what you've heard, but... It's tearing me apart."

There was a brief pause. Then she spoke, her tone still calm but laced with urgency.

"The rumor is that you got gangbanged... and that Kiko was there. I need to know what happened between you and him, B."

I broke. The sobs came fast, my voice crumbling under the weight of the truth.

"No, Amara. That's not what happened. I swear to you, me and him didn't do anything. He was there, yes, but... I was drugged. I was raped. And now, everyone thinks I wanted it. That I asked for it. But it's not true. I didn't ask for any of this..."

Her silence stretched, and my heart pounded. I could feel her processing. "I spoke to him," she said finally. "We're not exactly good right now, but I had to ask him. He gave me the same story you just did. Said he didn't touch you. But, B... people are talking. What's being said is nasty, and I need to be sure."

"I understand," I said, voice shaking. "But I need you to know, I didn't go there thinking that would happen. I saw them at the movies, and they invited me to a party. I just wanted to be included. I thought more people would be there. I didn't know. I didn't think."

I paused, my mind struggling through the fog of that night. "He actually helped me, Amara. When things got bad, he helped me get my keys and leave. It was... It was Umar and one of the others. They..." My voice trailed off, swallowed by grief.

Amara sighed. Not in frustration, but in that way you do when your heart hurts for someone you love. "I believe you," she said softly. "But B, you've gotta make better choices. You can't put yourself in situations like that. You should've left the second you saw there were no other girls. And never take drinks from people you don't really know. You've got to protect yourself."

Her words were a mix of love and accountability, and I appreciated both. They were hard to hear, but they were real. "You believe me?" I asked, barely above a whisper. "I thought... I thought you might turn your back on me."

"No," she said. "I'm still here. But I need time to think. You've got to promise me you'll start taking care of yourself. And please, go to the doctor. Make sure you're okay."

Despite her encouragement, I never went. I didn't go to the hospital. I didn't talk to the police. I buried it instead, let the shame eat away at me in silence. I told myself it was a one-time mistake. That it happened because of all my other bad choices. That I put myself in that position, so maybe I had it coming.

But when I started hearing other stories, other girls, same setup, same apartment, same name, I cracked all over again. I realized my silence hadn't protected me. It had protected them. And maybe, just maybe, it allowed them to do it again.

That thought haunted me.

The guilt of what I didn't say, what I didn't do, settled in my chest like a stone. I had been so afraid of what others would say that I forgot about what could happen to the next girl.

And that, more than anything, became the hardest thing to live with.

The fallout with Wes hit me harder than I expected. It wasn't just about the night I needed him, it was the deeper truth it exposed: the men I thought I could lean on, even someone as close as Wes, wouldn't stand by me when I needed them most. The loneliness that followed was suffocating.

It took months before we spoke again. We ended up reconnecting by chance at a birthday party. Neither of us expected to see the other, and the surprise threw us both. Small talk turned into a longer conversation, and somehow, that led to us texting again. Letting Wes back in wasn't easy. It felt fragile, like walking on cracked ice, but it was something familiar, and I missed the comfort of familiarity.

Not long after, I ran into Knox, though I hadn't planned on it. Wes and I had made loose plans to grab food, but he texted last-minute asking if I could meet him at Knox's grandfather's place instead. I paused before responding. Wes knew I wasn't ready to see Knox. I hadn't even fully forgiven him for what he didn't do, let alone process what his silence meant. Still, I went.

As I pulled up, I sat in the car for a moment, debating whether to stay. I called Wes to let him know I was outside. A few minutes later, I saw him walking out, and just behind him, there was Knox. I froze.

My gut instinct was to drive off, but I stayed, tightening my grip on the steering wheel. Music up. Doors locked. Eyes on my phone.

Then, *tap tap*. I jumped. Knox stood at my window. I didn't move at first. Then I glanced at Wes, who stood a few feet away, hands raised in a helpless gesture, like, *I didn't plan this*. I sighed and cracked the window.

"Long time no see, B," Knox said casually. "What, you don't wanna talk to me?"

I stared. "Not really."

He smirked, as if that didn't sting. "What's with the cold shoulder? I haven't seen you in months."

I blinked slowly. *Was he actually serious?*

"This isn't the time for that conversation," I said. "I'm just here to talk to Wes."

"Aight, B," he said, stepping back. "If that's the energy you're on, I'll fall back."

I rolled the window up without another word.

Wes and Knox exchanged a dap before Wes walked toward his car. I pulled up beside him. He rolled down his window, looking genuinely sorry. "I didn't know Knox was coming outside," he said. "I'm sorry. I wouldn't have asked you to come if I had known."

I nodded, not ready to unpack my anger. I followed him to one of our old spots, a steakhouse we used to love back when life was simpler.

We ate, we laughed a little, we talked. And when it was done, I told him it was nice catching up, then drove straight to Amara's. She had been watching my son and her daughter while I was out. I had already told her I was going to see Wes and promised to fill her in afterward.

Amara never hid her feelings about Wes. She saw him for what he really was, an inconsistent friend, someone who only showed up when it was easy. "That boy ain't loyal to anyone but himself," she'd remind me constantly. And deep down, I knew she wasn't wrong. Wes represented a life I couldn't quite let go of, chaotic, uncertain, but full of fire and familiarity. Amara, on the other hand, was my tether to something real. Something stable.

The tension between them was always thick. They didn't hide their distaste for each other, and each tried, in their own way, to pull me in different directions. One part of me longed for the hustle Wes brought, the danger, the excitement, the old me. But another part of me craved what Amara offered: peace, truth, growth.

Being in the middle of that tug-of-war left me exhausted.

Chapter 9

Fast Money Slow Death

Milani came back into my life at a time when I didn't realize how much her presence and her choices would shape mine. Venezuelan, with wild curls that bounced like they had their own soundtrack, she had that effortless kind of beauty you couldn't fake. Boys wanted her. Girls wanted to be her. But the thing about Milani was that she didn't seem to care about the attention; it was just part of the background noise in her life. What really set her apart was her loyalty.

We were just two girls in matching private school uniforms, whispering about crushes and swapping snacks at lunch. We drifted when we went to different high schools, but senior year brought us back together. And when it did, it was like the space between us never existed.

Her world and mine were built differently. Her mom, a strict, churchgoing woman, kept a close eye on her, steering her toward a "good girl" life. But we didn't need my living room to keep our friendship alive. We had Bush Gardens, mall food courts, and late-night phone calls. We had each other.

And Milani had a way of moving through the world that fascinated me. She didn't wait for permission. She made her own choices, her own money, her own rules. I didn't know it yet, but that independence, the way she seemed to call her own shots, would stay in the back of my mind. Later, when I was desperate and backed into a corner, I would think about Milani. About how she managed to get what she wanted without asking anyone for it.

For now, though, she was just my friend. My safe place. The one who didn't flinch when things got messy.

High school was brutal. Every day I walked through those doors, I braced myself for war. I had enemies: girls who hated me, spread rumors, whispered as I passed, and smiled in my face only to throw daggers behind my back. It felt like they lived for my misery. I carried the weight of every rumor, every sideways glance, every lie told about me. Most days, I showed up ready to fight. Not always physically, but emotionally, mentally, I was always on guard.

Despite the living hell that school was, I refused to give up on graduating. I had to go harder than most, day classes, night school, summer school. I pieced my credits together like a broken puzzle. But I did it. I walked across that stage with my class, wearing my cap and gown with pride and clutching a diploma that didn't just belong to me; it belonged to Amadeus. He was the reason I kept going when everything told me to quit.

My mother carried the weight of our survival. She worked as a supervisor at a market research firm, bringing in just enough to keep us afloat. She never relied on food stamps or WIC, no matter how much we needed them. Her pride wouldn't allow it. To her, government aid meant surrendering control, letting strangers into our business. And control was something she clung to fiercely, especially after everything we'd escaped.

That season of my life was a whirlwind, equal parts betrayal and love, regret and grit. But I had anchors. Amara, with her grounded wisdom. Milani, with her unwavering presence. They helped me hold on to the parts of myself that were still whole, even when I felt like I was falling apart.

At the time, I started dating a guy who had been pretty popular in high school. My mother didn't like him from the jump. She didn't even want him in her house. That led to arguments between us, over and over again. More often than not, I disobeyed her. I let him come over anyway, sometimes even sneaking him in to spend the night. Milani never liked him either. She could see through him in ways I couldn't, or maybe just didn't want to. Our relationship was on and off throughout my senior year, a toxic cycle that kept tightening its grip. Toward the end, the mask came off. He was cheating openly, flirting with other girls right in front of me at school, treating me with a level of disrespect so loud, it echoed.

Then came the abuse.

At first, it was subtle, pushing me during arguments, stonewalling me with silence, making me question my worth. Then it escalated.

The last time we were together, I finally reached my breaking point. I had packed up all of his belongings he'd left at my mom's house and was giving him a ride to his aunt's place. On the way, we got into a heated argument. He struck the back of my head while I was driving. Then, in a chaotic moment, he tried to jump out of the moving car.

I pulled over at Fadeos Bakery, heart racing, hands shaking. As soon as I stepped out, he came at me and shoved me to the ground. My body hit the concrete hard.

The people inside the bakery saw it all. They rushed out, yelling at him to get away from me and called the police. He took off before they arrived. I sat inside, trembling, but not surprised. I had seen this scene before. I had lived this scene before.

When the police showed up, I did what I'd learned from watching my mother: I didn't press charges. I didn't want to call her. I already knew what she'd say. She had warned me about him from the start, and I hadn't listened. But at that moment, I needed her. I needed the comfort only a mother can give.

She showed up at the bakery shortly after the police arrived, her face a storm of anger and concern. She was furious that he had laid hands on me, but deep down, I knew she was relieved I had called. Even through her frustration, she stood by me, like she always did when my world was falling apart. She took me home that evening. However, later that same week, she found me in the bathroom going through it.

"Ma, sutin's wrong with me," I said, tears spilling down my face, nerves making my hands tremble.

"Brandy, what is it?"

"I can't keep anything down. I keep throwing up everything. I feel so weak..." I groaned, the nausea twisting through my gut.

"Have you had your period this month?" she asked sharply, her instincts already kicking in.

I paused, trying to remember. "I think I have..." I scratched my head, unsure.

"Were you having unprotected sex with... I don't even want to say his name." Her voice cracked, fury rising again.

"Ma, come on, do I really need to say it?"

"Brandy Nichole." She wasn't in the mood for games. I knew that tone, knew what it meant when she called me by my full name.

My eyes dropped to the floor. "Yes, I did."

"Come on," she said, her tone urgent now. "We're going to the store. Get Amadeus ready, now. We need to get a pregnancy test."

I found out I was pregnant with his child. My mother drove me to the clinic. I had my first abortion. But it came with complications, excessive bleeding, pain that made my entire body feel like it was screaming at me. Something wasn't right. My mother could see it, too.

A few days later, she took me back to the clinic. That's when they told me the procedure hadn't been completed properly.

They had to do it again.

Beneath all of the pain, a quiet strength was forming. I couldn't see it clearly then, but it was there, growing in the cracks. I had been beaten down, humiliated, pushed to the edge. But I was still standing. And somewhere deep inside, a voice had started to whisper: *You will not be defined by your damage. You will survive this.*

Even with the turmoil swirling around me, I knew I had to keep going. My son depended on me, and I couldn't let my despair swallow us both. Each day was a battle, against exhaustion, against the version of myself that wanted to give up. But deep down, I clung to the hope that one day, I would emerge stronger. I had to. My son deserved a version of me that was steady, dependable, and whole, even if I didn't feel like any of those things yet.

After graduating from high school, I jumped straight into employee mode. I took a job at my mom's market research company. It wasn't glamorous, but it was something steady, and we needed the income. During the day, I stayed home with my son while my mom worked. Then at night, we switched, she would watch him while I was at work.

My job was to cold-call people, trying to qualify them for marketing surveys. It was a rotating mix of dull scripts, topics like fast food chains, insurance providers, liquor brands, even toilet paper preferences. I was tired, emotionally drained, and the work was monotonous. But I kept my head down and did it for a full year. I was quiet. Focused. Just surviving.

Around that time, Milani's life took a sharp turn, and it shook me. She started dancing at a bikini bar. When she first told me, my stomach sank. I was angry, at the world, at her choices, and at the distance that was growing between us. I tried to talk her out of it. Pleaded with her to reconsider. But Milani had made up her mind. The girl I had once walked home from school with, the one who cried with me when I found out I was pregnant, was now slipping into a world I didn't understand and couldn't follow her into.

Still, I couldn't cut her off. I owed her too much. She had stood by me when others left, and loyalty like that doesn't just vanish. But we started drifting. The phone calls got shorter. The visits became rare. It was like we were speaking different languages now.

Then she started dating a guy we used to crush on back in middle school, the popular one from the skating rink. He was good-looking, charismatic, and connected to that world in ways we used to joke about but never take seriously. His sister was already deep in the exotic dance circuit, and before long, Milani and her were taking trips to Miami. It stopped being about just making money. It became about fast living, status, danger, escape. I started hearing rumors about drugs, about pimps. The line between dancer and exploited woman was beginning to blur, and I didn't know how to help her without pushing her further away.

When she came back to Tampa and needed a place to stay, I let her crash in my room. I didn't think twice. Part of me just wanted to feel close to the Milani I used to know, the girl who once slept over at my place and stayed up with me talking about our dreams. Having her back, even temporarily, was a comfort I didn't realize I'd missed so much.

She brought her world with her, thick stacks of cash that didn't even look real to me. She'd sprawl across my bed, recounting wild nights, her eyes bright with the thrill of it all. Miami clubs. Celebrities. Drug dealers. Penthouses. But behind the glitter in her stories, I saw the wear in her eyes. Her spirit, once so soft and sweet, now had sharp edges. I could hear the fatigue in her laugh, the hollowness between the excitement.

Milani didn't see it yet, but I did, this life was eating away at her. And I didn't know how to pull her back from something that seemed to be giving her power, attention, and control.

While Milani was caught up in her world, everyone around me was hustling, grinding, scheming, trying to carve out their own piece of the American Pie. It wasn't about dreams anymore. It was about money. Power. Respect. Knox, with his deep family ties to the New York drug trade, quickly positioned himself as a street mentor to Wes and Benny. He had the experience, and they had the ambition. Together, they formed a dangerous alliance, and it didn't take long before Knox and Benny launched their own weed operation.

Back then, weed wasn't legal or easily accessible. If you wanted it, you had to know where to go, and that place was always the Trap House. Tucked deep in the projects, the Trap was infamous. If you were looking for anything, weed, pills, coke, that's where you went. But the risk? Sky-high. When the projects got "hot" with cops swarming, the whole operation would shut down in an instant, leaving dealers scrambling and buyers desperate. It was a risky game, but it was also necessary. That edge of unpredictability? It was the cost of staying in the game.

Knox was always watching for the next move. He got connected with a reliable supplier and convinced Benny to pool their money for a pound of weed. It was small compared to what would come later, but it was a start. From there, the business took off. They treated it like a convenience store, open all day, every day. Some days, they were pulling in over $2,500. Word spread fast, and customers lined up for everything from five-dollar bags to full ounces.

Back then, the weed world was all about tiers, "reggies" were the bottom of the barrel, "mids" were the norm, and "dro" was top shelf. Knox and Benny refused to mess with anything low-grade. They built their name on quality, and that choice quickly set them apart. They weren't sloppy; they were calculated. Focused. Ruthless when they needed to be.

Wes, ever the lone wolf, eventually broke off to do his own thing. That was his style, independent, self-reliant, never fully in sync with the rest of the crew. It was like he wanted the money but none of the entanglements. And maybe that's what kept him one step out of the line of fire, at least for a while.

The first trap house was Benny's mom's place, a modest three-bedroom home at the end of W Paris Street in Tampa. From the outside, it looked like any other home on the block: beat-up but lived-in, tucked into a noisy, vibrant, mostly Latino neighborhood. The air was always filled with the sounds of salsa or reggaeton, the smells of someone's grill, kids chasing each other through front yards, and neighbors chatting from porch to porch. It was a community that masked its bedlam well.

That noise, that motion, it was perfect cover. The constant traffic in and out of Benny's house never raised eyebrows. Everyone on the block had guests, music, cars, and noise. The trap blended in like camouflage.

Benny's mom and sister still lived in the house. His mom? She knew. Everyone did. But her protests, always in rapid-fire Spanish, lost their volume the moment the money started coming in. She didn't like it, but she didn't stop it either. Her main gripe was Knox. She hated him. She thought he was a bad influence, and she was right. But it was too late. Knox had sunk his hooks in deep, and Benny couldn't let go even if he wanted to.

On any given day, the yard looked like a block party. Five, ten cars parked on the lawn or curb. Blunts burning. Beats blasting. Guys posted up on folding chairs, laughing, watching, guarding. But business was business. Hand-offs were quick. Cash exchanged without a word. It was efficient, and for a while, it was smooth.

Then the inevitable happened, Benny got picked up with a QP (quarter-pound) on him. It was a wake-up call. He sat in jail for nearly three weeks before making bond, and though he came out tougher, the message was clear: the streets weren't loyal, and the cops were always watching. The hustle was profitable, but it came with a price, and it was only a matter of time before someone paid it.

Benny got out, and I was there the day Knox surprised him with a gift straight out of *Paid in Full*, a brand-new Jaguar XJ50. Sleek, silver-gray, and gleaming under the streetlights, it wasn't just a car, it was a message. The buttery leather seats, wood-grain dash, and the way it glided over the roads made it feel like we were floating above the chaos. In a neighborhood filled with beat-up Hondas and rusted-out Toyotas, the Jag was royalty. Heads turned. Streets whispered. Everyone noticed. So did I.

The Jaguar became more than a ride, it became an escape. On nights we didn't want to think, we'd hit restaurants that felt fancier than they were, throwing around the cash like it was endless. Then came the club nights, wild, electric, unforgettable. Knox, working the door at Club Yakaleo, gave us access to the scene's pulse. Some nights ended in laughter, others in fights that shut the whole place down. Violence was a frequent guest.

Benny and Wes never loved the club scene like Knox did. Benny didn't drink or do coke, he was strictly a smoker. Weed kept him mellow, kept him in control. Wes didn't even smoke; he preferred pills, just enough to take the edge off without dulling his thinking. Knox? He dived headfirst into it all: weed, liquor, powder, and adrenaline. He wasn't just part of the party, he *was* the party.

ADDICTED TO PAIN

They all had clean rides, another sign of their status. Wes had a smooth black Lexus. Knox and Benny flaunted Jaguars. But beyond the flashy whips, they shared a love for old-school Chevys, "dunks" and lifted trucks, tricked out with speakers and custom paint. Knox took it further. He loved speed and danger, riding through the city on his Yamaha Raptor ATV, tearing down blocks like the laws didn't apply to him. In his mind, maybe they didn't. He lived like he was untouchable.

After the Jag, Benny leveled up again, he got his first apartment out in Lutz, far from the chaos of the trap. It wasn't in his name, of course. He was smart, or at least careful. Bills were in his 17-year-old girlfriend's name. That's who he lived with, her and her older brother, Q, who I was dating at the time. The apartment was a modest two-bedroom, two-bath, decent but always tense. That place buzzed with energy, like something could explode at any moment. I visited a few times before Q, and I faded out. Each time, it felt like stepping into another world.

In that world, Wes was often the quiet anchor. When Knox got too hot-headed or reckless, Wes talked him down. He wasn't just the voice of reason, he was the conscience of the crew. Benny and Wes knew a side of Knox no one else did. Around them, he dropped the armor. He let his guard down. They were more than friends, they were his brothers. And Wes? Wes was the one he confided in the most.

Still, Wes kept a boundary between himself and the darkest parts of their world. He was about the grind, not the glory. He moved low, spoke less, and thought more. While Knox and Benny flexed, Wes played chess, he didn't want to go out like so many others. He watched how Knox's fire burned too hot, how Benny's solutions usually in-

141

volved violence, and Wes stayed in his own lane, hustling smart, not loud.

Knox, though, was the architect. The older brother. The general. He molded Benny into a dealer, taught him the code of the streets, showed him how to win and when to strike. Knox was calculated, strategic, always watching the board. But even Benny and Wes didn't know everything. Some parts of Knox's world were locked away, cold, brutal things he kept hidden. He wasn't without feeling, but when it came to business, he cut emotion out like a tumor. Protecting the crew meant keeping them in the dark about the ugliest truths. Not because he didn't care, but because he did.

Being the only female in the crew was like standing with one foot on each side of a fault line. I was included, but never quite *in*. The guys treated me like one of them, shared the laughs, the stories, the rides, but there was always an unspoken line I couldn't cross. I wasn't selling. I wasn't grinding like they were. I was the girl who hung around, not a player in the game.

But I rolled with it anyway. We all were searching for something, mentorship, brotherhood, success. We looked for guidance in the only place we knew: the streets. And even though I knew better, I couldn't walk away. I didn't want to be left behind, forgotten, while everyone else chased power and money. So I stayed, hoping I'd find belonging. But the deeper I went, the more I lost myself. I was chasing peace, but all I found was bedlam.

I remember the car incident like it was yesterday. I thought I was being smart, responsible, using my mother's income tax money to buy a reliable ride. It was supposed to be a turning point, a chance to build some independence. Wes and Knox introduced me to a guy they vouched for, someone they claimed was solid. He had a black '91 Honda Accord, and it looked perfect. I test-drove it, and it felt like freedom.

But my gut screamed at me the whole time.

There was no contract, no title, just their word and my desperation. I was tired of catching rides, tired of feeling stuck, tired of being broke. They told me this was the kind of opportunity people like us had to take. So I handed him the $2,500 in cash, and by the end of the week, the car and the guy were both gone. Just like that.

Calling the police? Not an option. That wasn't how we handled things in the streets. There was no justice, only street code. If you got, you took the L and moved on. But this one? This one felt different. It wasn't just the money, it was the betrayal. It was the silence from the people who brought me to him. Wes and Knox had nothing to say. No help. No answers. I was left to piece together the damage on my own.

I went looking for him everywhere. I knocked on doors. I called every number I had. I pulled up to Knox's grandfather's house, Wes's job, any place I thought might lead me back to the car, or my money. I begged. I yelled. I cried. No one cared. The more I searched, the more invisible I became.

That's when it hit me. I was never *really* one of them. I was just a mark, just a "lick." Someone they thought wouldn't fight back. Someone they could forget. Out of all of them, Wes seemed the most remorseful. Maybe he truly didn't know it was a setup. But even he couldn't do anything about it. In the eyes of that world, we were nobodies. And nobody stands up for nobodies.

That's when it hit me: *I was never really one of them.*

That betrayal cracked something open in me. I needed to fix this; I needed to get my mom's money back.

For the first time, I understood Milani. I mean, really understood her. The choices she made, the ones I'd judged so harshly, suddenly made perfect sense. Her world had rules. Consequences, yes. But also power. Control. She offered me an out:

"Work a few weekends. Stack fast cash. Then disappear," she said. Simple.

And I hated how tempting it sounded.

I had been so proud, so sure I was different. Better. But I wasn't. Not anymore. Not when I was carrying the guilt of losing my mother's *entire* tax return. Not when fear sat on my chest every time she asked about the car. My pride was screaming no. But reality? Reality whispered yes.

The betrayal wasn't just a moment. It was a mirror. And in it, I saw a version of myself I barely recognized, tired, scared, desperate enough to cross a line I swore I never would.

Chapter 10

I Became What I Judged

I didn't decide to start dancing because I wanted to. I did it because I didn't see another way.

Desperation has a way of redrawing your boundaries. After the robbery... after the inaction from Wes and Knox, who vouched for him... after I watched my mother's savings disappear like smoke, I realized the line I swore I'd never cross was closer than I thought.

And if I'm honest? The seed had already been planted. Milani never pressured me. She didn't preach. She didn't have to. It was the way she moved. The way she carried herself.

She'd always been pretty, but now she was *untouchable.* Designer bags. Hair always done. Nails always done. Victoria's Secret everything. That was *luxury* to us. While the rest of us were scraping up coins for gas, Milani was pulling up in a tricked-out truck with a subwoofer that rattled the block, tipping waiters, sliding her card without blinking, and paying for everyone's wings at brunch.

She bought ounces of weed like they were Tic Tacs. Ate out like it was nothing. Took spontaneous trips to Miami like it was just another Saturday. She didn't *need* anyone. She made moves. On her terms. No man. No middleman. Just her.

Meanwhile, the guys in our circle, Wes, Knox, and Benny, they had hustle, too. They were flipping weight, making street money. But I wasn't built for that world. I wasn't trying to be someone's runner. I wanted my *own* moves. My *own* power.

Milani showed me that it was possible.

I told myself I'd never sell my body. Never be *that* girl. But I still watched. And somewhere deep inside, I *wanted* what she had. So when the car deal fell apart, when I realized I had no way to fix it, no way to undo the damage, I didn't just feel regret. I felt something else I didn't expect: readiness.

I picked up the phone, hands shaking. "Hey, can you talk?" I asked.

"Yeah, what's up? You okay?"

"Not really," I said, voice cracking. "Remember the car I was supposed to buy? The one with my mom's tax money? It's gone. The guy disappeared. I got played."

"What? He just ran off with the cash?"

"Yeah. And the worst part? Wes and Knox co-signed for him. I trusted them."

Milani was quiet for a beat. "Did you have a bill of sale?"

"No. Nothing. Just his word." My chest tightened. "I feel so stupid."

I told her everything about the scam and the lie I was living every time my mom asked about the car.

After taking a breath, Milani responded, "I know this might sound wild, but... if it were me? I'd go to work. Just a couple of weekends. You'd make the money back fast."

I didn't say anything.

"No one has to know," she added. "You get in, get out. Nina's looking for someone new. I can make the intro?" She said it so casually. Because for her, it *was* casual. It was normal.

This was the road I swore I'd never take. But now? It was the only one still open.

Milani, ever calm, ever confident, was already on her way out of the scene, pregnant now, ready to pass the baton. But Nina? She *was* the scene. She'd been in the life for years and knew every detail like a blueprint. Stunning, strategic, and sharp-tongued, Nina was the kind of woman who could own any room without saying a word. With her as my guide and Milani by my side, they promised to teach me the ropes. How to move, how to dance, how to make money without losing your soul.

But I was still terrified. I didn't know what scared me more, being judged for stepping into the club, or admitting that part of me was already stepping in. Desperation had a way of stripping pride, and I had never felt so desperate.

Still, I listened. I learned. Nina taught me the basics, lap dance etiquette, club dynamics, and its rules. Milani let me borrow clothes, heels, and even makeup. They painted a version of myself I didn't recognize, confident, seductive, powerful. But under it all, I was just scared. Scared that once I stepped into this world, there'd be no turning back.

And yet... I stepped anyway. Because survival doesn't wait for permission.

The audition at the strip club was one of the most nerve-wracking moments of my life. I'd been through turmoil, through violence, through heartbreak, but this felt different. This was a kind of vulnerability I wasn't prepared for. I wasn't fighting anyone. I wasn't yelling or surviving some crisis. I was standing still, on a stage, waiting to be judged for nothing more than how I moved, how I looked, how well I could pretend I was okay.

My self-esteem was already threadbare. Years of feeling unwanted, unworthy, "too much" or "not enough," had hollowed me out. I had stopped believing I could be loved without pain, so lust became a language I understood. At least in lust, I could perform. I could disappear into a role that made people want me, even if it wasn't real. Love felt unreachable, something saved for the girls with fewer scars.

As I waited backstage, surrounded by mirrors that reflected a version of me I barely recognized, all those dreams I once clung to, college, a stable job, a quiet life, felt like they were slipping further out of reach. This wasn't the kind of decision you'd find in any life plan or textbook.

"Hey, B, have you picked a name yet?" Nina's voice echoed down the hallway. She was strolling toward me with her clothes bunched up in one hand, wearing nothing but a thong.

"I just got off stage," she laughed, catching the way I averted my eyes, clearly bashful about seeing her naked. "You'll get used to it, trust me. Has Jeff talked to you yet?"

"Yeah," I said, my voice shaking. "I signed the paperwork and gave him my ID. But Nina... I don't know if I can do this. He asked me to pick a name, went over the tip-outs, and told me I need to talk to the DJ about my songs. I don't even know what songs to dance to..." I was rambling, my words tripping over each other.

She chuckled again, placing a hand on my shoulder and locking eyes with me.

"Listen. You're a hustler, okay? There are men here who are going to want you and give you everything you need. You just have to remember what we taught you. Bitch, shake that money maker you got, and they will *make it rain!* The audition's coming up during the shift change between the day and night girls. We're gonna get you ready."

"Nina, I think I'm gonna throw up..." I blurted, turning on my heels and sprinting to the bathroom.

I was splashing cold water on my face when she came in and handed me a drink.

"Here. Whiskey," she said simply. "It'll calm your nerves."

I hesitated, then took a sip. The burn steadied me.

"Aight, bitch," she said with a grin, slapping my ass. "Let's get you dolled up and get this money!"

Nina didn't stay at the club for long. She left after the weekend, heading back to Miami, where she lived and worked. She told me she was the "bottom bitch" for the guy she was dating. I didn't fully understand what that meant at the time, just that it meant she wasn't coming back. I was on my own now.

Still, somewhere deep inside me, a small voice whispered: *This isn't the end of your story. It's just a chapter. Just a detour.*

I clung to that voice as I adjusted the borrowed heels on my feet, smoothed my hair, and reminded myself to breathe.

I had been told most girls start slow, bikini, then topless, eventually full nude. But I didn't have the luxury of easing in. I needed money. Fast. Shame was a currency I'd been spending for years anyway. What was one more transaction?

Milani had tried to coach me through it, what to wear, how to walk, what the club managers looked for. I remembered her voice telling me to smile, even if it was fake. "Confidence is everything," she said, even if you're falling apart on the inside. So I put on that smile. I stepped into the lights. And I danced.

It wasn't graceful. I stumbled more than once. My knees shook. I moved the way she showed me, trying to exude seduction, trying to sell a fantasy I didn't believe in. But I got through it. And by some miracle, or maybe because I was just desperate enough, they hired me.

***

My first night on stage was "amateur night." I wasn't ready, but ready didn't matter. The club was packed, the lights were blinding, and the music thundered through my body. And there I was, bare, exposed, terrified. But also... exhilarated. There was power in it. Twisted power, yes, but power nonetheless. For once, I was the one in control of how much I showed, how much I took, how much I earned.

The money came fast. Bills hit the stage like rain. And with every dollar, a little of the ache in my chest dulled. It wasn't healing. It wasn't love. But it was relief. And sometimes, that's all you have the strength to reach for.

And that night I became "Innocence."

As I started working regularly at the club, it didn't take long to see that the women who danced beside me were just as diverse as the men we danced for. Some glided through the room like goddesses, flawless, confident, always surrounded by high-rollers. They were the untouchables, the ones who wore their beauty like armor and moved like they belonged somewhere far better than here.

Then there were the grinders. Women like me. Women who didn't have perfect bodies or expensive outfits, but who showed up night after night to pay bills, feed kids, or climb out of debt. And then there were the hardened ones, the veterans. They weren't chasing dreams anymore. They were chasing paper. Cold, sharp, and strategic, these women had long stopped trying to be loved or liked.

Amidst this mix of glitz and grit was Nadia.

She wasn't flashy. She didn't work the room with exaggerated charm or flirt from across the floor. She moved with intention, with control. Unlike the others, she saw me. Really saw me. I wasn't just the new girl trying to fake confidence, I was a young woman drowning in low self-worth, standing at the edge of a world I didn't understand. And Nadia reached out.

She wasn't part of the club's elite, but she knew the system like a seasoned strategist. She became my mentor, the one who taught me what no manager ever would: the *real* rules of the game.

"Hey, is it Innocence?" she asked, catching my eye in the bathroom as we checked our reflections one last time before hitting the floor.

"Yeah. And you're Nadia, right?"

"Yup, that's me, the one and only." Her voice was coated in a thick Southern accent, playful but sharp. "I ain't heard that stage name before. It's got a real irony to it, you know? 'Cause there ain't a single chick in here who's anywhere near innocent. But I like it." She looked me up and down. "You new round here? To dancing?"

I felt exposed, like she was reading me page by page. "Something like that. It's not for long. I'm just trying to make some money for a car..."

She cut me off before I could finish. "This place runs on invisible lines," she said, bending over to check herself in the mirror. She adjusted her thong, eyeing her reflection for anything out of place. "Stray toilet paper, tags, a tampon string, glowin' in blacklight? Kills the fantasy in a second."

Standing back up, she applied a quick coat of lip gloss, then glanced at me. "There are squads, alliances, petty beefs. Play it smart, and you'll survive. Piss off the wrong girl, and you won't make it past next week." She pulled a mini shot bottle from her purple Crown Royal bag and downed it in one smooth motion. Then she handed it to me. I took a swig, more out of instinct than desire.

The club wasn't just about dancing, it was about politics. Seduction didn't just happen on stage; it lived in the locker room, in the way you navigated jealousy, in the alliances you formed on the floor. Looks helped, sure, but strategy? Strategy kept you fed.

"Innocence," Nadia said, her tone shifting to business, "here's the breakdown. Each song runs about four minutes. You've got 15 songs in an hour, that's sixty minutes. If you average $25 a song, that's $375 right there. But now subtract everything that cuts into that, walking from table to table, redressing between songs, making small talk, your three-stage sets a night, which eat up about 30 minutes total. Add in bathroom breaks, freshening up, grabbing food... If you don't manage your time right, you'll leave here broke."

She looked at me like she was handing down gospel.

And she kind of was.

Nadia taught me how to weaponize vulnerability. "You wanna make real money?" she said, watching me fumble to hold a client's attention. "Make them feel *needed*. Like they're rescuin' you. Not too much, just enough to tickle their ego."

She was right. Used the right way, vulnerability made men feel like heroes.

The tip-out was insane. Most people had no idea how expensive it was just to *show up* to work. The house fee alone was $30 per shift, just to walk in the door. Then came the rest: the DJ took 10% of what you made, no matter what. Even though Florida law didn't allow full nudity in clubs that served alcohol, we still had a bar, and the bartenders expected tips, usually $5 to $20 each, depending on the night. Most times, there were two of them working.

Then there were the fine cards. If you put yourself down on the schedule and didn't show up, they'd charge you a $100 no-show fee.

They'd clock you in anyway, then hunt you down for payment later. No excuses.

Security had to be tipped too, indoor and outdoor. That could add another $20 easily, and if the night got crazy, even more. Altogether, tip-out could easily run you $100 or more, and that was *before* you made a dime.

Then there were room fees. If I booked five private rooms in a night, that was $25 straight to the club. The customer already paid for the room, but the club charged *me* to use it. And if I didn't get a customer to buy me at least three drinks during my shift? I had to pay for those, too.

That's why it was tempting, risky or not, to meet certain clients outside the club. The rules were rigged, and the hustle inside didn't always add up. Outside, the money was quicker, easier, and came with fewer deductions.

Over time, I started to attract a different kind of customer. They weren't just there for a dance, they wanted something more. They wanted connection. They wanted softness. They wanted to feel like they mattered.

I gave them that illusion. Over and over again. I didn't have to lie. I just offered them the version of me they came looking for. And the money kept coming.

But behind the seduction, something else was happening. I was learning how to read people, how to shift energy, how to survive on instinct. I had never thought of myself as a hustler. But the club introduced me to a part of myself I didn't know existed. There was power in knowing what people wanted and how to give it to them in just the right dose. There was power in knowing how to disappear emotionally while remaining fully present physically.

I wasn't just surviving anymore. I was adapting. Calculating. Playing the long game. And in that transformation, I realized the club wasn't just a place that took, it was also a place that taught. It stripped away illusions and forced you to meet the rawest version of yourself. Whether you liked what you found or not was up to you.

Outside the strip club, my friends and I began craving more than success. It wasn't just about paying rent anymore, we wanted the shine. Our own apartments. Foreign cars. Designer bags. Jewelry that glittered under the streetlights like it had something to say. After our shifts, we'd sit around together, still in lashes and sweats, half-tired but wired, daydreaming out loud. We'd pass around takeout containers and blunt smoke while sketching out fantasy lives with real ambition. It felt harmless, even hopeful, like maybe if we said it enough times, those dreams would find a way to come true.

Sometimes, I even brought my son along when we gathered on weekends. He was too young to understand the energy around him, too innocent to recognize the low hum of danger in those environments. I wasn't dealing. I wasn't robbing or trapping. I was just there, buying a little weed, kicking back with my people, trying to feel something close to peace. But deep down, I knew how quickly things could go left. And every time I walked back through my door and tucked my son into bed, I wondered if I had gambled too much.

We were all still pretending this was temporary. A phase. A hustle we'd grow out of.

I told myself that I wasn't like the others. That I was just passing through this world. But every time I let the music and money numb the ache in my chest, I moved a little deeper into it. The dreams stayed big, but my options were shrinking. I was trying to live two lives at once: one chasing stability and self-respect, the other consumed by others' fantasies and seduction.

The more involved I got into club life, the more I uncovered how far the hustle stretched. Lap dances became a more seductive, theatrical layer to the lifestyle. The private rooms were like portals to alternate realities. Clients paid $200 for thirty minutes or $400 per hour in the opulent champagne rooms, each room with its own vibe: the red room, the vintage room, the gold room, and even a floral-themed greenery room. Plush couches. Dim lights. Fantasy. Illusion. The cheaper dances, $25 a song, happened in smaller, hidden rooms just off the main stage. They weren't as glamorous, but they were just as profitable.

Those rooms opened my eyes to the club's darker undercurrent, the fragile line between financial gain and physical risk. What started as a grind to make ends meet became a slippery slope into an identity I no longer recognized. I was trapped somewhere between who I had been and who I was pretending to be.

At first, I fumbled through it, walking out of dances, getting scolded by managers, and misreading cues I hadn't yet learned to interpret. I was clumsy, unsure, and nervous. Everything about the club felt foreign. But desperation has a way of accelerating your learning curve. Within a few months, everything shifted.

Nadia and I became a team. We knew how to work a room, how to read a man's mood before he opened his mouth. We made eye contact like it was a handshake. We moved like we belonged. Confidence came first, then strategy. I learned how to upcharge customers, stretch songs for every dollar they were worth, and sweeten empty promises just enough to keep them spending. If they were gullible or desperate, I leaned in. And once the money left their hands, there were no refunds.

The change in my lifestyle didn't go unnoticed. My mother saw it before I was ready to admit anything. The extra cash I always seemed to have. The late nights. The new clothes. The way I walked through the house was like I had something to prove.

One evening, while I leaned against the kitchen counter, she brought it up.

"I've just been hosting at a few spots," I told her, trying to keep my tone casual. "Sometimes I jump behind the bar too. The tips are good."

She gave me a long, steady look. "You don't have a bartending license," she said. "And why are you carrying around that big bag everywhere?"

My defenses snapped into place before I could stop them. "What, I can't carry a big bag now?" I fired back. "Since when is that illegal?"

Her eyes didn't harden with anger; they softened with disappointment. And somehow, that was worse. "I didn't say it was illegal," she said quietly. "I'm your mother. I notice things. I notice you."

That hit me. But I didn't let it show. I crossed my arms, heart pounding, suddenly ashamed and too proud to admit it.

She stepped back, her voice calm. "I'm not trying to fight with you, Brandy. I just want to understand what's really going on."

But I didn't want to be understood. I wanted space. I wanted control. I wanted her to stop seeing through me, stop asking questions I wasn't ready to answer.

"Well, maybe there's nothing to understand," I snapped. "I'm grown. I'm making my own money. Isn't that what matters?"

She didn't say anything. She just looked at me with that same quiet gaze, the one I used to find comforting but now felt suffocating. Then she turned back to the stove and stirred the pot like the conversation had never happened. No yelling. No lecture. Just silence and the soft scrape of the spoon moving in slow circles.

That was her way. She didn't push when she knew I wouldn't budge. She just finished cooking, made a plate, and left it on the counter for me, warm, covered in foil.

I grabbed my bag and left without saying much else.

By twenty, I was a machine. Driven by status, sex, and survival. I talked differently. Walked differently. My morals were distorted. My boundaries blurred. I was fixated on pleasure, power, and possession, because those were the only currencies that seemed to matter.

I had been dancing for about a year when Knox came to me with an idea. And I remember that night like it was yesterday.

It was after a long shift at the club. I pulled up to his grandfather's house just past midnight, the hum of the streetlights buzzing above the quiet block. I was drained, still smelling faintly of sweat and cheap perfume, but I needed to decompress, smoke a blunt, clear my mind. Knox was already outside, leaning against the fence like he'd been waiting.

"What up, B?" he called, that cool confidence in his voice like he already knew how the night would end.

"Hey! Nothing much, just working. Getting this money," I said, flashing a tired smile as I climbed the porch steps and dropped into the chair beside him.

He handed me the weed and a paper to roll. "Okay! I see you. How much you making these days, B?"

I didn't hesitate. I pulled out a fat wad of cash from my sling bag and held it up. "Rolling in it. Saving up for my own car. Maybe a new spot."

He nodded, smirking. "Aight, I see you. But... what if you could double that stack?"

I paused. Knox was no stranger to the streets, but I never figured him for the strip club type.

"My brotha, what do you know about the club? I ain't never seen you step foot in one," I teased, breaking down the blunt.

He chuckled. "I don't need to be in there to know what goes down. I see what the girls don't, and I see you. I see your hustle. And I know you could be making way more. Less work. More money."

I raised an eyebrow. "What are you getting at?"

He leaned back, locking eyes with me. He made it sound simple. "You're already there. You've got regulars. Trust. Access. You don't even have to do the dirty work. Just be the plug." His voice was smooth, hypnotic. "The money? It'll blow stage work out the water. You don't gotta dance harder. Just smarter."

I furrowed my brow, still not catching on. But Knox knew how to plant seeds. He spoke in riddles that unraveled over time.

"There's something I want to show you," he said. "I don't offer this to just anyone, but you're different. You've always been sharp. You got a kid to raise. A mom to support. And let's be real, respect doesn't come free. You earn it through money."

"Alright," I said slowly. "But you're talking in circles."

He grinned. "Let's burn this L, and I'll show you. But you gotta be all in. You say you're about your money? Then let's make some real money."

"Aight, bet. Don't test me. You know I get mine," exhaling the first puff and passing it back. But inside, something shifted, curiosity, desperation... maybe even hunger.

After we finished, we went inside. That's when I saw it, laid out on the table like it was nothing. Two fat ounces of cocaine. The room suddenly felt smaller.

That weekend, Knox pulled me into his world. No easing in. No half-measures. I learned how to test the purity, how to cut it with procaine and caffeine to make it stretch. He taught me everything, how to bag it, scale it, price it to the gram. Every detail was a lesson in precision.

But it wasn't just about product, it was about mindset. Knox drilled it into me: Never get too comfortable. Never trust too easily. Always keep your face clean. Move in the shadows. Keep your name out the streets. That's how you survive.

I told myself I was just learning. Just curious. But by the end of that weekend, I knew the truth: I wasn't watching the game anymore, I was in it.

Chapter 11

New Norm

This became my life in a world of hustle, danger, and survival. Every day, I grew more adept at navigating the treacherous waters of the drug trade. A single "bump" of cocaine, 20 to 30 milligrams, was just the introduction, often handed out freely to the girls at the club to get them hooked. Once the high gripped them, they transitioned quickly from half-grams to eight balls, 3.5 grams at a time, fueling their long nights and fattening my pockets. The more they realized how potent my product was, the more they sought me out. Word spread fast. I became the go-to girl for anything they needed to keep going.

No one in my circle warned me. They didn't remind me of the danger. Instead, they applauded me, feeding my ego, my drive, my

greed. The biblical wisdom that "bad company corrupts good character" echoed faintly in my mind, but I ignored it. I silenced it. I told
myself I was hustling, building, winning. What began as a short-term
hustle to save for a car spiraled. I traded my identity, my dreams, and
my innocence for cash, clout, and control.

My transformation was complete. I had gone from tomboy to
pin-up. From sneakers and bare skin to stilettos and makeup caked on
like armor.

The dressing room felt more like a studio, mirrors with bright,
round lights, lockers lining the walls, and benches scattered like islands. The air was thick with perfume and hairspray. Thongs, stilettos, weave, makeup, hot tools, everything either plugged in or strewn
across the room.

I had just arrived, a little late. Nadia was already working the floor.
I was still adjusting my clothes when her heels clicked around the
corner.

She stopped in her tracks. "Innocence! Oh my God...you cut your
hair?" Her eyes widened. "And look at your face... you using MAC
now?"

I turned slowly, gave her a pout. My long, wavy hair, gone. Now it
was sharp, shoulder-length.

"I don't know if I like it," she said, squinting. "It's cute... but not
for here. You need something that makes you stand out from these
other hoes." She dug in her bag, mumbling, "I got exactly what you
need, bitch."

"What is that? You think I'm putting that on my head?" I laughed,
a little scared.

"Girl, you good or nah?" she smirked. "Let me teach you something."

I sat between her legs. She clipped in a drawstring ponytail, tight, bouncy curls. When I looked in the mirror, I blinked twice. I didn't recognize myself. But I looked good.

"Girl, you look exotic," Nadia grinned. "This is the one. Wait, lemme get you some lashes too."

"We gotta hurry," I said, rolling my eyes. "Jeff's gonna come in with his clipboard like always. I'm already late, and I'm not tryna pay that damn fine."

"Girl, I hear you," Nadia said, focused. "He big mad this week."

As she finished gluing the lashes, Jeff's voice echoed down the hallway. "Innocence? You back here?"

Nadia slipped me a folded $50. "For the coke. Meet me in the side bathroom," she whispered, grabbing her top.

"Yes, I'm here, Jeff!" I called out.

He stepped in, clipboard in hand. "You got someone askin' for you."

"Can you let him know I'll be right out? Gotta scuff these new shoes first."

"Get out on the floor, Innocence," he snapped.

I slipped on the slick heels and ran outside to rough them up. Then I found Crash, the DJ.

"Hey, skip me in rotation. Client's waiting." I handed him a twenty.

As I stepped onto the floor, Nadia's name got called over the speaker. I met her in the side bathroom. "Took you long enough," she hissed, taking the baggie with the club's logo. She bumped two quick lines. "This is some good shit," she grinned.

I smiled. "Fresh batch from Knox."

She checked my nose. "You good!" I slapped her ass, and she ran out just as her stage song started.

I took a bump from my personal stash, just one. Too early to go all in.

Back in the club, I climbed the steps to the DJ booth.

"Damn, who do I have the pleasure of speaking to?" Crash joked.

I slapped his arm. "Stop playing."

"Nah, for real, you look like a new girl. Aight, killa!"

I scanned the bar, catching Nadia working a table already. Then Jeff pointed me toward the back.

That's when I saw him, Frank. The old man from last week who'd thrown hundreds at me. Demi had gotten to him first, but I remembered his name. That gave me an edge. As I passed, I caught the eyes of dancers and customers. Some with awe. Some with jealousy. For the first time, everyone noticed me.

I walked with confidence. But underneath the hair, the lashes, the heels... I was empty.

I kept hoping the next man, the next thrill, the next dollar would fill the void. But it never did. The lights, the money, the seduction, they were masks.

And behind them all, I had become a stranger to myself.

The club became a world unto itself, a microcosm where everything was exaggerated: the lights, the music, the allure. But beneath the glitter and excitement was a steady hum of hollowness. I was in a constant chase for the next big tip, the next thrill, the next numbing escape, but true satisfaction always eluded me. The confident, seductive dancer I had become was just a mask. Beneath the makeup and routines was still that same young girl who once dreamed of love, purpose, and a life far from the streets. Those dreams now felt like distant memories, buried under choices I never thought I'd make.

Meeting Raequan was a shift toward something even more emotionally draining. We met at a house party through a mutual friend, and from the moment I laid eyes on him, I was intrigued. He had a presence that pulled people in. I asked around, and the warnings were immediate: "He's no good." "He's got girls all over." But when we ran into each other again at a local club, all the noise faded. We danced, exchanged numbers, and from that moment on, something about him kept pulling me back.

Unlike most men, Raequan didn't rush into anything. He was more reserved, careful, and that only deepened my attraction. He came over to my mom's place a few times, and I even twisted his dreads. He moved differently, quiet, calculated, and I became infatuated. But our relationship was strange from the start. I was never his main girl. There was always someone else lingering in the background, a high school flame, someone his family and friends still mentioned with a kind of reverence. She wasn't loud or flashy like me. She was quiet, poised, the type of girl who seemed untouched by the lifestyle I had. I could never shake the feeling that she was the one he truly wanted, and I was just passing time.

Even at our best, things with Raequan were fragile. He was emotionally manipulative, cold, distant, and controlling. None of my friends liked him. They saw through the charm and warned me, but I didn't listen. I was too far gone. Every time he ignored my texts or vanished for days, I'd fall deeper. I'd blame myself. I'd do whatever it took to get back on his radar. I accepted being second, sometimes last, hoping that if I loved him hard enough, he'd finally choose me.

I lost myself trying to keep his attention, paying for dates, his tattoos, even helping him get a gun from a pawn shop. I covered car payments and nearly bought him a car outright. I thought love was something I could buy or earn, not realizing how much of myself I was giving away for nothing in return.

He never claimed me, and I never demanded he did, even though we spent nearly every day together. He'd drop me off at the club and take my car for the night, only to pick me up after my shift. I dressed up hoping he'd notice me, but more often than not, he'd be off entertaining someone else, sometimes right in front of me. His jealousy would flare if I so much as talked to another man, but when it came to his behavior, he didn't care who saw. He made scenes, started fights, and acted like I belonged to him, but only when it was convenient.

The worst part? I kept coming back. Every good moment we shared, the CDs he made me, the car rides, the laughter, felt like proof that maybe there was something real between us. But they were just breadcrumbs in a relationship built on imbalance and unmet expectations.

I was never enough for Raequan, but I kept hoping I could be. And in the process, I became a version of myself I didn't recognize, needy, obsessive, willing to endure almost anything just to feel wanted.

Looking back now, I see how much my mom carried for me during those chaotic years. While I was caught up in a toxic relationship with Raequan and chasing a life built on illusion and materialism, she was the one keeping everything together. She was the foundation beneath my feet, holding steady for Amadeus when I couldn't. But at the time,

I couldn't see any of it. I was too blinded by the noise in my own life, too wrapped up in seeking validation and affection from a man who never truly loved me, too distracted by the false promises of the lifestyle I had chosen.

When I first started dancing, Amadeus was around four years old and had just started pre-kindergarten. His father wasn't around much, and I was still dealing with harassment from Zara and her circle of mean girls. Despite everything, my mother and I shared the responsibilities of raising him. We coordinated school drop-offs and pick-ups, balancing our schedules as best we could. Even with my unpredictable nights at the club, I remained involved, talking with his teachers, attending school meetings, making sure he was doing okay.

My mom, who found peace and purpose in the kitchen, always had warm meals prepared. On the days she was feeling sick or had to take on a side job, I stepped in. But the truth is, most of the time, she was the glue holding our little world together. She gave me the space to stumble through my twenties while providing Amadeus with a sense of normalcy and love that I couldn't always offer.

Then there was my abuela, my father's mother, who was also an essential part of my son's early life. From the time Amadeus turned one until about two, she helped care for him. At first, I only asked for help occasionally, but slowly I began to lean on her more and more, taking advantage of her kindness. She was in her eighties then, and though her health was declining, she never hesitated to open her arms to us. Abuela had a calming presence, the kind that quieted calamity without saying much at all. My son adored her. And deep down, so did I.

But I didn't cherish her the way I should have. My mind was elsewhere, obsessed with the next club night, the next party, the next boy. I regret how I drifted. I didn't fully grasp that my time with her was slipping away. When she passed, it shattered something in me, but I didn't know how to grieve. So I avoided the pain. I buried it beneath everything else I was dealing with, letting time move forward while a part of me stayed frozen in that loss.

Her house, the property she once filled with warmth, became my refuge. It was the only place that still felt safe. I'd go there to feel close to her, to touch something real. I never really said goodbye. I held on to the house like it was a piece of her, a piece of the only real peace I'd known.

After she passed, my father moved in.

***

By the time my son was nearing six, life looked drastically different. I bought a Lexus LS 400, and I finally secured my own apartment, a modest two-bedroom that symbolized so much more than square footage. It was proof that I could stand on my own, that I was no longer dependent on anyone but myself. Getting approved was surprisingly easy. All it took was a letter from the club stating my income. Just like that, I was handed the keys to my own space, and it felt like the start of a new chapter in my life, one defined by freedom, self-reliance, and pride.

With that independence came the freedom to indulge in all the luxuries I had once only dreamed of. Every week, Wes and I made it a ritual to dine at upscale restaurants, where a single night out could run us upwards of $200. I didn't blink. I was in love with the rush of spending, of living like I had finally "made it." Jewelry became my addiction, an Avianne watch for $750, a $3,000 diamond ring, and dazzling earrings that sparkled like the life I was building. My hair was always styled by a professional, my nails were always done, and my makeup collection was a showcase of MAC's finest. I felt powerful. Untouchable. Like I had climbed my way to the top of the world, even if I wasn't sure what mountain I had conquered.

But it wasn't just about me anymore. My lifestyle fed off the energy of the people I surrounded myself with, especially Knox, Benny, and Wes. Image was everything. Our lives revolved around the nightlife scene: club entrances with no lines, VIP booths glowing under neon lights, bottles popping at every table. We weren't just going out, we were performing, constantly proving we belonged in the spotlight.

Even my Lexus became part of the show. I tricked it out with a custom sound system so loud it turned heads from blocks away. My apartment followed the same script: lavish furniture, brand-name everything, not because I needed it, but because I could.

The real hustle wasn't happening under the neon lights of the club, it was going down at the trap house. That's where the real money flowed. Weed moved 24/7, and the operation ran like clockwork. Our customers, "custies," as we called them, hit us up on prepaid Boost Mobile phones. Transactions were quick, no time wasted. "Come thru, come thru" was the daily chorus, as Knox and Benny managed the flow with precision. They kept the circle tight, only bringing in a few trusted guys from the neighborhood and a couple of Knox's cousins from Puerto Rico to handle deliveries and runs. It was all business. No friendship. No feelings. Just money.

But it didn't stop at selling weed. We weren't just peddling product, we were *producing* it. Long before cannabis became a billion-dollar legal industry, we were already ahead of the game. Knox had an obsession with growing, an almost scientific fascination that took him deep into the world of cultivation. He read everything he could, watched hours of videos, and dissected every detail of lighting cycles, nutrients, and hydroponics like his life depended on it. He wasn't just trying to grow weed, he wanted perfection.

His passion pulled us in. Benny, Wes, and I got swept up in Knox's dream. He made it sound so possible, so real, that we believed this could be the move that changed everything. Our next big come-up.

We found a specialty grow store tucked away in a forgotten industrial strip of the city. It felt like stepping into a secret world. The shop was packed with high-end equipment, irrigation systems, LED and HID lighting setups, digital timers, pH testing kits, and shelves of nutrients tailored to every stage of a plant's growth. Knox was like a kid in a candy store, running through the aisles, explaining the difference between veg and flower cycles like he was giving a TED Talk.

We started small. My bedroom closet became home to my first grow setup: just three plants. I watched over them like they were pets, learning the delicate balance of light, air, and water. Meanwhile, Knox and Benny leveled up fast. They converted a two-room shack behind Knox's grandfather's house into a full-blown grow room. The heat was intense. The smell was stronger. But it was progress.

Knox dreamed big, he saw himself running acres of farmland out West someday, becoming a cannabis mogul, a name people respected. And I believed him. I truly did. But dreams don't protect you from people. That's where it started to unravel. The new partners Knox brought in didn't match his energy. They didn't share his vision or discipline. Missteps turned into arguments. Miscommunication led to distrust. And just like that, the cracks began to show.

Benny, always the risk-taker of the group, made a reckless decision that would cost him everything. Although Knox repeatedly warned him, Benny insisted on stashing illegal items at his apartment. His girlfriend's mother already disapproved of their relationship, there were deeper issues there I never fully understood, but things truly fell apart when the cops were called to the apartment over a missing child report. Benny's girlfriend happened to be there when officers arrived. The smell of weed hit the air as soon as Benny opened the door, giving them all the probable cause they needed to search the place. And once they stepped inside, that was it. Game over.

What they found sealed Benny's fate: weapons, drugs, cultivation tools, enough to fill pages and pages of charges. He was only nineteen, and now he was facing over a decade in federal prison. Thirteen years. Q, one of our guys, wasn't there the night of the bust, but he was questioned. Benny, true to who he was, didn't name names. He took the fall without dragging anyone else down.

The news hit us like a punch to the gut. His sister was the one who told us, and a few days later, we met up at his apartment to clean out the place and look over the paperwork. Seeing Benny's full name in the news, slapped across headlines next to "million-dollar bond," made everything feel too real. The Feds had taken over the case, and they had everything they needed.

With Benny gone, the main trap house couldn't keep running out of his mom's house. Knox had never trusted her to begin with. Whenever product was low and we had to count up the money to re-up, Benny would sometimes come up short, hundreds missing with no explanation. Benny never had answers, just confusion. But Knox had his suspicions. He believed Benny's mom was skimming off the top, and if that was true, it meant she was stealing from all of us. That was all the motivation Knox needed to move on.

He started looking for something better and found it, two suburban homes, both owned by a Cuban landlord he knew through his uncle. The man didn't ask many questions, and Knox offered cash and an extra hundred a month to sweeten the deal. These homes weren't luxurious, but they were cleaner, quieter, and came with well-kept lawns courtesy of a lawn service Knox hired. Each had three bedrooms, two baths, and a layout perfect for running things under the radar.

The new spot at the dead end of a residential street gave us just enough privacy. Families filled the neighborhood, kids riding bikes, music playing through screen doors, neighbors barbecuing in their driveways. On the surface, everything looked normal. No one suspected that behind one of those doors, we were rebuilding the empire Benny's arrest had shattered.

With money flowing again, Knox started thinking bigger. The grow rooms in our closets and makeshift setups were no longer enough. He wanted real scale, whole houses dedicated to growing. And soon, he made it happen. Within a year, he had his first full grow house up and running.

But big dreams come with big risks. Managing a full-scale operation wasn't easy. Knox was juggling too much, equipment breakdowns, workers flaking, and the constant fear of getting raided. The stress was nonstop. He realized that to keep things going, he needed to move the grows out of the county, far enough to stay off the radar, but close enough to keep control.

That's when J-Money entered the picture, and everything changed.

Chapter 12

Addicted to the Hope of Him

J-Money wasn't like the others. He had experience running large-scale grow operations, something Knox needed if he was serious about expanding. Where others were reactive, J-Money was calculated. He wasn't just chasing fast cash or clout; he was playing the long game, thinking in terms of wealth, longevity, and strategy. Knox knew this was the kind of partner he needed to turn his vision into reality.

Unlike Knox's typical crew, mostly Spanish and street-savvy, J-Money was Middle Eastern, with a completely different energy. He never hung around the trap houses, never posted up outside, and didn't get involved in the day-to-day grind. That wasn't his world. Instead, we'd meet him at Knox's grandfather's house or at J-Money's place, always chill, always on point. He had a sharpness to him that set him apart. From the way he dressed to how he spoke, everything about him said precision and purpose.

What connected Knox and J-Money was their shared passion for marijuana, not just using it, but mastering the craft of growing it. To them, this was more than just a hustle; it was a science. They geeked out over strains, lighting cycles, nutrient blends, and optimal humidity levels like botanists. Knox had started small, experimenting in closets and backyard setups, but J-Money brought next-level expertise. He'd already built systems to maximize yields, avoid common pitfalls, and streamline operations. He wasn't just another street player; he was a cultivator with a blueprint, and with him in the mix, Knox's vision of grow houses became more than just a dream. It started to look like an empire.

While J-Money helped build from the top, Knox managed things from the ground up. That's where Ace came in.

Ace was one of many young guys Knox had taken under his wing, kids from broken homes, drifting through the streets with no real direction. Knox knew the game: the leaders never touch the product. You needed foot soldiers, hungry, desperate, loyal. He had an eye for spotting the right kind. Most of them were just 18, legal adults, but still too young to fully understand the danger they were walking into. And that's exactly what made them perfect.

Some of the boys even lived in the trap houses. Knox covered rent, food, bills, everything. In return, they ran the operation around the clock. For many of them, it wasn't just a job; it was a lifeline. A place to belong. A way to feel important. The risk didn't scare them. The reward, money, respect, and a sense of purpose, were worth it.

Knox made sure his soldiers were taken care of, especially when they got caught up. He'd pay for lawyers, bond them out, whatever it took to keep them loyal and quiet. He understood loyalty wasn't free; it was earned and maintained.

But Ace stood out from the rest. He wasn't just another recruit trying to get by. He looked at Knox like a mentor, maybe even a father figure. He wanted more than handouts and a place to sleep. He wanted to earn his place, rise in the ranks, and be someone in this world. You could see it in how he carried himself, eager, observant, always trying to prove himself. He wasn't content being a runner. He wanted a seat at the table.

And Knox? He saw the hunger in Ace and respected it.

Even with all the money Knox was making and the loyalty he commanded, he remained a prisoner of his past. As a convicted felon, he couldn't get a passport, a driver's license, open a bank account, or legally own property. Years of run-ins with the law, stretching back to his teenage years, had stripped him of access to the basic tools needed to build a legitimate future.

Though he wasn't legally allowed to drive, that never stopped him from getting behind the wheel, or from paying others to do it for him. But it was often behind the wheel where trouble found him. Traffic stops became traps. One wrong move, one missed taillight, and the police had all the reason they needed to stop him, search him, and pull the thread on whatever else he had going on.

Like many caught in the cycle of street life, Knox faced major barriers when it came to building real, sustainable wealth. Without access to banking or credit, everything was cash, untraceable but limiting. There was no way to grow legally, no path to equity, no safe investments. He was hustling nonstop, but always on borrowed time. The legal system made sure of that. It didn't matter how smart he was or how much he stacked; the rules of the game were never designed for him to win.

The threat of arrest, betrayal, or violence was always just around the corner. The same streets that gave him his power could take it all away in a blink. Even as he built his empire, Knox remained shackled to a system that refused to let him rise above it.

As I became more immersed in that world, the clubs, the streets, the hustle, I felt myself slowly detaching from my family. The connections I once had with my cousins and extended relatives faded into silence. The laughter and familiarity that once filled holidays and birthdays were replaced by awkward conversations and strained smiles, like we were strangers pretending to still know each other. The distance wasn't just physical, it was emotional. It felt like the only people left in my family life were my son, my mom, and me. And even then, we were each carrying our own weight, silently drowning in our separate battles without knowing how to reach for one another.

Yes, the money was steady, and from the outside, it might have looked like I was winning, but it was coming at a price I hadn't fully calculated. I believed I could live a double life without consequence, that I could keep the truth from my family. As far as I knew, neither side of my immediate family had discovered I was dancing or dealing. But the streets knew. Word always gets around. Friends knew. Enemies, too. And once the truth was out, it became another weapon they used against me.

The DCF started knocking again, responding to false reports made by people with vendettas, people who wanted to see me fall. It was another wake-up call that no matter how hard I tried to compartmentalize my life, the pieces were starting to bleed into one another, unraveling the illusion of control I had worked so hard to maintain.

Through all of this, I searched for comfort in my love life, though love was the last thing I truly found. Raequan had an unshakable grip on me, an emotional and physical pull that defied logic. No matter how many red flags waved in my face, something about him kept me tethered. His narcissism chipped away at my spirit, and yet, I stayed. He made me feel small, insignificant, always chasing something just out of reach. And somehow, I let him. I mistook his dominance for passion, his manipulation for desire. The truth was, our connection lived somewhere between lust and emotional dependency, and it blurred the line between pain and pleasure.

He broke me down, brick by brick, and I let him, convincing myself that if I could just become the woman he wanted, maybe he'd finally choose me. Around him, I twisted myself into a version I thought he couldn't resist. I suppressed my ego, fed his, and wore the shape of his approval like a mask. The most unsettling part? A piece of me liked it. I liked how he controlled me, how he made me feel like I needed him to feel complete. He didn't have to tell me I was worthless, I already believed it. He just confirmed it.

Raequan never objected to me being a stripper. In fact, he embraced it, even accompanied me to clubs, just not the one where I danced. That place was mine. During this chapter of my life, I also began to explore my attraction to women. There were flirtations and moments of curiosity, mostly shared in Raequan's presence, often encouraged by him. We pulled women in together at clubs, but it never became anything deeper for me. Still, those moments revealed a different side of me, one I didn't fully understand but was drawn to. A side that longed to be seen, even if it was only ever halfway recognized.

Through all of this, Raequan remained a stranger to the most important part of my world, my son. He met Amadeus only a few times, and the indifference was unmistakable. He never asked about him, never showed interest in his life. And truthfully, I never pressed it. I kept that part of my life cordoned off, calling Raequan just a "friend" when my son asked. From the way Raequan spoke, it was clear he wasn't ready for kids, especially not someone else's.

That's why what happened next caught me completely off guard.

I remember it was a Saturday night, and we hit up Oasis, a nightclub in Brandon that had a totally different vibe than our usual city spots. It was classier, more upscale, and that night, everything felt a little more magical. I'd met up with a couple of girls from work, and Requan was there with his crew. Together we created memories that, for a few hours, made me forget everything else. The music pulsed through my veins, the drinks flowed, the lights danced across the room, it felt like a dream.

But dreams end.

When the club let out at 3 a.m., it was time to take Raequan home, our routine. He drove, and I slid into the passenger seat, still riding the buzz from the night. My head was light, my spirit even lighter, until he turned the music down. That was my first sign.

"Hey, you good, B?" he asked, glancing at me with that smile, gold teeth flashing under the glow of the dashboard. I had always loved his smile, even when it masked the truth.

"Yeah, I'm good," I replied, leaning over to rest my head on his shoulder.

But he shifted. Moved my head off him gently. "I gotta tell you something," he said, his voice suddenly serious.

"What's up?" I asked, confused by the shift.

He hesitated, then, "Rhea's pregnant."

Everything in me stopped. My breath. My thoughts. My world.

"What?" I sat up fast, turning to face him fully. "What the hell are you talking about?"

"She's having my son," he said, so casually. Like it was nothing. Like I was nothing.

The words hit harder than any punch ever could. The tears came without warning. Hot, relentless, full of disbelief and heartbreak. I flinched when he reached for me, pressing myself against the passenger door like I could disappear.

I stared out the window, the night suddenly colder, emptier. Rhea? The name I'd buried, ignored, pretended didn't matter. She wasn't some side girl, she was the one. And now she was carrying his child. Not me. Her.

The rest of the drive was a silent funeral for what I thought we had.

When we got to his place, he didn't pull into the driveway like he usually did. He parked down the street. My heart sank even lower. "Is she inside?" I asked, barely above a whisper. "Is that why you parked here?"

Silence. He didn't need to answer.

He got out, left the door open. I slid across the seat, wiping my face, trying to gather the pieces of myself.

"B, call me when you get home," he said, leaning into the door frame. "Did you hear me? I know we need to talk. Just... tonight ain't it."

I looked up at him, shaking with rage and grief. "Really? Tonight wasn't the night to talk, but it was the night to drop this on me and leave me broken?"

His face didn't move. No apology. No emotion. Just closed the door.

I hit the gas and tore out of there, tires screeching. I wanted him to hear it. I wanted the sound to haunt him.

I turned the music all the way up, but it couldn't drown out the sound of my own heartbreak. I screamed out the window, over and over, until my voice cracked. Slammed my fists against the steering wheel, each hit a cry for everything I had lost.

The drive home was a blur. I don't remember the turns, the lights, the streets. Just pain. Consuming, raw, and endless.

Inside, the house was silent, but my mind was anything but. The shock from earlier still echoed inside me, louder than any music or scream. I moved like a ghost through my own home, heading straight for the kitchen. I poured myself a drink, something strong enough to numb the ache in my chest. Then I remembered the leftover cocaine from the other night, tucked away in a drawer. I looked at it. It looked back at me.

But it was 5 a.m., and I couldn't bring myself to do it. Instead, I rolled a blunt, lit it, and let the smoke fill my lungs. I exhaled slowly, trying to push out the pain, the confusion, the heartbreak, but nothing left with the smoke. I didn't want to feel. I didn't want to cry. I didn't want to care. But there I was, doing all of the above. Sitting in the quiet, wrapped in a blanket of sorrow I had worn too many times before.

Am I addicted to pain? The thought crept in like a whisper I couldn't shake.

I didn't call him.

I eventually passed out on the couch, my half-smoked blunt still in the ashtray, the taste of heartbreak lingering in my mouth.

When I woke up, the sun was already creeping in through the blinds. My phone buzzed.

RAEQUAN: ?

That was it. Just a question mark.

No, "I'm sorry." No, "Are you okay?" Just the bare minimum.

I stared at it. No words. No reaction. Just... emptiness.

ME: ...

I didn't respond. Not that day. Not the next. Not for several days after that.

I told myself I was strong enough this time, strong enough to finally choose myself. I wanted to believe I was done chasing someone who only ever showed up when it was easy for him. I wanted to believe I could break the cycle, stop shrinking myself just to be seen. But the truth was simple and painful:

I wasn't ready.

Eventually, I went back. Back to the man who never really held me. Back to the chaos I called home.

About a week passed in silence before his name lit up my phone again. This time, it wasn't a vague emoji or some cryptic message. It was real.

RAEQUAN: Where you at?

I stared at the screen, heart thudding. He had a baby on the way. He had chosen someone else. Rhea.

I had told myself I wouldn't go backwards. I had told myself it was over. I had promised myself that this was the end. And yet... here he was. Still checking for me. A part of me lit up, and I hated that it did. *Why is he reaching out? Does this mean I still matter? Am I still the one he thinks about?*

My fingers moved before I could stop them.

ME: Hey... didn't think you'd be texting me.

RAEQUAN: Why?

ME: Because of our last conversation... you know, the baby and all.

RAEQUAN: WYA?

ME: Home.

RAEQUAN: Come to my cousin's crib.

ME: When?

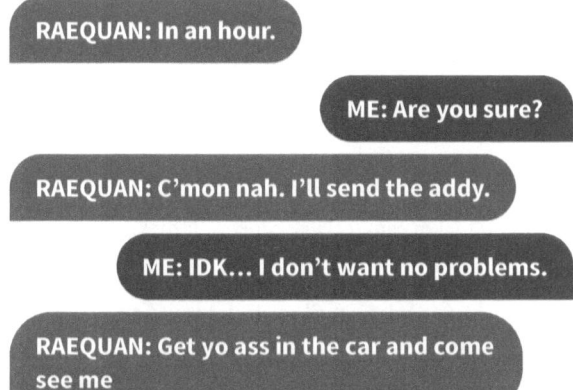

I hesitated. My stomach flipped. Butterflies didn't just flutter, they swarmed.

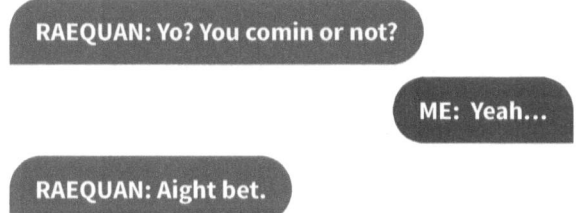

And that was it. I didn't just respond to the message; I responded with everything I hadn't healed.

The silence. The longing. The parts of me still hoping that if he came back, maybe we were still something. Honestly...I wasn't addicted to him. I was addicted to the *hope* of him. The version I created in my head, the one who might choose me if I waited long enough. If I stayed available. That hope was my drug. And I kept relapsing.

I chose him over and over again, over my growth, over my healing, over my peace. Every time he resurfaced, I opened the door. Because I didn't know how to stop needing someone who only needed me when it was convenient.

And I convinced myself that if a baby couldn't keep him from reaching out to me... maybe I still had a place in his heart. Maybe we had something unfinished. Maybe I wasn't supposed to close the door just yet.

That's what trauma does. It lies. It tells you that inconsistency is proof of love. It makes pain feel like passion. It makes longing feel like connection.

By the time his birthday rolled around, I was already drowning in mixed signals. He was throwing a party at Empire, the same club we used to hit in Ybor City. I figured he'd be too wrapped up in his own life to even think of me.

But he texted again:

> **RAEQUAN: Pull up. It won't feel right without you.**

That one line undid everything. I hadn't learned yet that when someone says it won't feel right without you, they're not always saying you *matter*. Sometimes, they're just saying they're used to your *availability*. And I was still learning how to stop being convenient for people who were careless with me.

I worked the day shift so I could make it that night, but before heading home, I stopped by Nadia's. She was hosting a little kickback, drinks poured, lines already cut on the table. I told myself I'd only stay for a few, just long enough to still get to the club.

I didn't plan on getting as lit as I did. Time slipped away. I was supposed to get ready at home since the club's dressing room had nothing but a basic shower setup. But one line turned into a few drinks, and before I knew it, it was 1 a.m. I was too intoxicated to drive, so I went home.

Later, a friend from the club called and said Raequan was clearly upset, grilling her, asking where I was.

When the club let out, he called. "Yo B, where you at?"

"I'm real sorry, I lost track of time, "

He cut me off. "Where are you at?"

"Home."

Click. He hung up.

I figured he'd sleep it off. So did I, until I was yanked awake in the dark.

He was in my room, pulling me up by the arm. I was disoriented, heart pounding. I had never seen him like this. He was angry, interrogating me, eyes wild. I told him he was scaring me, but he didn't care. He gripped my shoulders, shook me, then threw me onto the bed.

And then, just like that, his energy flipped.

He lay down beside me, his tone suddenly softer, like the storm had passed. He told me how hurt he was that I hadn't shown up. He thought I was with someone else. I cried, trying to explain, I had just gone home, lost track of time. But he wasn't really listening.

Next thing I knew, he was kissing me. And we ended up having sex.

Over the next week, he started coming around more often. At first, I thought maybe he missed me. Maybe he realized he cared more than he let on.

But things started to shift. What Raequan didn't know was that I was living a double life.

He had no idea about the business I was doing with Knox, Benny, and Wes. I told him they were like family, kids I grew up with, nothing more. In reality, they were part of my other world, one that Raequan couldn't be part of. His crew ran with people who were enemies of

187

Knox and his circle, and if they all found out it wouldn't be good. There was tension in the streets between their sides, and even though Knox, Benny, and Wes didn't like that I was dating Raequan, they left it alone, and he never asked too many questions.

Maybe he didn't want the answers.

One night, I was in the shower. I'd left my phone out on the table. When I came out, towel wrapped around me, I had no idea he had invited people over. I crossed the hall toward my room, minding my business, and suddenly, he rushed me. His grip was tight as he grabbed my arm and shoved me hard onto the bed. "What the fuck you doin', bruh? I got my people out there. You tryin' to show them something?"

"What is your problem? I didn't even know they were here!" I snapped, snatching my arm back. "Don't grab me like that."

He stared at me, hard. "Aight, B. You like to play games, huh? Okay. So who the fuck is Corey?"

The name caught me off guard. "Corey is a dude I used to smoke with back in high school. We barely keep in touch. He has a girl now. There is nothing there. He just hit me up earlier to smoke...Did you go through my phone?" I asked, stepping back.

He shoved me down again, harder this time, pinning me to the bed. "You keep playing games with me. I'm gonna find out who he is, and if you lyin', B, I swear to God."

I started to panic. "Get off me!" I shouted.

He finally let go and stood back while I got dressed, watching my every move. "Call him," he said.

"What?"

"Call him."

"Oh my God. Are you serious? He has a girlfriend. We don't even talk like that."

"I said call him."

I hesitated, but dialed. Corey answered, of course, the one time I didn't want him to. Before I could speak, Raequan snatched the phone, cursed him out, made threats, and hung up. Then he deleted the number and kept my phone for the rest of the night.

Weeks later, I ran into Corey at Empire. I apologized for the bullshit.

He just shook his head. "You need to stop dating men like him."

Chapter 13

Life Be Lifeing

Another person I couldn't seem to escape was Zara. Just when I thought I'd put enough distance between us, she reappeared, in the worst way possible.

One night, I walked into the dressing room after a long shift, exhausted, ready to change and dip. And there she was.

Zara.

Smirking like she owned the place. Like she hadn't spent years trying to ruin my life.

"What the fuck? I know this ain't real," I said, half-laughing, trying to steady my nerves.

Nadia, right behind me, froze. "What's the problem?"

"Wassup, bitch," Zara snapped, her voice sharp and mean. This wasn't casual banter. It was meant to cut.

"Fuck you, Zara. Who the hell do you think you are coming to my place of work?" My voice rose. My heart raced. The whole room stopped. Girls turned, eyes locked on us.

Zara crossed her arms, fake calm. "Hoe, please. Don't make me tell these girls how scary you really are. You still pressed over old shit? That's not my fault."

"Old shit?" I laughed bitterly.

"I don't need your permission to get a bag," she snapped, stepping closer. "Can't handle the pressure? Clock out and go cry somewhere."

Nadia slid between us. "Innocence, chill. You've been drinking, remember? And you got stuff on you."

Zara smirked. "You ain't gonna do shit. You know who I run with. You don't want those problems."

The room gasped just enough to send me over the edge. I shrugged off Nadia's arm and stepped into Zara's face. "You're gonna get what's coming to you, I swear."

"Ladies!" Jeff's voice cracked through the tension as he stormed in. "You wanna fight, take it outside. I don't have time for this shit, there's money to be made. Now get to work!"

We stood there, breathing heavy. Zara locked eyes with me.

"This ain't over," I muttered.

"I'll be waiting, bitch."

Later, I barged into Jeff's office.

"She can't fucking work here, Jeff."

He didn't even look surprised. "You need to calm the hell down, barging in like you own the place. Why don't you go home and cool off?"

"You don't get it. She's made my life, and my son's, a living hell."

"As long as she's making money and not throwing fists on the floor, she stays," he said flatly. "You wanna leave, leave. But I need dancers. Honey and Lexus already left for Miami."

I slammed the door. "Heartless fuck," I hissed. I stormed into the bathroom and broke down. Nadia followed.

"Yo, you good?" she asked gently. "Is that the chick from the voice-mails? The one who's been messing with your mom and your son?"

I nodded, tears falling. "I'm scared, Nadia. I can't fight her. She's in a gang, she knows how to scrap, and she wants me to pop off. I'm not safe, and now she's here. In *my* space."

"You're right. It's a lot. But you can't let her win. Your son needs you. I got you. You're not alone."

My name was called over the speakers, my stage cue.

"I can't go up right now."

"I got you," she said. "I'll tell Crash to put me up."

I hid in a stall, wiped my tears, and took a bump. Just enough to level out. I had another hour to finish. No way I was paying a fee to leave early.

I avoided the dressing room and found Kevin, the night manager.

"She in there?" I asked.

He radioed. "She's in the manager's office. Dressing room's clear."

I rushed to grab my stuff, wild thoughts racing, trash her things, hide her heels, mess with her money. But I didn't.

Not because I didn't want to. Because I couldn't afford to bring that mess back to my son or my mom. I walked out calm, head high, even if my hands were shaking.

Jeff's solution? Split shifts. She'd work different nights. It helped. For a while.

She didn't last long. A few months, maybe. But even in that short time, she left a scar. One more wound in a long list I hadn't asked for.

Shortly after she left, the visits from DCF increased. More frequent. More invasive. One caseworker showed up one afternoon and started reading from a report filled with disturbing accusations:

"Do you use drugs? Do you use them in front of Amadeus?""Do you sell drugs? In front of your son?"

I stood frozen, rage and fear twisting in my chest. It was clear someone was feeding them lies, deliberate, targeted lies. And I knew exactly who it was.

The caseworker asked me to take a drug test on the spot. My heart raced. Thankfully, Knox was there. Calm, composed, and sharper than anyone gave him credit for, he stepped forward and asked one simple question: "Do you have a court order?"

The answer was no.

"Then she's not doing anything," he said firmly, arms crossed.

The caseworker didn't push. They couldn't.

But the damage was done. My nerves were shot, and paranoia followed me everywhere. It wasn't just about keeping my job a secret anymore, it was about protecting my son, my home, my life. And now, Zara had crossed into territory that felt like war.

My relationships with other dancers, dealers, and club regulars resembled something like family, not in the traditional sense, but in the way trauma-bonded people look out for one another. We weren't close, not really. We didn't know each other's secrets or hold one another accountable. But we lent clothes, gave rides, shared tips, and made small loans. That kind of loyalty was our currency. I stayed loyal, even though deep down I knew many of them wouldn't do the same for me.

Over time, my views on men hardened. I stopped believing there were any good ones left. Most were selfish, manipulative, and untrustworthy. I grew disgusted, yet I still entertained shallow connections, using them as tools, for pleasure, for money, for distraction. I never stepped into full-blown prostitution, but I was adjacent to it, helping other women move in that world and sometimes taking a cut. For many of them, it wasn't a choice. It was survival.

My heart was off-limits. I guarded it like it was made of glass and fire, fragile, yet capable of burning anyone who got too close. I kept my private life completely separate. No man ever learned my real name. I never revealed that I had a son. I never let them near my home. My life outside the club was mine alone, and I made sure it stayed that way.

When Raequan and I weren't speaking, I shut down emotionally. Sex became purely physical, a performance. I avoided pictures, affection, or even eye contact that lingered too long. If a man got too close, if he started showing signs of caring, I ghosted him. Feelings weren't allowed. Love was weakness, and I couldn't afford to be weak.

Instead, I leaned into lust. Lust was clean. It had no strings. It gave me a sense of power when everything else in my life felt out of control. I liked the chase, the control, the way I could make a man feel wanted one moment and insignificant the next. My mouth was sharp, my standards high. If a man didn't look good, had no money, or couldn't satisfy me, I'd cut him down with words that left bruises. I was called intimidating. Too cold. Too independent. Too much. But I didn't care. Power was my drug.

For two years, I even had a "sponsor", Frank, an older man in his late 60s or early 70s. He was wealthy, physically incapable of sex due to health issues, and perfect for the version of me I had become. He wanted companionship. I wanted luxury. He'd take me to upscale restaurants, buy me gifts, and tell me stories of his past. I gave him my time, and he gave me his wallet. There was no romance, no pretense, just a mutually beneficial transaction wrapped in expensive dinners and polite laughter.

Other times, I'd go out with men who paid me just to be seen with them, to accompany them to a gala, a dinner, a VIP lounge. These weren't dates. They were deals. I gave them my presence, and in return, they funded my lifestyle. No feelings. No intimacy. Just me, in control, never letting them get close enough to see the cracks.

And there were cracks. But I had gotten good at hiding them.

In the strip club, I met men with every imaginable fetish. Over time, I learned how to exploit their desires without flinching.

One client paid me $50 to $100 just to urinate in a cup so he could drink it. Another booked the champagne room just to beg me to crush his testicles beneath my heels, twisting them like I was putting out a cigarette. He paid well for the pain. Then there was the European attorney, Benjamin. He reeked of sweat, refused deodorant, and indulged in cocaine-fueled binges and sadomasochism. He'd strip naked, hand us his tools, nipple clamps, pinchers, tasers, and pay me and another dancer hundreds, sometimes thousands, depending on how long we stayed and how much coke we brought.

"Innocence, our guy just showed up," Nadia called as she found me in the dressing room, wiping myself down with baby wipes, trying to erase the last dance.

"Daaang, bitch, was it that bad? How many wipes you need?" she laughed, catching my expression.

"Ugh, it's disgusting. Like... how do you not smell yourself? Then he put my titty in his mouth, I almost slapped him. Charged him an extra fifty just for that. I still smell him."

"Listen, did you hear who's out there? Our dude, what's his name again?"

"Benjamin. How could you forget?" I laughed. "That's your favorite dollar bill, ain't it?"

"Hell yeah. I forgot, you right," Nadia smirked. "I sat on his lap waiting for you. He doesn't want dances here, but he's down to chill, and there's candy."

I knew what that meant. Cocaine. He always came with a stash. "I need to make some money," I said. "It's been slow. These dudes are broke and extra. If he's down to meet after, at least we won't have to tip the club."

"Exactly. And maybe he'll want more candy, and book the suite again. Easy money, bitch."

I nodded. "Let me change outfits. Go sit with him before one of these other hoes gets any ideas, today ain't the day. I swear I'll pop off."

Nadia dipped. I got ready fast.

When the club closed, Nadia and I were already plotting. We got Benjamin to pay for the hotel suite, easy. I had to re-up with Knox first. Dancing only pulled $200 that night, but flipping coke brought in another $400. Not bad for a slow shift.

I met Nadia at the suite. Benjamin answered the door with a sloppy grin.

"Heyyy, my beautiful girls!" he beamed, already high.

"See? Told you we'd come," Nadia purred. We each kissed a cheek like dark little promises.

"I brought you candy," I teased, laying out a few lines on the table.

"Hell yeah!" he dove in, nose to the table, snorting deep.

When he came up, sniffing and buzzing, he pulled out a plastic bag of crumpled bills and tossed it like confetti.

"Let's make it rain, girls! Y'all ready to beat me like I owe you rent?"

"You know we are," Nadia laughed, slipping off her jacket.

I reached for the clamps, smirking. "Which toy first, baby?"

By the end of the night, we'd made over two grand just for playing his twisted little game.

Pain for pleasure. His... mine... both.

"Damn, we cashed out tonight," Nadia said, thumbing through the bills on the bed. "Should've brought the ball gag. He's gettin' mouthy."

I didn't laugh. I was staring at the bruises on his thighs, the red welts across his chest. The things this man begged us to do. The fact that I didn't flinch.

I used to think I did it for the money. But the truth was, I liked it. I liked using men like him. Men who begged for it. Men who made it easy to turn power into profit.

"You good?" Nadia asked, already rolling a blunt.

I nodded, still staring at Benjamin, out cold, drooling into the couch, toys scattered like broken weapons. "Yeah," I said. "I'm great."

The room reeked of sweat, powder, and smoke. Sin had no shame here.

"He said he's in town till the end of the month," Nadia said. "Think he'll call again?"

I didn't answer at first. I looked at my reflection in the black TV screen, makeup smudged, eyes hollow, smile gone. "Yeah," I finally said. "He'll call. After tonight? This was our best night yet." I laughed, counting my cut.

No stage. No grinding. No hands on me. Just control. Just games. And way more money than a lap dance ever paid.

These men weren't people. They were walking wallets. Just another income stream to feed the lifestyle I couldn't let go of. They came for fantasy. I gave them exactly that.

But behind the lashes and painted smile, I was numb. Compartmentalizing every degrading moment like it was just part of the job. Because it was.

As the months passed, I stopped hiding my love for money. I didn't just want it, I needed it. I couldn't feel like I had accomplished anything unless I made close to a thousand dollars a day. Money fed my ego, my habits, my identity. It bought me everything I thought I needed, status, beauty, drugs, alcohol, power. And most dangerously, it gave me the illusion of control.

My self-worth was no longer tied to who I was, but to how many dances I sold, how many bills I picked up off the floor, how much desire I could stir in a man's eyes. The club became my stage, and I played my part to perfection. Nobody knew my real story, and I liked it that way. Reinvention came easy when you had a new alias, a fresh wig, and the money to back it up.

But behind all of it, I was unraveling.

Drugs, which had once been occasional, became my daily routine. When painful memories crept in, when I thought about my childhood, my father, the assault, the betrayal, I drowned them out with a high. I stopped being able to dance sober. Being intoxicated made me feel fearless, seductive, untouchable. I wasn't partying anymore, I was self-medicating. Every pull, every line, every drink numbed the parts of me I couldn't bear to face.

I was trying to fix the brokenness inside me with everything outside of me. But nothing worked. And still, I couldn't stop.

I totaled my first Lexus in a car accident. Thankfully, no one was hurt, but the emotional hit was heavy. That car had become a symbol of the life I was building, and losing it felt like a personal failure. So I did what I always did when life knocked me down: I got up and hustled harder. I picked up extra shifts at the club, pushed more coke, and within a month, I was behind the wheel of a new Lexus. That insatiable hunger, for more money, more recognition, more material success, never left me. It fueled everything I did.

Knox and Wes were still living the fast life, too. Wes had carved out his own corner of the hustle. He sold weed and coke independently from Knox's operations, while keeping his job at the jeweler, an odd but effective cover that helped legitimize his income. His apartment became our escape from the grime of the chaotic trap houses. It was his sanctuary, and eventually, it became mine too.

Wes's place was styled like a bachelor pad pulled straight from a rap video. Framed posters of Scarface and Big Pun hung on the walls, flanked by images of dollar bills and opulence. His furniture was all sleek leather and glass, black, chrome, clean. Every cushion fluffed, every surface wiped down. It was the kind of place that gave off the illusion of order and success, even when everything outside those walls was in disarray.

I felt a strange sense of comfort there. It became one of the few spaces where I could exhale, even if just for a little while. Milani happened to live in the same complex, and I often found myself bouncing between her apartment and Wes's. I'd stop in to spend time with her and her son, then drift back to Wes's place to hang out, decompress, or crash after a long shift. That small triangle of spaces gave me the closest thing to peace I could find during that time.

Through it all, my mother kept showing up for our family in all the ways that mattered. She had recently landed a job at Medco, a steady 9-to-5 that offered more security than her previous work. Around the same time, she moved into a house in Wellswood. It belonged to my Tia, who had offered it to her as a way to give her more room and stability. Despite everything she was dealing with, financial stress, family burdens, and her own exhaustion, she never dropped the ball. She was still the one who made sure my son had what he needed. She was still the one holding our fractured family together.

My father, on the other hand, was still living a double life. He worked under the table as a plumber, collected Social Security Income, and hustled pain pills on the side just to stay afloat. Around that time, he started seeing someone new. His world remained chaotic, messy, and familiar in the worst ways. Still, despite everything, he began making an effort to reconnect, mainly through my son.

The reconnection caught me off guard. After years of keeping my father at a distance, I found myself opening the door again. That crack in the wall between us seemed to extend to my mother, too. They started speaking again, minimally, and suddenly, he was showing up at her house, hoping to see my son. Whatever remnants of their old relationship had once existed didn't rekindle, they remained who they always were with each other: civil until it turned into shouting, and then distant like strangers under the same roof. The only difference now was that my father would leave when the tension got too thick, instead of letting it boil over.

His temper hadn't gone anywhere. My mother, soft-spoken and composed, would hold back until she couldn't, and then her words would cut deep. They moved like seasoned dancers through their old patterns, predictable, tired, and sad. And yet, she still cared for him in quiet ways. She'd cook extra food and save a plate for him, even when he hadn't come by. Her peacekeeping was habitual, almost automatic. They coexisted in the same house on different islands, my father glued to the television, my mother buried in a book, and my son lost in his Xbox.

But there were rare moments of warmth. On good days, they'd take my son out for Cuban sandwiches at the West Tampa Sandwich Shop or stop by Mr. Empanada. It was a fleeting illusion of normalcy, a brief breath in a long-held exhale.

My son called my father "Nano," and in his young eyes, Nano was larger than life, the closest thing he had to a dad. Nano told stories the way he once told them to me: wild adventures, rules broken, crab traps set at sunrise, and movies snuck into without tickets. He never missed a baseball game. He cheered from the bleachers like it was the major leagues, his pride loud and unfiltered. They had their rituals, especially during mango season on La Salle Street, picking fruit straight from the tree, juice dripping down their arms, like it was their little secret. Nano spoiled him with everything, time, gifts, money, and never asked for anything in return.

But Nano's love came with a sharp edge. One afternoon, my son fell off the monkey bars and hurt his arm. A loud pop echoed through the playground. Another child ran for help, and Nano showed up within seconds, red-faced and raging. "Son of a bitch, Amadeus!" he shouted. "How the hell did you fall? What were you thinking?" My son, already in pain, was now frozen in fear. He tried to hide, but Nano followed, unleashing a storm of insults and shame.

Even on the ride home, the berating didn't stop. The car filled with his anger, each word louder than the last. My son shrank into the seat, holding back tears, until a concerned bystander, watching it all unfold, called the police.

When they pulled into the driveway, flashing lights weren't far behind. My stomach dropped. All I could think about was the stash in the house, my drug operation was suddenly on the edge of exposure. I walked out to meet the officers, doing my best to stay composed, to appear like any other concerned mother. They asked questions, scanned our faces, and pressed gently to see if there was mistreatment. I gave them what they needed, just enough to walk away. But even after they left, the air stayed thick with fear.

My son's arm was broken. He wore a cast for weeks, sidelined from baseball, his joy paused. But it wasn't just his arm that ached. The incident with Nano had shaken more than his body, it had rattled the fragile life I was trying to keep intact. My father's explosive love, my hidden hustle, the constant threat of everything crashing down, it was a house of cards, and I could feel the wind picking up.

Chapter 14

Guns, Roses, & Money

By this point, I was neck-deep in the grow operation. Knox had talked me into staying on board, convincing me that backing out now would be a waste, stupid, even. And he was right about one thing: I was already in too deep. I put the water bill in my name, signed on for upkeep, and even added myself to the lease for one of the grow houses. My commitment was official, legal, and traceable. There was no turning back.

Trips to the grow houses became routine. They were hours away now, tucked far from the city where prying eyes might notice too much foot traffic or too many lights. My days were long and grueling, cleaning, checking on systems, tending to the plants. What I thought would be glamorous, profitable, maybe even fun, turned out to be relentless work. Growing marijuana wasn't just throwing seeds in soil and waiting for cash to sprout. It required precision, patience, and care I didn't have. I wasn't a green thumb, I was a hustler out of her element. But Knox? Knox lived for it. His eyes lit up every time he talked about yields, nutrients, and strains. This was his world, and he was in it for the long game.

To avoid detection, we had to be smart, really smart. The electric company kept tabs on usage, so we worked hard to make our numbers look "normal." That meant cycling the lights during off-peak hours and using energy-efficient setups wherever possible. But that wasn't always enough. We got bold, reckless even. Some meters didn't have locked covers back then, and through a few trap house connections, we knew electricians who were down to help. They'd rig the wiring or slide magnets over the meters to lower the readings. It was risky, illegal, but necessary. Every watt counted.

There was one boundary I tried to hold: my father. I didn't want him involved. He wasn't reliable, and I knew if things went south, he'd either bail or blow up. But Knox needed someone, someone to stay at the grow house, keep eyes on things, feed the pitbull we left there as our built-in alarm system. My father volunteered. Against my better judgment, I agreed.

One of the grow houses was near Gaither High School. A nice neighborhood, clean, quiet, the kind of place where nosy neighbors could ruin everything. We had to make it look like someone actually lived there. Trash had to go out on time. Lawns had to be cut. The lights had to flicker on and off like any normal house. My dad helped with that, did some minor plumbing, maintenance, and played the part of a low-key resident.

For a while, it worked. The operation was running smoothly. We were finally seeing returns on the heavy investment. But deep down, I knew it was only a matter of time before something gave.

As I became more entrenched in the drug world, the boundaries of my life blurred. What had once been whispered about in shadows was now my new normal. The money flowed in, more than I'd ever imagined, and the thrill of it became a drug all its own. But with every high came a crash, and one night, reality came barreling in harder than ever before.

That night, I had a friend staying over. My car had recently been wrecked, so we'd decided to lay low and stay in. She'd fallen asleep in the living room with her son in a car seat nearby, and I was resting in my bedroom. Everything was quiet, until...

I was jolted awake by the cold press of a pistol against my forehead.

In that split second, my life changed. I was being robbed at gunpoint, the quiet of my home shattered by the consequences of the choices I'd made. At first, it felt unreal, like a cruel, twisted prank. But that illusion dissolved when I saw my friend being held at gunpoint too, tears running down her face as she tried to shield her baby. She had answered a knock on the door, thinking it was Raequan. But it wasn't.

The men rushed in and tore my living room apart, searching for drugs and cash. My re-up, worth about $2,000, was gone, along with $700 in savings. But more than the money, they stole my sense of safety, my illusion of control.

They forced me back into the bedroom, yelling, demanding more. I had nothing left. I cried as they tore through drawers, clothes, everything, while my son slept just feet away, untouched by the nightmare swirling around him. One of the gunmen pressed the weapon back to my forehead, his eyes daring me to lie. But there was nothing to give. He didn't believe me.

When they had taken what they could, they herded my friend and me into the bathroom. We clung to each other, sobbing, begging. I thought it was over. The gunman aimed and pulled the trigger.

Click.

Nothing.

The gun jammed. We gasped. His partner screamed, "Come on!" and in the next breath, they were gone.

Miraculously, my son slept through it all. The gunshots never came, and we were left, shaken, stripped, and still alive.

They took everything, our phone batteries, IDs, house keys, even the keys to my car. We were trapped. Desperate, I searched and found a spare key to my totaled Lexus at the far end of the complex. It was our only shot. My friend and I debated staying, but our fear decided for us.

We got out.

I dropped my son off at my mom's sometime after midnight. I didn't have the words to explain what had happened. She didn't ask. She just took him, worry heavy in her silence.

From there, I drove straight to the only safe place I could think of: Knox's grandfather's house. I needed shelter. I needed answers. Mostly, I needed to feel like I hadn't lost everything.

I had almost been killed over $2,700. That number haunted me, not because of its size, but because of what it almost cost me. The weight of it all pushed my anxiety to a breaking point. I wasn't just shaken, I was unraveling.

When I got to Knox's grandfather's house that night, I broke down. Knox, always quick to move in a crisis, started making calls. Almost immediately, suspicion turned toward Raequan. It wasn't just paranoia, tension between Raequan's crew and Knox's had been simmering for a while, and this felt like it could have been a setup. The rivalry wasn't new. This was just another spark in an already volatile fire.

An hour later, Wes called with a lead. He'd tracked down Knox's younger cousin, Cash, and his sister, both of them had some of my stolen belongings. The betrayal cut deep.

Cash had been living with Knox ever since a falling out with family in Puerto Rico. I had only seen him a handful of times, mostly in passing when Wes and I were still close. He'd been training to become a boxer under Knox's father's guidance, but a family dispute forced him back to Tampa, where Knox reluctantly took him in. Knox tried to guide him, but it was clear Cash was slipping between the cracks.

I remembered Cash being at my apartment a few weeks prior during a re-up. I hadn't thought twice about it, he was family. But that's how he knew where I lived and what I had stashed away.

We found Cash and his sister at Benny's mom's house. When we arrived, Knox didn't hold back. The betrayal burned too hot. He beat them both, venting his fury in fists while I stood numb. I got my ID and my phone battery back, but everything else, my savings, my product, was gone.

The next day, they came to my apartment to help clean up the wreckage they'd left behind. The space was unrecognizable, drawers emptied, furniture overturned, and broken glass everywhere. But it wasn't just my apartment that was in shambles. I was, too.

I couldn't stay there. The fear lingered in every corner. The shadows held too many memories. I broke my lease and moved back in with my mom. It was the only place that still felt like a sanctuary, though even there, the trauma followed me like a shadow I couldn't shake.

I was haunted by the image of the gun pressed to my forehead, by the betrayal, by the illusion of safety shattered in seconds. What I'd built wasn't a life. It was a trap. And for the first time, I could see the truth: I wasn't in control. I had never been.

I wish I could say that was my last brush with death, but it wasn't.

Not long after the robbery at my old apartment, I found myself in the middle of a shootout inside Raequan's cousin's house. I had stopped by briefly before heading to my mom's to get ready for a night out. Raequan was on the phone, his voice low but tense. There was beef, something about one of his cousins and a guy on the other end of the line. I didn't ask questions. I'd learned by then to stay out of things that didn't concern me.

Less than an hour later, I was told to go to the back room and take Raequan and Rhea's baby with me. I sat on the bed, cradling the infant in my arms. Then the first gunshots rang out.

The windows shattered. Screams tore through the air, raw, panicked, agonizing. The baby started crying, and I rocked him, trying to keep him calm as my own panic surged through me. I was frozen, my heart hammering, ears ringing, as the chaos unfolded just feet away.

Time slowed. I sat there, paralyzed, until the door burst open. One of the men stumbled inside, his face torn open where his eye used to be. Blood streamed down his cheek, his screams slicing through the air. I clutched the baby tighter, terrified, until I heard Raequan yelling my name. The police were on their way.

I handed the baby to him and stepped into the living room. The scene was like something out of a nightmare, one of his cousins lay on the floor, riddled with bullets, gasping for breath as his life slipped away.

Adrenaline took over. I was shoved into my Chevy Caprice, the car I'd gotten after totaling my Lexus, and we fled the scene. My car, now riddled with bullet holes and a shattered back window held together by flimsy tint, bore the physical scars of the night. I drove home in a daze. Somehow, miraculously, I was unharmed. But I couldn't shake the feeling that my luck was running out.

That night marked a turning point.

Up until then, I had ignored every red flag with Raequan. I convinced myself the passion made it worth it, that the highs could somehow excuse the lows. But this, this wasn't just another low. This was a line I couldn't pretend I hadn't crossed. I was risking my life in the name of love, in the name of loyalty. And for what?

The truth was, I stayed with Raequan because it was familiar. Because I had gotten attached to the chaos, to the toxic jealousy, to the way he made me feel like I wasn't worthy of anything better. Deep down, I believed it. I believed I didn't deserve more.

After that night, I confronted him. I demanded to know why he hadn't protected me. Why had he left me to fend for myself in a war zone, literally and emotionally? I had shown up for him in every way, emotionally, financially, physically. I had been ride-or-die.

When things got real, when the bullets actually started flying, he disappeared.

We fought. Loud. Raw. Unfiltered. Everything we'd been pushing down finally erupted: his detachment, the manipulation, the empty promises, and his silence when I needed his voice the most. I had carried our relationship on my back for too long. And I was done.

"I almost got killed," I shouted, pacing the living room floor, heart pounding. "What the hell was that, Raequan?"

"Yo, both my cousins are in the hospital, one who might never see again and the other on a ventilator. You think I fucking knew about that shit? You think I would've had my baby there if I knew? Get the fuck outta here with your feelings."

"My feelings?" I laughed, bitter and stunned. "Oh, let's talk about feelings. You have none. You don't care about me. You don't care about us. When have you ever cared? I was in that room holding Rhea's baby, hearing gunshots, not knowing if I was going to die. And where were you?"

He stepped closer, voice rising. "Yo, what the fuck you want from me, B? You knew the truth. You know what it is and what it isn't. You know who the fuck I am!"

I backed away, shaking my head. "Not this time. You're not going to start twisting this again. I'm done playing that game."

"Wow. You on some other shit right now. I ain't never made you be with me. You chose this. You wanted me. And now you mad at yourself for it? So you blame me?"

"Yes. Because you never truly wanted me," I snapped. "You just used me. You only came around when it was convenient. You strung me along while giving someone else your child."

"Aight," he said, arms thrown wide. "So all the times you came to my family's crib, that was nothing? The earrings I bought you? I don't just buy any bitch that shit. All the nights out, all the times in my hood, you think I do that for someone I don't care about? Get the fuck outta here with your dumb shit. My cousins are in the hospital. My baby moms is trippin'. And now you wanna bring up the past like I'm the bad guy?"

I could feel it breaking, all of it.

"You bought me those earrings after four years, Raequan. Four years," I said, voice trembling. "Do you know how much I've done for you? You wrecked my car, never paid me back. Now my new one is trashed after this shit, and you're still not taking responsibility. I want you to be honest. Just once. Be honest."

He looked at me, jaw tight. Then he shrugged. "Aight... you want honesty? Here it is. I don't give a fuck." He walked out and slammed the door behind him.

That was the last night I ever saw him.

The connection we once had, intense, magnetic, consuming, had vanished. And all that remained was grief. Grief for a girl who had believed, too deeply, that this kind of love was better than being alone. That pain was just part of the package. That loyalty could make someone stay.

There are moments in life when you wonder where God is. Back then, I didn't know how to pray. I didn't know how to thank Him for sparing me when I didn't even know I needed saving. But now, looking back, I see His fingerprints all over my survival. Every close call. Every heartbreak that could've broken me, but didn't.

I was being protected. I just didn't know it yet.

.

Chapter 15

Lines Crossed

After ending things with Raequan for good, Wes and I decided to move in together, with my son, as roommates. It felt like a fresh start, a moment of peace. Having a male figure around brought a sense of security I hadn't felt in a long time, especially after everything I'd been through. Wes, for his part, was cycling through casual relationships. I met a few of the women, but none ever stuck around long enough to leave a lasting impression. Truthfully, I wasn't home much anyway. I was focused on stacking cash, hustling hard so I could finally afford a place for me and Amadeus.

Then Knox reappeared.

He'd been back and forth between here and New York City, lying low since the robbery at my old apartment. When he finally stopped by, I was taken aback. He looked different: leaner, more muscular, and with a quiet confidence that caught my attention in a way it never had before. His hair had grown out, and I've always had a weakness for long hair. He carried himself with a maturity, a presence that stirred something in me. For the first time, I saw Knox not just as the homie but as a man.

By then, I was spiraling: deeper into cocaine, heavier into drinking. The pain of the breakup with Raequan and the turbulent life I was living it all pushed me further into the void. And Knox? He became my new escape. My new partner in crime. We'd party all night, ride the high into the early morning hours, lost in a blur of smoke, liquor, and shared self-destruction. One of those nights, the inevitable happened, and we ended up in bed together.

It was awkward. It was impulsive. And yet, it felt strangely natural.

Wes noticed the shift between us. He was suspicious, but we kept it low for a while, sneaking off during group hangouts, linking up at Knox's place when we needed space. But nothing stays hidden for long.

Before we became official, I was still entertaining others. I wasn't ready to be anyone's girl. Some of the men I messed with recently were associates of the crew. Some of them had beef with Knox. That didn't sit well with him. I'd tell him I wanted him, but my actions said something else. I didn't expect to like Knox that way. I never thought we'd cross that line, sex, emotions, relationship, it was a lot to process. When we were together, I wanted just him. But when he wasn't around? Out of sight, out of mind.

Eventually, though, it became clear we weren't just friends any-more.

The feelings crept in, complicated, real, and impossible to ignore. Unlike the men I danced for or entertained, Knox had already made his way past my defenses. This wasn't about lust or money. He'd seen the worst of me and stayed. We weren't kids anymore. And Knox? He had grown into a man I couldn't deny. I realized he'd been waiting for this chance all along. When I finally told him I was ready, really ready, to be his, he didn't hesitate.

Once the cat was out of the bag, the whole crew knew.

Overnight, I stopped being "one of the guys." I became "Knox's girl." And with that label came all the judgment, whispers, and disappointment I hadn't prepared for.

Wes was the first to make his thoughts known...

"Yo, you heard that *American Gangster* album?" he asked, as I slid into his car one evening. Jay-Z was his favorite rapper, and he was visibly hyped. "B, you gotta hear number three, *American Dreamin'*. Yo, this album is hard!"

I smiled, trying to match his energy. "Yeah, Knox was just playing it inside... I haven't heard the whole thing yet, though."

But instead of pressing play, he paused the song and looked at me. Not with the usual warmth. But with something sharp. Something disappointed. "What are you doing, B?" he asked flatly. "Of all people... Knox?"

I looked down, trying to keep my voice steady. "Wes, come on, it's complicated. Can we just listen to the track?"

He didn't budge. "The fuck it is. You and Knox? That makes no sense. You two are not compatible. Anyone with eyes can see that. What about the crew? What about *us*?"

"I get it," I said. "I really do. I didn't expect this either. I'm confused too..."

He cut me off. "You're making one of the biggest mistakes of your life. And you've made some big ones. But this?" He shook his head. "This is the craziest shit I've seen you do. I'm trying to help you not blow everything up."

"Why does it have to be that extreme? We're friends. Why does this change anything?"

"Stop smoking," he snapped. "You sound dumb right now. Everything's already changed. And not for the better. Remember who Knox is, B. You *really* know what you're getting into?"

His voice dropped, the anger giving way to something closer to heartbreak. "Out of all the guys who would've treated you right... You chose the one who's gonna wreck you. And this crew? It won't survive this."

I stared out the window, my hands balled in my lap. "I get your point of view," I said quietly. "I do. But this... it just *happened*. I didn't plan it."

He didn't answer. Just shook his head, started the car again, and turned the music back on.

The rest of the drive was quiet. Heavy. I could feel the shift, the invisible fracture forming between us.

And it wasn't just Wes. The bond I had with both him and Benny started to fray almost immediately. Years of hanging out all together, it all felt like it was on pause. Or worse, erased.

Benny, who was locked up in federal prison at the time, went cold. If he called Knox and I was around, he wouldn't talk to me. The letters he sent were short, curt. They read like warnings, not updates. He questioned what we were doing and made it clear that, in his eyes, I had crossed a line. It didn't matter how close we'd all been. In their world, there were rules. And I had just broken one.

With Knox over more frequently, the tension in the apartment grew. Eventually, Wes decided he didn't want to be my roommate anymore. That left me with no choice, I had to move back in with my mom. Again.

Another shift. Another beginning. But this time, I wasn't moving alone.

I was losing not just their friendship, but the sense of belonging I'd fought so hard to find. Even my mom, Amara, and my son seemed off about it. The tension was subtle, but it was there, watchful eyes, quiet disapproval, a shift in energy I couldn't ignore.

The truth is, I wasn't just looking for love, I was searching for safety. Safety from Zara and her crew, from the threats, from the DCF visits. I craved the kind of protection I never had growing up. But I kept searching in all the wrong places, clinging to people just as broken as I was.

Knox gave me a version of that protection. Once we became official, the harassment stopped. Zara and her "Queens" backed off. The visits from DCF ended. But that protection came wrapped in the same violence and drug-fueled chaos I was already drowning in. Our relationship wasn't the cure to my pain, it was a mirror of it.

The gang's grip had already begun to loosen, some locked up, others moved away, their unity breaking apart from the inside. But their presence still lingered.

One day, while shopping at the mall with my mom, my father called. "You got friends at the house," he said. "I think their names are Zara and Tiny." I knew they weren't there for anything friendly.

Tiny had always been in the mix, even if unofficially. She was Asael's baby mother, and that made her part of the problem. Knox had recently seen Mateo at the corner store and made it clear: the drama needed to end, or there'd be consequences. I wondered if Mateo had passed that warning on to Zara.

I told my father, "Don't talk to them. Just tell them to leave." My mom and I rushed home, Amadeus was there, and I wasn't taking chances.

Once home, I called Tiny. She'd left her number with my dad. I told her to come by if she wanted to talk. She pulled up in her car with three kids in the back seat. I was outside waiting with Knox and my mom.

"What is this about?" I asked", "Why are you still bothering me and my family after all these years?"

"This ends tonight," Knox started, "But I'll give y'all the floor. Say what you need to say. After this? No more bullshit. Or there will be problems."

Tiny nodded, tension thick in the air. "I came to ask if you've done a DNA test."

Before I could respond, my mom cut in, "What's your concern?"

Pointing at me, "She slept with Asael." then pointing to herself, "I'm his baby mother."

"So what? Are any of you raising Amadeus?" my mom's voice now raised, "It's been years of this mess, Tiny! Grow the hell up and leave us alone!"

I stepped in before things escalated further, "First off, we didn't sleep together. That's a lie Zara and you cooked up. Second, Mateo's been asked to take a DNA test multiple times, and he hasn't. So what's this got to do with you?"

"Because I have three kids with him. I need to know if there's another. I'm not here for drama, I just want answers." Tiny's voice started to soften revealing her true intentions.

My mom wasn't moved by the apparent sincerity, "What's Asael gonna do? Send child support from prison? Raise Amadeus from behind bars? You need to focus on the kids he already has. Let Mateo handle his own business."

"This isn't your fight." I interjected, "Mateo knows where to find me if he wants answers. Otherwise, all of you, Zara, you, everyone, stay the fuck away from me and my family. You feel me?"

"Zara and Mateo aren't together anymore. We're here to talk, not cause trouble." Tiny persisted.

"So where is Zara?" I looked down the road to see if she was approaching and was just late to this ridiculous party.

Tiny followed my gaze, "I don't know."

"Then what's the point of this? Why now? Mateo's not here! Asael is NOT here! The people who should be here aren't, so why are you?" I was incredulous.

"Because I need answers. This has been hanging over my head for too long."

"This conversation's done. Don't come back," my mom was fed up. "Mateo knows what to do if he wants a test." My mom turned on her heel and walked back into the house.

Knox gave Tiny the nod. She wasn't worth a single word to him. She got in her car and drove away, and that was the last time we ever saw or heard from any of them.

What Knox and I had looked like love, loyalty, laughter, moments of unity. But beneath it all was pain, unhealed wounds, and a desperate attempt to fill voids we didn't understand.

Knox moved in with me at my mom's place in Wellswood. We lived in what we called "the box", a converted garage that served as our bedroom, bathroom, and laundry room all in one. It became our world. Our bedroom, our safe space, even our trap base. We met plugs, made deals, it felt like we were building something together.

But that excitement didn't last.

Knox started pushing me to quit dancing. He didn't want me at the club anymore. He didn't want me seeing my sponsor, Frank, or getting paid to indulge men's fetishes, or making money in any way that didn't fit his image of respectability. He said it was about love and loyalty, but to me, it felt like control. I wanted out too, in some ways. I was tired. But I couldn't just walk away. The club wasn't just money, It was my fallback. My safety net. I didn't know how to stop hustling when I didn't know how else to survive.

I found myself wondering how other women did it, how they balanced a serious relationship with a lifestyle built on hustle. I felt torn between Knox's expectations and the demands of the life I was still neck-deep in. I was giving up pieces of myself, one shift at a time, one argument at a time, and it was starting to chip away at who I thought I was.

Every time I came home from the club, the interrogation bega:

"Are you drunk again?" "You high?" "You really came home to me like this?"

His questions would kill my high before I even stepped in the door. I hated it. The anxiety would build on the drive home, thinking of ways to mask my breath, make my pupils look normal, act sober when I wasn't. I'd try to rush into the shower to avoid his gaze, but it never worked. He'd follow me in, start picking at me, making me feel like I was dirty, like I was an addict. His words didn't come from love, they came from resentment.

The arguments became constant, over how I made my money, whether I was really dancing or tricking, what I wore, how many men saw me naked that night. He'd throw out slick comments like, "So they all get to see my girl naked before I do?" or "You ever wonder what that makes me look like?" Sex was one of the last reliable ways in which we could express our connection to each other, but because of his insecurities, even that got poisoned. He would ask, "Was I just putting on a show? Was I being fake?"

I could feel people getting in his ear. Whispering. Judging. Making him think he deserved better than me. That he needed a "classier" woman. A woman with less baggage. A woman with less history.

It broke my heart because I thought he knew me. I thought he understood where I came from. But somewhere along the way, he stopped seeing me. And just like that, he became like everyone else, another man telling me I wasn't enough.

At times, when it was just the two of us, Knox was attentive, gentle, even. He'd rub my feet, roll our blunts, talk to me like I was the only one who really got him. In those moments, I could believe in us. But as soon as we stepped outside, everything shifted. I was no longer his partner, I was just his homegirl again. He stopped taking me to the places we used to love, the restaurants we'd frequent, the late-night drives with music blasting. It was like he wanted me close, but only behind closed doors.

His ego kept me at a distance, and so did his silence.

At the same time, I started noticing a shift in how he interacted with the girls around the trap houses. The way they looked at him. The way he didn't stop them. My intuition screamed at me, telling me something wasn't right. I couldn't prove anything, but I didn't need to. I felt it in my bones. The betrayal. The lies that went unspoken. It left me feeling like I was losing him, like I was losing myself.

Any time I questioned him about where he was going or who he was with, he'd flip the script. Suddenly I was the problem. The insecure one. The nag. His go-to answer? "I'm going to the streets, B." As if that explained everything. As if I didn't have the right to ask.

Those moments spiraled into screaming matches that always ended the same way: with me feeling unheard, discarded, like I was just something he'd picked up along the way. The streets had no curfew, no loyalty, no boundaries, and being with a man like Knox meant I was always fighting against a ghost. He didn't answer to anyone, and yet here I was, foolishly expecting him to answer to me.

Sometimes he'd let me tag along. And those moments gave me hope, made me feel like maybe, just maybe, I was back in. But then he'd drop me off somewhere and disappear for hours. Once, he left me at a random house in the middle of the hood with no car, no explanation. When I refused to stay, he told me to leave. So I walked. Two hours. No call, no text. Nothing.

Other nights, he'd show up at my place long after midnight, stumbling drunk or high, while I'd been pacing for hours, my phone in my hand, calling him over and over. He never answered. When he finally walked through the door, all he ever said was, "the streets." Like that was supposed to make it okay.

I'd snap. I'd throw his stuff out into the yard, scream at him to get out. He'd ignore me, walk past me like I didn't exist, crawl into bed, and go to sleep like none of it mattered. When he felt like it, he'd pack his things and disappear to his grandfather's house. But it never lasted. A couple days later, we'd reconnect, usually over drugs, a party, or some other distraction. We'd pick up like nothing happened, pretending everything was fine, but inside, I felt like a damn fool.

The girls at the trap houses didn't help.

They were always too flirty, too bold, laughing a little too loud, leaning a little too close. And Knox never shut it down. Not once. He let it ride, like I wasn't even there. Like I was invisible.

I started to feel like I was slipping backward. Like I was becoming that girl again, the one who just wanted to be seen, to be chosen, to feel like she mattered. But this time, it was worse. Because I *had* been chosen... and I still felt like a ghost.

We argued constantly. Loudly. Shamelessly. Sometimes in front of the very people I was competing with for his attention.

"Knox, can we talk?" I said one night, standing just feet from the table stacked with weed and pills.

He didn't even look up. "Wassup?"

"In private," I said, glancing over at Ace bagging up orders and two girls in skintight outfits, openly flirting. They looked at me like I was in the way.

"Man, hold up. I'm busy. Can't you see I got high-paying clientele?" He finally glanced my way, just long enough to let one of them know she had his full attention.

"Knox," one of the girls chimed in, "don't forget to add that special to my order like you promised on the phone earlier."

"Oh, we giving out specials now?" I asked, half-laughing, but not really joking.

He grinned. "The Best for the best-paying clientele."

That word. *Clientele.* It always felt like a jab. Like a code word for women he was messing with behind my back.

"Knox, Ace, before we head to work, can we light up real quick?" the other one said, already pulling a blunt from her purse.

"Man, light that shit up," Knox said, waving it off.

I didn't say another word. I just turned and walked into one of the rooms in the back, my chest tight.

Seconds later, Knox followed, slamming the door behind him. "Yo B, what is your problem? Why you actin' out in front of my custies?"

"Custies now? Just a minute ago, they were 'clientele.' Don't play with me, Knox. They're out there in hoochie dresses, flirting in my face, and you're just eating it up."

"Do I go to *your* job?" he snapped. "Do I cause a scene when I'm sure there's more than just conversation going on? Nah. I stay in my lane."

"Oh, so we're using my job again. That's the line now?"

"Listen real close, B," he said, his voice low and cold. "I'm not stopping what I do here just 'cause you feel a way. Those broads? They spend money. That money? I spend it *on you.* So cut the shit you about to cause at my trap."

I stared at him, my heart pounding. "You're fucking one of them, aren't you?"

He shook his head. "Yo, calm yourself before I *really* embarrass you in front of those bitches."

That was it.

"You can have that bitch. Fuck you." I shoved past him and stormed out.

"Yo, where that blunt at?" I heard him yell just as I slammed the door behind me.

Tears spilled down my face before I even made it to the car. I sat there shaking, pulled out my cocaine stash, and hit a few bumps, numb was the only way I could function. Then I called Nadia.

It was time to make money.

***

Around that same time, I found out I was pregnant.

It didn't seem real at first. With all the drugs I was doing daily, weed, coke, and alcohol, didn't even think it was possible. I hadn't been careful, hadn't even thought about it. But it happened.

We talked. We agreed. We'd end the pregnancy.

But when the day came, he dropped me off at the clinic like I was an errand. No comforting words. No waiting. No "are you okay?" Just silence.

I sat there alone in that sterile, cold room, wrapped in a paper gown, mind spiraling. There were other girls there, some with friends, some with boyfriends holding their hands.

I had no one.

And no matter how justified the choice felt in my mind, my body grieved. My heart grieved. Another difficult situation and I carried the weight of it by myself. Even now, I don't remember the nurse's name. But I remember the way she looked at me, not with pity, but with softness. Like maybe she knew what it was like to be left behind.

That day carved a space inside me that no one could fill. Not Knox. Not the drugs. Not the money. Just emptiness. And shame.

But also... the faintest spark of something else A whisper that maybe, just maybe, I deserved better.

No matter how hard I tried to suppress it, the truth stared me in the face, I was nothing to him now. Once, I had been the girl he chased, the one he joked with, rode with, built dreams with. But now? Now, I was just "the stripper." Just another chapter in his street story. A shadow of what I once was to him.

I believed Knox loved me, in his own way. But it was street love, the only kind we knew. Love that was conditional, fragile, and tangled up in ego. He could never fully stomach what I did to survive. He hated that other men saw me naked, that I was desired in ways he couldn't control. It bruised his pride to know people saw "his woman" as someone who was easy, not respectable.

He couldn't move past it.

It wasn't just our relationship that was falling apart, our business was unraveling, too. One night, after a long and draining shift at the club, something in my gut told me to check on the trap house. I tried calling, first the runners, then the clientele line, but every phone went straight to voicemail. Silence. That's when the dread crept in.

As I pulled up to the neighborhood, red and blue lights bounced off the walls, painting the scene in flashing warning. My stomach dropped. It felt like a scene out of the movie *Belly*. I didn't wait to process it, I hit the gas and got out of there fast, calling the crew to try and salvage whatever product we had left. But it was already too late.

The raid had been catastrophic.

The charges were serious: drug trafficking, weapons possession, and even animal cruelty. One of the pit bulls we'd been breeding for extra cash had been left in poor condition. A pregnant female had gotten loose the week before and fought with another dog, leaving a bloodied scene for the cops to stumble upon. It only made things worse.

The fallout was brutal. Knox's vision of building a self-sustaining weed empire was crumbling. The crew, once tight-knit and full of ambition, began to splinter under the pressure. Everything became riskier, and trust started to erode. For a while, we shut the trap house down, trying to clean up what was left after the police tore through it. Strangely, the landlord never said a word, if he even knew. Maybe he didn't want to know.

When we reopened, everything went underground. No one was allowed to come directly to the house anymore, pickups happened off-site, away from prying eyes. We had one burner phone the cops hadn't found during the raid, and that single device became our lifeline. At first, customers were hesitant. But addiction always wins. Within a week, they were back.

Knox ended up doing a three-month bid after the bust. With him gone, Cash and Kato were put in charge. I had once promised myself I'd never be the woman waiting on a man in jail, especially after watching my mom suffer through my dad's time behind bars. But here I was, breaking my own rule. Never say never.

Chapter 16

The Chimichurri Incident

While Knox was locked up, I took on a role I never expected. I ran point, visiting the trap to collect money, managing his cars, overseeing things he never wanted me touching. He hated the idea of me driving his cars or lingering at the trap. He told me to get in and get out. But I didn't listen. If I wanted to stay, I stayed.

I visited him when I could. Sometimes we talked, sometimes we fought. I clung to the sound of his voice during those collect calls, trying to ignore how cold and transactional our conversations had become. They were mostly about business, coded updates, legal news, and vague plans for when he got out. The subject of "us" only came up when we were pretending things were fine.

Meanwhile, Cash and Kato were a disaster. They weren't running the trap right, starting fights, robbing people, and letting girls stir up drama that slowed business down. I kept dancing, because I had to. The money Knox left behind was drying up fast, and neither Cash nor Kato respected me. Especially Cash.

I started noticing product missing during pickups. Money that didn't add up. Knox, even from jail, saw it too. He cut them off and brought in Q, my ex, and Ace to handle things. It was a risky move, but we didn't have a lot of choices. Q was dating someone else by then, a girl I'd once given stripping advice to. We kept it strictly business, but I knew how it looked to Knox. He'd call while I was sitting next to Q, and the interrogations would start. It was ironic, I had once been the one asking the questions.

Those three months were tough. But I showed up. I held it down. And a part of me liked the power, the control, the title. I was "bossed up," calling shots. But behind that tough exterior, I was falling apart. The drugs became my crutch, my escape from the pressure, from the fear, from myself. I was barely hanging on.

Amadeus asked me about Knox, wondering where he had gone. I didn't sugarcoat it. I told him the truth, Knox had gotten into trouble and had to go to jail for a while. My mother had never hidden the truth about my father from me, and I decided I would do the same with my son.

When Knox got out, he moved fast to reclaim his territory. He won back his clientele by slashing prices, practically giving the product away at first. Robberies followed, targeting his competitors, and standoffs erupted on the block with guys who didn't have the smarts to take him on. For Knox, it was a quick comeback. Ruthless, efficient.

With things back on track, I found myself spending more time at the trap. But even with me, Knox drew lines. Some nights, he'd tell me to stay home. Other times, he'd send someone else to drop me off if he didn't want me lingering. And the drugs I was using? They were all coming from him. That began to wear on me. I had cut off all my other plugs once we got serious, and now I had no access when he wasn't around. I didn't want to disrespect him, but part of me regretted ever giving up that independence.

Reality hit in waves: I needed to get sober. For my mother. For Amadeus. But the grip drugs had on me ran deep. Some days, I couldn't tell if I was craving Knox or the high more. I was a functioning addict, keeping up appearances while falling apart inside.

A few months after Knox got out, things seemed to settle, at least on the surface. But under that calm was a powder keg. I could feel it.

We stopped by one of the trap houses in Town & Country to collect earnings and check inventory. Knox had reclaimed the block since his release, and not everyone was happy about it. Cash, in particular, carried a quiet grudge. He'd been running his own crack spot while Knox was locked up and had no intention of giving up that control without friction. Add Kato to the mix, already under fire for allegedly stealing a gold chain from Knox's brother, and the air was thick with tension.

I remember the energy in that house. It buzzed. Something was about to pop off.

"Yo Kato," Knox started, his tone low but firm. "You were the last one in the crib when the chain was still there. Now it's missing. And Cash, I got words for you too, always stirring shit."

"I ain't take no chain, Knox. I swear on my life," Kato said, his voice already defensive, nostrils flaring from the coke he'd been sniffing.

Cash didn't take kindly to being looped in. "What the fuck is your problem? You always treatin' us like we kids or somethin'."

Knox lit up. "Let me say this real clear. Stop making the block hot. Cash, you and your crack operation? It's gotta move. I can't have overdoses drawing five-O around here. And Kato, you better find that chain. That was a family heirloom. You hear me? Let me get that blunt."

He snatched it from Cash, taking a hit like it was the only thing keeping him from exploding.

Cash scoffed. "It ain't my fault the custies OD. I can't babysit every junkie. I got a business to run."

"Don't 'cuz' me," Knox snapped. "I had this block before you ever cooked a damn rock. And something's wrong with your product if they're dropping like flies. You ever think of that? Dead customers don't bring money."

Kato stayed quiet, sniffing lines at the kitchen table, his hands jittery.

"And Kato," Knox turned, eyes narrowing. "What you wanna say?"

"I didn't steal no chain. I don't know how to fix somethin' I didn't even do," Kato muttered.

Knox just stared at him, then walked slowly into the kitchen.

"So what you sayin'? You callin' my brother a liar?"

The room fell silent.

"I see y'all chillin', bitches passed out in the other room, music blasting. Who's product is this?"

"Uh... we got it from a friend," Kato lied badly.

"Nah. This ain't from no friend. Y'all better not have hit a lick," Knox said, voice rising.

Cash tried to calm it. "It ain't like that. We just got a little blessing, ya mean?"

"A blessing?" Knox stepped in close, his voice a razor's edge. "So now robbin' folks is called a blessing?"

Cash looked away, chuckling nervously. "Man, it wasn't even like that. It was just a quick come-up. Nobody even got hurt."

Knox shoved him, hard. "You stupid or just bold? You bringin' heat on my name, stealing from crews we break bread with? You know what kind of war that starts?"

Kato, eyes wide, finally stepped forward. "We didn't know, aight? We didn't know it was one of your connects. We thought it was just some out-of-town crew..."

"You *thought*?" Knox grabbed him by the collar. "You don't think when my name's on the line. You *ask*. You check in."

Cash tried to intervene. "Ayo chill. We didn't mean no disrespect."

Knox let Kato go with a shove, his chest rising and falling like a loaded gun. "Y'all out here stealin', overdosing the block, and now my chain's gone? I should light this whole crib up. Don't move until I get back. And get them bitches outta here. *Now.*"

We left. The air felt thinner when the door shut behind us. A few hours later, the streets exploded.

Cash and Kato had taken Ecstasy and, high out of their minds, ended up at The Chimichurri, one of the busiest Dominican food trucks in the area. Words were exchanged. Egos collided. And then bullets started flying.

I watched the news that night in disbelief. Just hours earlier, we'd been in that very house with them. Now, it was a warzone on live television.

That night confirmed what I already knew: Cash and Kato were dangerous liabilities. Their judgment was trash. Their pride was lethal.

They didn't get caught. But they didn't stay. They vanished into the streets, ducking retaliation, dodging the fallout.

To make matters worse, a serious beef was brewing between Umar and Cash, and it was spiraling fast. Those nights stay with me, sleeping with one eye open, AKs lying next to us, knowing any second could turn deadly. What started as a simple disagreement over cocaine supply became personal when a woman got involved. Lines were crossed, egos flared, and the streets started whispering.

Knox was caught in the middle, trapped between two men he cared about, both stubborn, both dangerous. Desperate to stop things from spiraling, he flew his father in from Puerto Rico, hoping he could help mediate with Cash, cool things down. But Cash wasn't interested in peace. Instead, he escalated the beef, going so far as to shoot at Umar's little brother.

That was the final straw.

"You wildin' the fuck out, Cash," Knox said, jaw tight, pacing in front of him. "I flew my pops in to talk to you, try to keep this shit from spiralin'. And you go shoot at Umar's little brother?"

Cash didn't flinch. He snapped back, eyes hard. "Fuck peace, Knox. Ain't no peace when a motherfucker been movin' funny behind your back. You wanna sit down with everybody, hold hands and shit. I don't play like that."

Knox's voice rose, frustration bleeding through. "Nah, fuck all that tough talk. This ain't the same block we grew up on. We got eyes on us. You think shootin' his brother ain't gonna spark a fuckin' war?"

Lighting a blunt, Cash smirked, calm in a way that was almost chilling. "Let it spark. I don't fear fire, I walk through it. You out here tryin' to be mayor or some shit, talkin' strategy while these opps plottin'. I ain't Umar. I don't forgive, and I damn sure don't forget."

Knox stepped in closer, lowering his voice but not his intensity. "You think this is loyalty? This is ego. You makin' choices that don't got no return. You crossed a line even I can't defend. You ain't thinkin' 'bout nobody but yourself. And you puttin' all of us in a war."

Cash leaned in too, eyes locked on Knox's. His voice dropped low. "Then don't defend me. But don't get in my fuckin' way either."

Knox didn't budge. "I already am. Ain't gon' be no peace talks next time. You better be ready to stand on all that."

We all knew what was next. If Umar retaliated, it would spark a war. If Cash struck first again, same outcome. Both men had deep connections, loyal crews ready to ride without question. No matter which way it played out, it was going to be bloody.

While the tension boiled between Cash and Umar, Kato's time finally ran out. He'd been ducking warrants for months, bouncing between hotel rooms while we tried to smuggle him out to New York or Puerto Rico. But Kato was stubborn. He refused to leave Tampa. "I just wanna go back to the hood," he'd say, like it was calling him home. We left him at one of the traps with a warning to lay low.

Less than 48 hours later, they got him.

Soon after, the Feds caught up to Cash, too. It might've been a traffic stop, maybe a tip, we never knew for sure. But the outcome was the same: Cash was locked up, and the feud with Umar fizzled out. Still, the damage lingered. The trust between Umar and Knox never fully recovered. Knox somehow talked them out of retaliation, but that silent tension never went away.

Once Cash got locked up, the streets turned cold, and darker. His pregnant girlfriend and he, both desperate for protection, made a decision that would shift everything: they started working with the Feds. They flipped on everyone. Knox. Kato. Even Benny.

The betrayal sliced deep.

As the investigation grew, young members of Cash's crew were picked off one by one. Every arrest added pressure. And soon, the paperwork started circulating. Paperwork that named Knox as the ringleader, using his government name, Isandro Reyes.

One of Knox's street partners came by the house with a stack of legal documents. His face said it all before he even spoke.

"My brotha, I'm telling you...they all snitching."

I was on the other side of the room, twisting a blunt. Knox called me over, "Yo, B, come here."

I walked over and looked at the papers laid out on the table. "Wow... they're saying you're a manager at McDonald's. That you handle the money, set up all the deals. Wait, who is this? I don't recognize the name they have listed." I pointed to it.

"Damn," Knox muttered. "That's that dumb youngin' from Miami, Looney. What else he saying? Light that L."

I flipped through the pages. The paperwork read like a movie script, dialogue, statements, accusations. I couldn't believe what I was reading. "He says he works for you. That you're the boss. That you've hurt people. He names Cash and Kato, too. He's *singing*, for real. And he's listing trap houses, says you run them."

Knox took a long drag, lost in thought.

"Knox, say the word. What do you want to do? We can locate this lil' youngin'..." his partner offered.

"Nah," Knox interrupted, his voice steady but sharp. "Don't talk like that. I'ma hit you up later. Don't make no moves. Let Ace know, shut everything down early. Stash in the backwoods."

After he closed the door behind his partner, he turned to me. I could see the paranoia in his eyes. "B, I'm not stressing this too hard. Looney didn't know enough to really hurt me. But somebody's feeding him info. The question is, *who?* Who else is talking?"

"And how did your boy even get that paperwork?" I asked.

"You don't need to know all that," he replied, brushing it off, then chuckled, "Damn. They said I'm like a McDonald's manager? Let me see that shit."

"It's on page 26," I told him. "But seriously, what are you going to do? How are you gonna stay in the streets now? I think you should stay here, with me." I hugged him tightly as he sat, flipping through the pages, his mind clearly racing.

"You just want me home, B. That ain't me." He smirked. "I'ma call the lawyer, Alex, tomorrow. Roll another blunt, let's watch *John Gotti.*"

What we didn't know was that law enforcement had been watching us, closely, for months. They weren't just circling the block anymore. They were building a case, and it was no longer a game. It was war.

I had warned Knox, I didn't want my father involved. He was unreliable, hotheaded, and not built for pressure. But when the warrant went out for Cash after the Chimichurri shootout, Knox made a reckless move: he brought Cash to the grow house. The one with my name on the lease. The one tied to my father.

That decision shattered everything. The Feds were already watching that house. My father and Knox had been at odds for months, but this crossed a line. I'd told Knox my father is not reliable long-term, but he didn't listen. When my father found out Cash had been there, with a warrant hanging over him, he lost it. He wanted out, and I didn't blame him.

It felt like deception was coming from every direction.

One night, I was at home with my son. My father was visiting, and we were each in separate rooms, wrapped in our own routines. The quiet didn't last. My son appeared in my doorway, wide-eyed and unsure.

"There are people outside with vests knocking on the door," he said. "I don't recognize any of them."

My heart dropped. I moved slowly toward the door, just enough to peek out the window. My worst fear was confirmed, it was the cops.

Everything blurred. A thousand thoughts spun through my mind, but nothing prepared me for what happened next. They forced their way in, flashing a warrant for my father. His ties to the grow house had finally caught up to him.

They separated us immediately. My son was taken into another room, where they questioned him illegally. Meanwhile, I was dragged into my bedroom. They tore through the house like they knew exactly where to look, rifling through stash spots with surgical precision.

The interrogation was aggressive and relentless. Questions came rapid-fire, about murders, drug trafficking, weapons. Then they found my dance bag and a calendar from the club, and the judgment shifted. It wasn't just about my father anymore, it was about me, my choices, my world.

After two exhausting hours, they hauled my father out of the house in handcuffs. Watching him being led out from our living room like that, a man I'd once feared, then tried to forgive, was surreal. Another reminder of the world we were caught in.

Before the cops left, a few lingered and insisted I call my mom. When I hesitated, they contacted her boss themselves. She arrived 45 minutes later, her face heavy with worry, but the questioning didn't stop.

Around 9 PM, Knox called. They let me answer, and I had to play it cool. He asked how my day had gone and whether I'd seen the lawyer yet, referring to Benny's case. Speaking in code, he warned, "Don't tend to the tomatoes right now."

I kept my tone steady, pretended everything was fine. As soon as I hung up, they pounced.

"What did you talk about?"

I told them nothing.

Though they found a small stash of weed in my room, they didn't have enough to charge me. Still, they used every scare tactic, threatening jail time, court dates, and child services. But they got nowhere.

Before leaving, they let me know just how deep they were. They knew everything, about pill mills, weapons, drug routes, and stash spots. They even knew about the black bag of illegal firearms. We were more exposed than I could have imagined.

Once they left, my mother and I exchanged a look, there was no time to waste. We packed up my son and left for West Tampa. We didn't know what our next move was, just that we couldn't stay still.

I found an old payphone and made the calls. Knox. J-Money. I told them everything. Knox always played it safe, but even he was blindsided by how close the cops had gotten. I called Ace, urging him to relocate everything to a safer spot, one I was sure they didn't know about.

But it was too late. As Knox and J-Money scrambled to move the rest of the stash, time ran out. J-Money got caught en route, and within an hour, the cops raided both properties. It was like they had been waiting for my calls to spring the trap.

Knox was sentenced to a year. My father caught probation, narrowly escaping worse. J-Money, caught with more than just weed, got four years.

As for me, I walked away with a minor charge. The officer never showed up to my hearing, and just like that, the case was dismissed. But the damage had already been done.

The raids wiped everything out. All our product was seized. Even my dog, who had been staying at one of the grow houses, was picked up and taken to a shelter. I had to scrape together whatever I could to bail her out.

The fallout was more than financial. It was emotional. Trust fractured, friendships strained, and the vision of the life we were building collapsed overnight. Everything we'd worked for was gone. We were left to pick up the pieces in a game that was no longer played by our rules.

***

A year later, Knox finished serving his time and returned home. But the tension kept rising. Cash had turned on Benny, too, the same Benny who took him in, fed him, sheltered him, welcomed him as family, gave him a home. Benny was already serving thirteen years, but Cash's testimony only tightened the noose. People in the streets began picking sides, and not everyone saw Cash for the snake he was. Looking back, the red flags had always been there. But loyalty has a way of blinding you, especially in our world.

It all came crashing down the day we watched Cash take the stand. A case from years earlier, buried under time, was now resurfacing with Cash pointing the finger. It was one of the hardest things I've ever witnessed. Knox and I were there in court, sitting behind Benny, doing our best to show up for him. But nothing could dull the sting of disloyalty, not when it came from someone who once sat at your mother's dinner table.

The courtroom felt like a cage. The air was heavy, almost sticky with judgment. Everything about it was suffocating, the cold benches, the whispers that never seemed to stop, the sense that even the walls were watching. You could feel the power in the room, but it didn't belong to us.

The judge presided high above, expression unreadable, glasses sharp enough to cut glass. Her gavel sat like a threat, and the flags behind her stood tall but meaningless. There was no justice here, only decisions made behind stiff suits and practiced lines.

The jury sat off to the side, twelve strangers holding Benny's fate in their hands. Some looked bored, others curious, a few even sympathetic, but who knew what they were really thinking? To them, maybe Benny was just another case. But to us, this wasn't a story. This was his life.

The prosecutor was slick and confident, every word carefully chosen, his presence filling the room. He walked like he owned the outcome. Benny's defense attorney, paid for, in part, by Knox, sat close, speaking in low tones, offering calm where there was no calm to be had. But even he looked uneasy, like he knew what we all feared, this wasn't a fight we were going to win.

Time dragged. Each minute stretched into a slow ache. Everything echoed in that room...every whisper, every breath, every lie.

Benny, locked away for years already, had no idea what had gone down since. He'd been shuffled from Florida to New York to Mississippi. While he sat behind bars, the streets kept moving, Knox's empire, the grow houses, the trap houses, Kato, Cash, it all evolved. And now, Benny was being dragged into a murder pinned on him by three men desperate for lighter sentences: Cash and two other inmates, scheming behind bars to save themselves.

The trial lasted about a week at the courthouse in St. Petersburg. They brought in Kato from lockup, though he never testified. Knox and I visited him briefly while he was held in Pinellas County, but even seeing his face did little to ease the weight pressing down on us.

I missed the first few days, but Knox didn't. He showed up every single morning, dressed sharp, committed to being present. When I did sit in, I watched a kid from the block, Silas, take the stand. I didn't know him personally, just recognized the name. He looked nervous, but he did what the court asked: said his name, and then started telling their version of what happened that night.

Then something unexpected happened.

"I would like to plead the Fifth, Your Honor," Silas said, voice trembling.

A gasp swept through the courtroom. The prosecutor, clearly caught off guard, leaned forward.

"Pleading the Fifth? Is there a reason you won't testify? Have you been threatened? Is someone in this courtroom intimidating you?"

Silas didn't look at anyone. His gaze stayed fixed on the floor. "I don't recall what happened that night," he muttered. "I plead the Fifth."

The victim's family looked stunned. Knox, Benny's mother, and I exchanged confused glances. The prosecutor wasn't done. He reminded Silas they had a recording, his own statement, recounting everything in graphic detail. He warned that refusing to cooperate could result in additional charges. But Silas stood his ground, head bowed, visibly shaken.

Nobody knew what changed. Still, the prosecution moved forward and played the audio anyway. It was brutal, Silas' own voice, scene by scene, naming names, pointing fingers. He painted Benny as the shooter, implicated himself, and even recounted details that only someone present would know.

Benny's lawyer argued it was all fabricated, Silas and Cash, locked up together, piecing together a false narrative to cut themselves a deal. There was no DNA, no murder weapon, no direct evidence, only that recording. But it was enough to feel like the walls were closing in.

Benny's mother sat near us, surrounded by her church family who had been praying outside the courthouse all week. She barely looked at

Knox. I never fully understood why, but her distrust of him was deep. She didn't want him near Benny, let alone in the courtroom.

I sat there feeling helpless. The system was chewing Benny up, and no matter how present Knox and I were, we couldn't stop what was unfolding. Watching Cash turn on him was gut-wrenching, betrayal of the highest order.

Knox sat beside me, his eyes locked on the courtroom doors. You could feel him hoping, pleading silently, that Cash would walk in and remember what they all used to be. That family would mean something.

But when Cash walked in, he didn't even glance our way. His jaw was set, his eyes forward, his demeanor cold, like a soldier marching into war.

The judge's gavel cracked through the room. "Mr. Salazar, please take the stand."

Knox tensed beside me, his hand clenching the bench until his knuckles turned white. He leaned toward me and whispered, "He won't do it. He knows what this means. Blood's thicker than water."

But Knox was wrong. Dead wrong.

The prosecutor began, and Cash answered every question with ease, clear, calm, deliberate. It was like he had rehearsed it all. "Mr. Salazar, what did the defendant say when he returned home the night of April 14th?"

Cash leaned into the mic, glancing briefly at Benny before turning back. "He said he 'took care of it.' That he 'did what needed to be done.' He even described how it went down."

Gasps rippled through the courtroom. My stomach turned. Knox didn't move, but his whole body radiated fury. His silence screamed.

Benny's attorney jumped up. "Objection, hearsay!"

"Overruled," the judge responded firmly. "The witness may continue."

Cash kept going, offering specific, intimate details. Things no one would know unless they lived with Benny, unless they'd shared his secrets. Each word was a dagger.

Then came the final blow.

"Mr. Salazar, can you identify the defendant?"

Without pause, Cash raised his hand and pointed, "He's right there."

He locked eyes with Benny, as if daring him to deny it. The silence was deafening. My heart raced. I turned and looked at Benny. His expression was hollow, but behind the stillness, I saw it. The disloyalty. It was a grief deeper than words. I watched loyalty shatter right before our eyes.

I could feel the bile rising in my throat. I wanted to get up, to walk out, but I couldn't move. I was frozen, paralyzed by the weight of what we had just witnessed. This was it. The moment that shattered everything we thought we knew. Knox's cousin, his own blood, had driven the final nail into Benny's coffin.

Next to me, Knox was breaking down. His face, usually so unreadable, was now contorted in disbelief and fury. When he finally spoke, his voice cracked.

"I can't believe he did this," he muttered, almost to himself, like he was trying to make the backstabbing make sense.

The rest of the day, he said almost nothing. His silence spoke louder than any outburst ever could. The pain was too deep for words.

Across the courtroom, Benny's mother broke down. Her grief morphed into rage, her eyes narrowing into daggers aimed directly at us. Knox and I stayed back, what could we even say? One wrong word, one wrong glance, and the whole thing could have erupted. Nothing good would've come from a confrontation.

When we left the courtroom, the air felt heavier than ever. It wasn't just disappointment. It was devastating.

I missed the day the next witness took the stand, but I heard enough to piece it together. The prosecution had gained ground. Benny was no longer just another name in a lineup, he was being painted as a violent mastermind. They twisted every shred of evidence to fit their story, casting him as someone who ruled with fear. By the time closing arguments were made, the defense was backed into a corner. They even hinted at intimidation from inside the courtroom, accusing someone of trying to silence witnesses. It was one more nail in Benny's image, one more step toward conviction.

Still, despite everything, there was no physical evidence. No DNA. No murder weapon. And in the end, that lack of hard proof was what saved him. Benny beat the murder charge.

The news broke across Hillsborough County and stunned everyone who had followed the case. He had dodged the harshest sentence, life or worse, but there were no celebrations. The damage was done. He still had to serve the rest of his original sentence. And even worse, the emotional scars, ours and his, ran deep.

From what I later heard, Cash didn't last long in general population. Not long after returning to prison, Cash was stabbed. It didn't kill him, but it was a clear message: no deal, no testimony, no name-dropping could shield him forever.

He ended up with around 25 years total after the federal case wrapped up. All the names he gave, all the time he spent on the stand, none of it saved him. And no one, inside or out, had any sympathy left for him. His health was declining, and so was his relevance.

We had survived the trial. But the doublecrossing, especially by Cash, left a fracture that would never fully heal. What had once been a brotherhood built on loyalty and code had become a battlefield of distrust. Knox and I walked away from that courtroom not as victors, not as survivors, but as people who had just watched their family implode.

Chapter 17

The Making of a Double Life

We didn't allow customers at the house, and for a while, things felt manageable. The hustle stayed in the streets, never at our doorstep, and that was how we liked it. It had been about a year since my mom, Knox, my son, and I had moved across town. Around that time, Knox's grandfather bought a couple of properties for Knox and his brothers, far from the drama we had left behind in Wellswood.

When Knox first brought up the opportunity to my mom and me, it felt like divine timing. My Tia had been talking about selling her house, but she wasn't going to leave us homeless. So, when this came up, it felt like everything was falling into place, a clean break, a chance to finally plant roots.

One evening, Knox walked into the house with a look I'd come to recognize, calm, serious, like he had something important to say.

"Hey, B, can we talk? Like, me, you, and your moms?" he asked, leaning in the bedroom doorway while I was getting ready to head out.

"Yeah, let's go into the kitchen," I already felt the weight of something big about to shift.

As we entered the kitchen, the familiar aroma of my mother's cooking filled the air, warm, comforting, grounding. Knox's mood immediately lifted. "Oh man, I smell something real good! Momma, what are you cooking up?" he grinned, wrapping her in one of those warm, playful hugs that always made her laugh.

She smiled knowingly, wiping her hands on a dish towel. "What do y'all want?" she asked, half-joking, already sensing something was up. We hadn't even sat down for dinner, but the seriousness of how we were all gathered said it all.

I shrugged, glancing over at Knox. "Don't look at me. Knox is the one who wanted to talk."

He leaned forward in his chair, getting straight to it. "Look, I know your sister's been talking about selling the house, and I think this is the right time for a new plan. My grandfather's been buying property for me and my brothers, and he just found one out in Lutz, a mobile home on over an acre of land. It needs some work, but it's better than any other option we've had in a while."

My mom paused, curiosity flickering across her face. "Have you seen it?"

Before Knox could answer, I jumped in. "And what exactly does 'some work' mean?"

He chuckled softly, nodding. "I haven't seen it yet. My grandfather's on his way now to pick me up. But from what I've heard, it's in decent shape. No rent, no payments, just the sweat equity to get it livable. The inside is outdated; it was built for someone with a disability, so it's got that '80s vibe, but nothing we can't handle. I'm ready to put in the work. If y'all are too, we can make this something special. A real fresh start."

The idea was tempting. A place of our own. No rent. No constant fear of eviction. My mom looked over at me, then back at Knox. I could already see her weighing the possibility, the chance to finally rest, to build, to stop just surviving.

"It does sound like an opportunity," she said, slowly but sincerely.

And with that, we agreed. It wasn't a perfect option. But it was ours. And in a world where nothing had ever come easy, that alone made it worth saying yes.

When we finally saw the trailer, reality hit. It needed serious work. Knox hadn't exaggerated. The layout was functional but awkward, designed for someone with limited mobility, and the decor looked like it had been frozen in the 1980s. Faded wallpaper, cracked linoleum floors, and outdated cabinets it was all a far cry from what Knox envisioned. But with his eye for aesthetics and expensive taste, he saw potential. What started as a few minor upgrades quickly turned into a full-blown remodel.

Knox wanted everything to be perfect, the kitchen, the bathrooms, the bedrooms. No corner was left untouched. The remodel dragged on for months, turning our supposed sanctuary into a never-ending project. Even after we moved in, the work wasn't done. We lived in a space that felt more like a construction zone than a home, the smell of fresh paint lingering in the air as new flooring was laid room by room.

With every improvement, the place began to reflect us: our hopes, our hustle, our need to create something stable in our world. But it wasn't easy. Living amid drywall dust and torn-up rooms wore on my nerves. There were nights I'd lie in bed, exhausted, surrounded by tools and half-finished walls, wondering if peace would ever come.

This was our first experience as real homeowners, and it came with hard lessons. We had well water and a septic tank, and the house didn't even have central air, just individual A/C units we hoped wouldn't fail. It felt like something always needed fixing, and the pressure of maintenance crept into our relationship. Knox and I clashed often over bills, repairs, and responsibilities. We had different priorities, and that difference showed in how we argued, how we handled money, and how we processed stress.

Amid all this, I decided to leave the club. I was tired of the emotional whiplash and the lifestyle that drained me. I started distancing myself from everyone who still lived in that world. I cut ties, stopped returning calls, and slowly faded from the club scene that had once consumed me.

Even friendships started to feel like a threat to Knox. "Clubbing" isn't the right word for what we did. Amara and her girlfriend would hit up a bar, a lounge, or a pool hall just to play games and have a few drinks. We were all extroverts, so casual conversations with strangers, guys or girls, happened naturally. But for me, even those innocent interactions triggered paranoia.

If someone said hello, I worried Knox would find out, twist it into something it wasn't, and show up unannounced to make a scene. That constant fear kept me in a bubble, isolated, anxious, always second-guessing every move I made.

I wasn't just trying to start over, I was trying to erase the past, to reinvent myself from the ground up. But what I didn't understand back then was this:

Leaving one world behind doesn't guarantee peace in the next.

A quiet shift had begun within me. I found myself revisiting a long-abandoned dream, going back to school. Determined to carve out a different path, I enrolled in a technical college for a 15-month Medical Assistant program. It was affordable, structured, and most importantly, it felt doable. Amadeus was growing up fast, entering fifth grade, and I knew the questions would soon follow. I couldn't stomach the thought of him learning that his mother had been a stripper. I'd heard stories from other dancers, children asking questions too grown for their age, and I didn't want to be one of them, lying or telling a truth that might break something in him.

I wanted out, desperately. But fear held me back, fear of how I would survive, how I would provide without the club. That world, as toxic as it was, had given me power, purpose, and identity. Stripping wasn't just a job. It was a mask I'd worn so long that I didn't know who I was without it. The thought of applying for a "real" job made my stomach turn. What did I have to offer? A high school diploma and years of hustling? I hadn't clocked into a 9-to-5 since I was eighteen. Knox had no answers for my doubts. His silence felt like a void, deepening my fears that I was losing both my independence and my sense of self.

Knox wasn't opposed to me going back to school, if anything, he encouraged it, but he was clear: the strip club had to go. Eventually, I gave in. I started juggling school during the day and cut my dancing to just a few nights a week. Then Knox pulled a string, he got me a retail job through a connection he'd made while locked up. It was his way of easing me out of the club, though it stung more than I let on. I wasn't ready to leave dancing, not entirely, but the pressure from Knox and the dread of Amadeus finding out forced my hand.

It was my first *real* job in years, and it was brutal. The hours dragged. The pay was insulting. The uniforms were itchy and unflattering, and the smell of the store clung to me like disappointment. My coworkers were kind enough, but they didn't know my past, and I had no intention of explaining it. I was starting over, but it didn't feel empowering. It felt like punishment.

"What time are you going to lunch?" my coworker asked, leaning on the counter like we weren't both seconds from a breakdown.

"Three," I muttered, eyes glued to the computer screen.

"You always go so late," she said, stretching like she'd just finished a marathon instead of stacking tiles all morning. "I couldn't do it. I need my food by one or I'm hangry."

I gave her a tired half-smile, the kind you offer when you're too drained to fake anything better. "Guess I'm used to late nights and skipped meals." It was the truth, but not in any way she'd understand.

"You okay today?" she asked, softer now, noticing the way I shifted weight off my aching feet.

"My feet hurt from standing all day. I'm dreading closing. Watch, someone's gonna roll in at 6:58 and want a full consultation like they didn't see the sign."

She laughed. "Ain't that the truth. Folks act like we don't have lives outside this place."

I didn't respond. My life outside the store? Complicated. Knox. School. The constant pull of slipping back into what I knew best. But that wasn't a story I was about to unpack on this sales floor.

"Look on the bright side," she said, trying to be positive. "You got a steady check, you're in school, working toward something."

"Mmhmm." That word, *steady*, sat wrong on my tongue. *Working toward something*, I echoed in my head, thinking how I'd already lived three different lives before ever putting on this uniform. Every shift felt like detox, like I was withdrawing from a life that, for better or worse, made sense to me. I knew how to survive. But this? This felt like suffocation in fluorescent lighting.

Right then, Ralph, our manager, popped around the corner, clipboard in hand, voice full of corporate cheer.

"Hey, ladies," he said, peering over his glasses. "Let's pick up the energy a bit, yeah? Smiles. Greet the customers. Quotas to hit."

I clenched my jaw. The pep talks, the forced smiles, it all felt like a bad sitcom I couldn't turn off.

"Absolutely, Ralph," my coworker chirped.

I forced a grin. "Got it."

As soon as he walked away, the smile dropped like dead weight.

"You good?" she whispered.

I let out a short laugh and shook my head. "Just counting down the minutes until I can breathe again."

She nodded, not really understanding. And that was fine. Not everyone needed to know what it meant to go from hustling in the streets to being boxed in behind a register, just trying to keep it together long enough to reach the next chapter.

She hummed her way to the back, and I stayed rooted at the counter, watching the clock like it owed me answers.

Still, I showed up. For my son. For my mother. For the version of me that still believed I could be something more.

The one bright spot in my week was Amadeus' baseball games. Sitting in the bleachers, watching him swing the bat with such joy, it reminded me why I was doing all this. That was my heartbeat, my reason. Knox, on the other hand, rarely showed up, and when he did, he was buried in his phone, his mind still tethered to the streets. He wasn't a bad man, but he had never known how to be fully present.

Even so, I tried to give him what I thought he never had, a taste of normalcy. Vacations. Birthdays with cake and gifts. Christmas mornings with wrapped presents under the tree. I worked hard to create a home filled with love and laughter, hoping it would heal some of the wounds he carried.

But no matter how much I gave, the ghost of my past always stood between us. Knox couldn't fully let go of who I had been. He couldn't see the woman I was becoming without bringing up who I used to be. His insecurities clung to us both, whispering doubt, stirring resentment.

And yet, I loved him. I admired his hustle, his unapologetic ambition, the way he loved his family with a fierceness few could match. I adored his laughter, his dreams, and the vulnerability he only ever showed to me. I believed, maybe foolishly, that we could make it work.

That we could push through the darkness together and come out on the other side with something beautiful.

I believed that if I just held on long enough, it would all be worth it.

After I graduated from the Medical Assistant program, I landed a job with a Nigerian doctor I had interned for during my externship. It was a personal victory, my first legitimate career step, but the paycheck was humbling. It didn't come close to the kind of money I used to make dancing. No more drugs, no more late nights at the club. I was clean, and I was proud of that. Still, part of me missed that girl. The fast life, the power I had in those rooms, the thrill of making money like water. There were days when the stress of my new job hit me so hard, I'd catch myself wondering if it would really be so bad to go back.

But I didn't.

Meanwhile, Knox was still neck-deep in the streets. He hadn't changed. He was still selling drugs, robbing grow houses, and clinging to his dream of building his own marijuana empire. I tried pushing him toward something different. I suggested trades, told him maybe he could become a locksmith, something stable. But the truth was, Knox struggled with reading and writing in English, and that reality crushed any hope he had of ever pursuing a more traditional path. He felt like he didn't belong anywhere outside the hustle.

That divide between us started to widen. I was trying to evolve, and he was staying the same. I had sacrificed friendships, distanced myself from people like Wes and Benny, all in the name of our relationship. But Knox? He wasn't losing anything. Not really. And I started to feel that imbalance...deeply.

Then, at 28, I found out I was pregnant with my second son, Justice. I was still working at the doctor's office, juggling the pressures of work, parenting Amadeus, and now carrying another child. I was exhausted, physically and emotionally. But I was committed to keeping our family afloat.

Knox, though, was falling apart.

The pressure was mounting. The man who had once sold me a car, and never delivered, had been arrested. Rumors swirled that he was planning to cooperate with law enforcement, offering Knox's name as leverage for his own deal. The walls were closing in again. On top of that, Knox's grandfather, his guiding light, was quietly dying of cancer. No one had told the grandkids. When Knox finally found out, it was like someone ripped the ground out from under him. There was no gentle buildup. Just a blunt truth: your grandfather is dying. That was it. Another fracture. Another piece of him.. gone.

We had planned a trip to Puerto Rico, my first time on the island. I'd dreamed about it, imagined the beaches, the food, the history. Knox had been many times without me, but now it was finally supposed to be our time. A fresh start.

But the night before our trip, Knox had been gone all day, making what he called "money moves" with people from a different crew, some of them from Benny's neighborhood. A lot was weighing on him: his pending case, the sting of Cash's betrayal, the complicated loss of two people who'd once been like brothers to him. You could see it in his eyes, in the way he moved. That day, something shifted.

He came home late that night, and the second I saw him, I knew something wasn't right.

His energy was off, sharp, restless. His eyes wouldn't settle on anything. His movements were jerky, his body coiled like a spring. At first, I thought maybe he'd been partying. But then he looked at me, and the way he looked at me... it sent a chill straight through my bones.

I started asking questions. "Where have you been?" "What's going on?"

That's when he snapped. The accusations came fast, without warning.

"B, are you wearing a wire?" "Are you working with the Feds?" "Are you setting me up?" "Why are you asking so many questions?" "Are you working with everyone else? Are ya'll plotting against me?"

His words came out like bullets: rapid, paranoid, nonsensical. His fists clenched and unclenched, his breathing grew shallow, his whole body buzzing with fear.

I had never seen Knox scared like this before.

My mother came in, alarmed by the escalating argument. She tried to soothe him, but he wanted nothing to do with either of us. Without warning, he stormed out of the house and walked straight into the neighbor's yard.

I followed. I was terrified of what he might do, not just to himself, but to someone else.

I called his father in Puerto Rico, hoping he could calm him down. But he brushed it off, assuming Knox was just high. I knew better. This wasn't drugs. This was something else...something deeper, darker.

His paranoia only grew. He started pacing the neighbor's yard, muttering about being watched, about people trying to kill him. One minute he was angry, the next panicked, then heartbreakingly quiet. I stood there, crying, begging him to come back inside, to let me help him.

But he wouldn't even look at me.

He started telling the neighbors to keep me away, like I was the threat. At one point, I saw him clutching a green folder, whispering that his lawyer wanted him to cooperate with the police. That's when I knew, this wasn't just paranoia. He was unraveling.

Eventually, the police were called.

I stood in the middle of the road, sobbing, begging him not to do this, not to push us to this point. "Please, Knox," I cried, "please don't do this to me. Don't do this to yourself." But he looked right through me, like I was a stranger.

His face was blank. His eyes lost focus. He didn't recognize me.

When the officers gently placed him into the back of the squad car, I knew he wasn't in control anymore. The man I knew would *never* willingly get into the back of a cop car; that man wasn't there. Not fully.

Knox was taken in under Florida's Baker Act. What was supposed to be a voluntary 72-hour hold turned into an involuntary stay. They deemed him a danger to himself, and from what I'd seen, they were right.

HIPAA laws kept me in the dark. I wasn't allowed to know anything, not even what medications he was on. I was shut out while the man I loved crumbled behind closed doors. I wanted to help him. But no matter how hard I tried, I couldn't save someone who didn't want, or know how, to be saved.

Chapter 18

When Hope Left

The facility felt like something out of a nightmare, dimly lit with flickering fluorescent lights that cast eerie shadows on the peeling off-white walls. The air was thick with the sterile bite of antiseptic, layered over something stale that clung to my skin like a warning. The small, barred windows near the ceiling let in only the faintest slivers of light, cold and distant, like hope itself had been locked out.

When I finally saw Knox, my heart broke in a way I wasn't prepared for.

He looked like a ghost: pale, sunken, hollow. His body had thinned, his eyes were vacant, and his speech came out slow and fragmented, like someone was forcing the words through a broken machine. He wasn't himself.

Then it happened. I felt it before I saw it, his eyes widening, his chest tightening, breath caught in his throat. Panic washed over him like wildfire. I reached out, desperate to hold onto any fragment of him still present, but it was gone.

Suddenly, staff rushed in.

"He's hallucinating," I yelled, stepping forward, voice raw. "He doesn't understand..."

A staff member barked, "Step back or we'll have to remove you."

"Remove me? I'm the only person who knows him," I shot back, panic flooding my voice.

But when another staffer wheeled in a syringe, I dropped to my knees in front of him, arms outstretched.

"No...please don't do that!" I cried. My tears fell as his gaze flicked to mine, terrified.

"Babe... what's happening?" he slurred, voice strained. "Why are they doing this?"

"I'm here. I'm right here," I sobbed, hitting my chest. "Don't leave me."

Still, they jabbed the needle into his arm. His body stiffened, then went limp. His face dropped into a blank mask.

"Get off him!" I screamed, lunging forward. Nurses held me back like a child.

One of them spoke quietly: "He'll be sedated for a while... he was a danger to himself."

"They made him worse!" I cried. "You don't even know him!" My fists balled, helpless.

They dragged his body away. I collapsed against the wall, breath ragged and chest tight, a void growing in my heart.

In that moment, I watched my man slip away, physically silent, mentally absent. I screamed and begged, but all doors closed behind him. That was the last time I saw him. Not as a partner, not as anything more than an empty shell in a padded room.

I wasn't his wife. I wasn't recognized as family. I was just the pregnant girlfriend, locked out, shut out, and utterly powerless.

His father arranged for his stepmother to fly in and take care of him. For a week, I drove her to the facility, waiting outside each time while she went in. Eventually, the decision was made: Knox needed a complete change of environment. He was going to Puerto Rico to recover. His stepmother would take him.

The day of his release, I sat in the car, hands resting on my pregnant belly, trying to steady the storm inside me. When he walked out, he didn't even recognize me.

At first, he refused to get in the car. It took his stepmother speaking softly to him in Spanish, reassuring, coaxing, before he finally climbed into the back seat, silent and distant. The drive to the airport was quiet, the tension so thick it was hard to breathe.

We pulled up to Tampa International a little after nine; the departure lane was a swarm of brake lights and blaring horns. Knox's step-mother sat rigid in the front seat, both hands clenched around her purse strap, while Knox rocked back and forth behind her, mumbling half-sentences I couldn't catch. The closer we crawled to the curb, the faster he rocked.

"Suave, papi... tranquilo," she whispered in Spanish, stroking the back of his hand like you'd soothe a skittish animal. He wouldn't meet her eyes. Wouldn't meet mine either.

I found a spot near the far end of the curb and threw the car into park. The second the engine shut off, Knox snapped upright. "Don't leave me," he hissed, voice sharp, eyes darting.

"I'm not leaving. We're just getting your bags," I said, forcing calm.

His stepmother opened the door first. "Come on, mi amor, rápido." She tugged at his elbow. He hesitated, then followed her out, shuffling the way he did when the paranoia stole his stride.

The humid night hit us like a wet blanket, diesel exhaust, cigarette smoke, the citrusy tang of janitorial cleaner all tangled together. A skycap's cart banged behind us; a toddler cried somewhere up the sidewalk. Ordinary airport chaos, but in Knox's head, every sound was a threat.

While I muscled the luggage from the trunk, he stood on the sidewalk, arms folded tight across his chest, eyes scanning the crowds like he expected an ambush. His step-mother spoke to him in a low, urgent stream of Spanish sentences. I caught fragments: *confía en mí... solo un vuelo... todo va a estar bien.* He nodded, but each nod was smaller than the last.

I slammed the trunk and turned to lock the car. In that split second, maybe three seconds total, I lost sight of them.

Panic rose so fast it made my vision swim. I spun around, scanning the curb, dodging a family dragging neon suitcases. Nothing. Another step left, still nothing.

Then, thirty yards ahead, I spotted him: Knox, alone, weaving through parked shuttles in a slow zigzag, expression blank and eyes wide, like a child separated from his mother in a grocery store. His stepmother was nowhere.

My breath hitched. I bolted.

"Knox!" I shouted, but my voice dissolved into the airport din, rolling luggage wheels, announcements echoing off concrete, the low thrumming engines. I closed the gap and grabbed his forearm. He flinched hard, almost swung at me. "Where is she?" I asked, heartbeat throbbing in my ears.

He stared past me, confused, lost. Didn't answer.

Somehow, I convinced him to come inside with me. We searched for her amid the crowds, desperate and disoriented. When we reached the JetBlue counter, I explained the situation to the woman behind the desk. She tapped her keyboard, scanned the screen, then looked up.

"She's already boarded," she said. "The plane just took off."

She was gone. She had left him behind, taking with her all his belongings, all his medication.

I could hardly breathe.

Knox was still deep in paranoia, unable to trust me, unable to grasp what had just happened. I immediately called my mother, my voice coming out in gasps.

"Ma, she's gone, and Knox is trippin' on me. We're at the airport, and like, I can't do this."

"Brandy, hold on. Who's gone? What's going on?" she asked, trying to make sense of my panic.

"His stepmother!... wait..." I looked up to see Knox walking away from me, headed straight for a security guard.

"Mom, I need you to come to the airport. Now. I'm on the JetBlue side." I hung up and hurried after him.

Knox was speaking rapidly to the guard, eyes wild. "She's trying to hurt me," he said, pointing in my direction. "I need to get away from her."

"Sir, sorry for all this," I said quickly, trying not to sound desperate. "He's mentally ill. His caregiver just abandoned him and boarded the flight."

The guard's eyes narrowed. "Ma'am, who are you to him?"

"I'm his pregnant girlfriend," I replied, my voice cracking. "I've known him since we were teenagers. Please, my mom and my son are on the way. I just need to keep him safe until they get here."

"Ma'am, I need you to take a seat over there while I speak to him."

I nodded and sat, watching as Knox paced and repeated himself. The minutes dragged like hours. I kept calling my mother over and over just to track how close they were.

When they finally arrived, I was still seated, tears streaming silently, my arms wrapped around my belly like a shield. I was trying to stay strong, for myself and for our unborn son.

Then Knox saw Amadeus. Everything changed. His face softened, lit up even. Amadeus still believed, in that innocent child way, that we were all going on a family trip to Puerto Rico.

His dream broke the moment he found me.

"Mom, are you okay?" he asked, his voice tight with concern. "Are we still going to Puerto Rico?"

Before I could answer, my mother gently stepped in. "No, baby. There is no trip."

Amadeus lowered his head, the disappointment sinking in, but he walked over to Knox anyway.

"Hello, who are you?" the security guard asked, cautiously.

"He's my son," Knox answered without hesitation.

Amadeus smiled, wrapping his arms around him. Knox hugged him back, calmer now, grounded by the familiarity of his touch.

"Can we go home now?" Amadeus asked softly.

"Yes, we can, son," Knox replied.

He took Amadeus by the hand, and together they walked back toward me and my mother. That walk, those few yards, felt like an eternity. The same kind of slow-motion stretch that happens in dreams and disasters.

Knox let Amadeus lead him to the car. They got in the back seat together. There was no way I could bring Knox home. Not in the state he was in. Not with Amadeus in the same house.

We exchanged no words. Just the hum of the road, the weight of choices, and the ache of a heart doing its best to hold everything together.

I drove us to his grandfather's and left him there.

Knox had always been mentally strong. But now, paranoia gripped him, creeping into every corner of his mind until it consumed him. He became convinced I would betray him, despite everything I had done to stand by his side. The fear in his eyes when he looked at me, the one who had his back the most, shattered me.

I went to see him a few days later, desperate to regain a sense of control, he came up with a plan: we should get married. In his spiraling mind, becoming my husband would protect him through spousal immunity. He believed marriage would make me more respectable in the eyes of the court and legally unable to testify against him. But more than that, it made our relationship more respectable in his own eyes.

For Knox, it wasn't love. It was fear.

But for me? It felt like a seed of hope. A flicker of possibility, that maybe we could still build a life together, far from everything that had broken us.

In my heart, I believed marriage could anchor him. I thought if we just crossed that line, if we made it official, something would shift. And maybe, once his mind was stable again, we could become all the things we were meant to be, but never had the chance to become.

"Hey B... we should get married," Knox said suddenly, looking at me from across the room. His eyes were locked on me, but they weren't steady. They weren't all the way there.

I paused, unsure I'd heard him right. "Huh? Are you for real?"

"Yeah. I am," he nodded, his tone calm but detached, like he was halfway here... and halfway somewhere else.

"Like... for real, for real?" I sat up straighter, my heart fluttering, part hope, part warning. Part of me wanted to believe this moment was real, romantic, even, but deep down, I knew better.

He leaned forward, resting his elbows on his knees. "You're becoming the mother of my only child. I want to make you a wife. A person of high respect."

I searched his face, trying to read between the cracks. "Honestly, it would make sense. If we were married, I could help more with your health. I could speak for you when you can't. Sign for things."

"Exactly," he said quickly. "And with all this legal shit going on, I don't want them coming after you."

I tilted my head, confused. "Who's coming after me?"

"The FEDS," he whispered, lowering his voice as he glanced toward the window. "They watching. They been watching. That's why I can't trust nobody."

I started imagining a new chapter: leaving Florida behind, disappearing into a place where no one knew our names. A place where Knox would leave the streets, where drug dealing and violence would be memories we escaped instead of a reality we were living. I was willing to do whatever it took to save him. If marriage was the price, then so be it. Forget the dream of a perfect proposal, a white dress, or a fairytale. This wasn't fantasy. This was real life.

As Knox slipped deeper into himself, I started losing pieces of who I was, too. My wedding and the pregnancy, both experiences that should have been times of joy, were clouded by fear and unpredictability. Every day became a mission: keep him grounded, keep him safe, keep him from vanishing completely.

I poured every part of myself into saving him. Believing love and being present could anchor someone who was already untethered. But with each passing day, it became harder to ignore the truth.

Two weeks later, we got married.

The ceremony was simple. We held it in the backyard of the double-wide trailer. Knox had bought a gazebo long ago, and that became the heart of the wedding. We lined it with string lights and fire torches, trying to create something beautiful.

A pebble path led to the gazebo, where we arranged chairs and tables under the shade of the oak trees. It wasn't extravagant. I was three or four months pregnant, dressed in a $500 gown from David's Bridal. I smiled, I entertained, and I did everything I could for people not to notice any of the differences in Knox's personality, not sure any of it was working. It was exhausting.

My mom, Amara, and a few close friends helped organize the day. As always, my mom gave it her all, handmaking decorations, cooking alongside my cousin, Bella. The meal was simple: pork, black beans, salad, and Cuban bread. The cake, a modest two-tier from Publix.

Our rings came from the same jeweler Wes once worked for. Knox's brother stood by him as best man, and Amara was my bridesmaid, her daughters the flower girls. Amadeus was the ring bearer. We wore purple and white. We rented chairs to make the space feel more formal.

There was no honeymoon. No bachelor or bachelorette party. No reception.

Just a desperate vow between two people trying to hold on to something that had already slipped through their fingers.

The day came and went, a small, intimate gathering of about fifty people. None of the original squad was there. Benny, Kato, and Cash were all locked up. Wes had drifted out of our lives completely. The only person from Knox's past who showed up was a guy who brought his girlfriend, who worked at a salon and had helped me with my hair that day.

I chose the wedding song. Knox wasn't involved in much of the planning. The stress was relentless. I constantly feared that the emotional weight of it all might cause me to miscarry. I felt like I was carrying everything, running the house, caring for Amadeus, navigating my pregnancy, and trying to manage Knox's deteriorating mental health.

I worked through my entire pregnancy because I had no other option. I was the only one keeping us afloat, and we were barely making it. Knox wasn't making money from the streets anymore, and after Medco let my mom go, I became our sole source of income. Once again, my mom stepped in as she always had. She cooked, picked up Amadeus from school, and made sure he was cared for when I couldn't.

Knox, when he was home, would try to contribute, fixing up parts of the house, remodeling, but his efforts were scattered and inconsistent.

I had learned from my first experience. I knew more about what to expect, what signs to watch for, and how to advocate for my own health. But that didn't make it easy. I was still sick all the time, battling relentless nausea, morning sickness, and the constant struggle to keep food down. My weight had to be closely monitored. I returned to the same OBGYN practice but saw a different provider this time. And even though I was physically healthier than I'd been during my first pregnancy, the emotional toll was far worse.

I mourned the life we had once dreamed of together, the laughter, the passion, the promises of a future we would build side by side.

But most of all, I grieved the man Knox used to be. The one with vision. The one who made me laugh until I cried. The one who once made me feel like the center of his world. That man was gone. In his place stood a stranger, paranoid, broken, lost.

And I didn't know if he was ever coming back.

Justice was born without any complications. Knox was there, along with my mother and Amadeus. In a moment that should've felt sacred, Knox gave Amadeus the honor of cutting his baby brother's umbilical cord. It should have been filled with love, with unity. But something inside me knew we weren't whole. Not really.

Knox's mind wasn't what it once was, but it was better. He'd been seeing the Nigerian doctor I worked for, following up on his mental health, taking prescribed medication. There was progress, slow, but real. Still, Knox, being Knox, decided the meds weren't necessary anymore. The cost was too high, and his trust in the process was too low.

For almost a year, he kept away from the streets. He focused on getting better. That case, the one built on 15-year-old information, fizzled out. Maybe the source wasn't credible. Maybe the system just moved on. Either way, for the first time, it felt like we had a shot at peace.

But peace, for Knox, never lasted.

When the pressure started creeping in, bills piling, money running low. He sold anything that could make money. Without asking me, he sold his ATV, his chains, and his jewelry. And worst of all, he sold my 1977 Chevy Malibu. That car meant something. And he gave it away like it was just another sacrifice to survive.

Then came the weed. Then the calls. Then Wes.

Chapter 19

The Final Goodbye

I t started slow. A few conversations. A few "small" moves. But it never stays small with Knox. Suddenly, he wasn't just back in the game. He was deeper in it than ever. Pounds of weed. Eight balls of cocaine. This time, no trap houses. This time, it was bigger, riskier. He had evolved in the worst way.

And me? I had fought for him...for us. I'd stood beside him during his breakdown, helped him pick up the pieces when the world walked away. I carried our family. I carried him. And still, he went back to the only thing that had ever truly betrayed him: the streets.

The love I had? It began to rot into resentment.

Our intimacy dried up. Not all at once, but slowly. Quietly. Like a faucet tightening itself shut over time. The chemistry faded. The connection we used to fight for felt... gone. I didn't see him the same anymore. I couldn't.

While he chased dreams that never held him down, I held down everything else. The house. The kids. The bills. My sanity. I was stretched thin, surviving while he stayed stuck, promising progress but delivering silence.

So I turned cold.

I stopped asking for partnership and started building walls. I sharpened my tongue until it cut without thinking. I humiliated him with my words. I stripped him of the little dignity he was still holding onto. I wanted to hurt him because of the way I had been hurting.

"Car's still in the driveway. Not fixed. Just like everything else around here," I snapped one morning as I passed him in the kitchen. "What's the point of having you around, again?"

He looked up, groggy. Confused.

I didn't wait. "Same pile of dishes. Same tired excuses. Same sorry excuse of a man. And like always, Brandy'll clean it up. Because that's what I do. I clean up your messes while you sit around playing pretend."

He sighed. "Yo, I told you. I've been handling things. You act like I don't carry pressure too."

"Pressure?" I laughed bitterly. "You don't carry pressure, you carry failure. You walk around with it like a badge. Every dream you've ever had? Just that. A dream. No follow-through. No growth. Just more talk."

"Yo, chill."

"No, *you* chill. You want respect? Be someone worth respecting. You can't fix a car. Can't fix the house. Can't fix your own damn self. And every time I look at you, I wonder how the hell I ended up here, lowered to this."

He pushed his chair back. "You're doing the most right now."

"You think you're a man? A man doesn't choose the streets over his family. A man doesn't leave his woman to hold up the entire goddamn world while he sits on the couch watching it burn. You call yourself a provider? All you've ever provided is *pain*."

He clenched his jaw. "You really think I'm not trying? You don't think I have to carry losses? You don't think I regret shit every day? I've done more for you than anybody ever did."

"More for me? You gave me broken promises and some sad little hope I'd be the one to change you. That's not love, that's *leverage*. And I fell for it. Like a fool."

"You better stop with where you're headed with ya words, B. I'm telling you now."

"Oh, you're 'telling me now'? Please. All you ever build are problems, stress, and paranoia. I'm telling you this because I'm *done*. Done begging. Done hoping. Done watching you rot in your own potential while I drown in responsibility."

His voice dropped. "You've already made up your mind, huh?"

I nodded, breath caught in my throat. "You're a fantasy, Knox. A dream dressed up in ambition. But it's all lies. And I'm done paying the price for your delusion."

Silence.

"I want relief," I whispered. "From this house. From this weight. From you."

And then one night, when Justice was just a few months old, I woke up to Knox whispering that he was leaving.

"Just for a bit," he said. "Texas first. Then New York. Some business with my cousins."

I sat up in bed, blinking. "*What?*"

But by the time I gathered my words, he was already packing a bag.

No goodbye kiss. No clarity. Just the echo of the door closing behind him, and the silence of a new kind of betrayal settling in the crib next to me.

Things were supposed to be different now. We were married. We had a child. I thought things would change, that he wouldn't just disappear without a word like he used to. But here he was, doing exactly that. No conversation. No consideration. Just a whisper in the night and a bag in his hand.

The illusion I had built in my head shattered.

I cried. I begged him not to go. I argued, pleaded, poured out everything I had left in me. But he just stood there, expression blank, like I was background noise. And then, without another word, he walked out the door.

Days passed. Nothing.

His phone went straight to voicemail. No texts. No updates. No clues. My mind spiraled. I checked hospital records between Texas and New York. I called jails. I reached out to bail bondsmen. I searched for him like he was missing, because to me, he was.

Then, I got a call.

Knox was locked up. In North Carolina. I had to take off work, lie to my boss, pack the kids into the car, and drive eight hours to pick him up.

I wasn't relieved. I was exhausted. Furious. Broken.

Knox was changing, and not in a way I could support. His dreams started sounding more like excuses. His business tactics were reckless. The woman who once adored the hustler in him? She was gone. Now, I hated it. I hated the lies. I hated how easily he could disappear.

The weight of our relationship began to physically manifest in my body. My skin erupted in hives daily for months. Doctors told me it was stress. My weight plummeted. I was drinking more. Smoking more. Doing coke more. Just to numb the pain.

But walking away wasn't simple. We were married. We had a home. Kids. A life. Leaving meant undoing everything we'd built, everything I had sacrificed to maintain.

At the same time, I was trying to build something for myself. Amara and I joined a network marketing business centered around travel. My nine-to-five wasn't cutting it, and I needed more. To get traction in the business, I created social media accounts for the first time ever.

And with that, everything changed.

My inbox flooded with people from my past. Suddenly, the whole world had access to me. It was overwhelming, but it was also an awakening. I realized I had a voice. A presence. And opportunities.

When Knox saw one of the photos I took for the business, he flipped. He accused me of cheating. Questioned everything. Even blamed Amara, calling her a bad influence.

That was my breaking point.

After everything I'd done, everything I'd endured, he still couldn't recognize my loyalty? I had held this man down through jail time, breakdowns, betrayal, and street shit, and now that I was trying to win for myself, he couldn't take it?

This time, I wasn't folding. I had been losing for years, standing beside him. That was over.

I was built for more. I wasn't meant to work a dead-end job building someone else's dream while my husband ran the streets unchecked. I had protected his image for too long, wearing a smile for the world while dying inside. And when I finally tried to step into my power, he tried to dim it.

But then I got a message on Facebook Messenger from a name I hadn't seen in years. The guy who had scammed me out of the car I tried to buy at nineteen.

And in that message, I learned the truth I never expected: *Knox had been involved.*

To this day, I don't know why he chose to tell me after all those years. Maybe it was fate. Maybe it was karma. Maybe he was bitter because he got locked up, and Knox didn't. But the moment I read that message, I lost it.

Had my addiction to pain led me to sleep with the enemy? Had I given my life, my love, my loyalty, to the very person who betrayed me first?

That revelation broke something in me. I was waiting, simmering in rage.

I didn't know exactly how the conversation was going to go, but I knew this much: I had no patience left. No more space for lies. No more tolerance for gaslighting, guilt-tripping, or manipulation.

Tears streamed down my face, not from sadness, but from pressure. The kind that builds slow, steady, boiling just beneath the surface. My body trembled as memories played on loop in my mind.

Had I really given this man *years* of my life?

I didn't know where Knox was, but I knew he had to come home eventually. And when I heard the car pull into the driveway, my heart pounded in my chest like a war drum. The sound of his keys, his voice on the phone as he stepped through the door, it all made my skin crawl.

Even his voice disturbed me. He walked into the kitchen like everything was normal, grabbed a drink from the fridge, and ended his call. That's when I confronted him.

"Knox, don't lie to me," I said, my voice calm but razor-sharp. "I'm going to ask you something, and I need the truth."

He looked up, confused. "B, what's the problem *now*?"

I clenched my fists. *The problem?* He had no idea. "Did you have anything to do with that car scam when I was nineteen?"

His face twisted in confusion, like I was speaking another language.

"Don't give me that dumb-ass look," I snapped. "Yes or no. Did you help set me up?"

"Yo, B... you need to calm the hell down," he replied.

"The *hell* I do!" I yelled. "Answer the question. I heard some foul shit, and I need to know what *really* happened. Did you rob me?"

His body tensed. The truth was in his silence. And then, he flipped it. "Who the hell you think you talkin' to like that? You accusing me now? Gettin' disrespectful? You out here on social media, acting brand new with your little business and your new energy. Who *knows* what *you* been up to?" He turned his back and walked away.

That's when I saw it, the brand-new 70-inch TV he'd just mounted on the wall.

I snapped.

The curtain rod was leaning in the corner, left there by my mom after washing the drapes. I didn't even think. My hands moved on their own, grabbing it, lifting it, bringing it down hard. Glass shattered. The screen split down the middle like a lightning strike.

Amadeus remembers the noise. Waking up to the commotion. He saw Nanie rushing from her room, panicked. Heard the yelling, the rage, the sound of glass meeting metal.

Knox exploded. My mom tried to calm him and me, but it was too late. I had never been the one to destroy things.

It terrified me. It terrified my son.

But in that moment, one thing became clear. It was time to go. We all have a beast inside of us. And instead of taming mine, Knox had fed it. I turned to Amadeus, my voice shaking but clear. "Start packing. Whatever you can carry, for you and your brother." Then I looked at my mother. "We're leaving."

And the wildest part? Knox didn't stop me.

Amadeus was scared, rushing to grab clothes, throwing things into bags, heartbroken. Everything was changing in an instant. He wasn't just leaving the house; he was leaving the only home he'd ever known.

And truthfully, so was I. I didn't know where we were going, but I knew one thing for sure: I wasn't going back to him.

I called Amara, frantic, tearful, my voice shaking with rage. No hesitation. She opened her doors that night, like she always did. We stayed with her for about a month before reconnecting with the family on my father's side. They welcomed us into their home in Land O'

Lakes, a quiet two-story house on a few acres. Bigger than Amara's apartment. A better fit for all of us.

Starting over wasn't easy. This time, it wasn't just me. I had two boys and my mother, all depending on me.

The drive between Land O' Lakes and Tampa was long, exhausting. But we made it work. Amadeus stayed in the same school. I kept my job. My mom stayed home with Justice. And we had just one car between us. Still, we kept going. Day by day.

I threw everything I had into building a side business with Amara in a direct sales company called DreamTrips. I wanted it to work. I *needed* it to work.

But the return never matched the energy I was pouring in. Eventually, I had to let it go.

But what I gained? It was bigger than money.

DreamTrips introduced me to a whole new mindset. For the first time, I was exposed to the concept of *residual income*, money that worked while you slept. I heard names I'd never heard before: Warren Buffett. Robert Kiyosaki. Napoleon Hill. I read books like *Rich Dad Poor Dad* and *Think and Grow Rich*, books filled with financial truths no one in my family had ever known.

Not my parents. Not their parents.

We had always lived in a cycle, poverty-driven, negative, surviving paycheck to paycheck. But now, I am learning differently. I was learning how to *use* money instead of letting it use me.

I saw people my age winning, people who came from where I came from. They weren't just talking about dreams. They were building legacies. And they weren't stingy with the game. They shared it.

This wasn't just about selling travel. This was about breaking generational curses. This was about shifting mindsets and rewriting the script.

I took the hustle that once served the streets and flipped it into something new. I started networking, hosting travel parties, speaking in front of rooms full of people, leading conversations about money, opportunity, and success.

I wasn't just learning, I was transforming.

I had always wanted to travel. I'd watched Knox fly across the world for years without me. But through DreamTrips, I finally got to see the world for myself, Colorado, the Grand Canyon, Arizona, Miami, and beach towns up and down Florida.

And for the first time, I wasn't a spectator in someone else's story. I was living my own.

The money didn't flow like I wanted it to. But it wasn't a loss, it was an *awakening*. The experience gave me access. Access to knowledge, to people, to truth. I learned things no classroom ever taught me. I learned that wealth wasn't just for the lucky. It was for the bold. It was a choice. A mindset.

And once your mind shifts, there's no going back.

The relationship was over. But Knox? He still wanted his family back. Talking to him during the separation was unbearable. Every conversation was laced with tension and resentment. I didn't trust him. I barely wanted to leave Justice alone with him. People we both knew kept the gossip alive, carrying messages between us like poison. We barely spoke. We barely saw each other.

Eight years invested, and I was left with more broken pieces than I had started with.

Eventually, Knox accepted that I was serious about the divorce. He hired a lawyer to handle everything. My only cost was $500 to change my name back to my maiden name. Knox paid for the rest. We sat together in the lawyer's office, signing papers and discussing details that no longer mattered. We weren't going to fight, not over custody, not over child support, not over alimony or property. I didn't want a single thing from him.

Not the house.Not the money.Not the memories.Nothing.

Before we even got a court date, Knox was picked up by the Feds. We both saw it coming. Everyone who walks that path either ends up in prison or in a grave.

The lawyer proceeded with the divorce anyway. When the court date came, I went alone. Our attorney represented us both; there was nothing left to dispute. Knox wasn't required to be there. And just like that, I was divorced.

I was free. The details of his federal case were unclear, except for what I heard from his cousin Knowledge, Cash's younger brother. Knowledge reached out one day, asking me to stop by.When I did, he told me Knox was facing serious time. I wasn't surprised. I wasn't even shaken. If anything, I felt relieved. I felt free from the weight of him. But my heart ached for Justice. He would grow up without a father. And I had a choice to make.

I decided right then: I wasn't bringing my son into the jail system. No visits. No phone calls.He would know his father through photos and memories...good ones. Ones I would share when the time was right. If Knox ever got out, we'd cross that bridge when we got there.

Until then, I was moving forward.

Chapter 20

Dancing for Survival

I was unmarried. Single again. On the prowl. Same face, same game.

I was still drawn to street men, their confidence, their toughness, the unspoken power in how they moved. But I wasn't looking for love. I was back to my old ways: sexing and ghosting.

The 9-to-5 at the Nigerian doctor's office wasn't cutting it. Eventually, I made a decision. It was time to start dancing again.

When I left the strip club the first time, I thought it was for good. But the truth? It took more than one try to really leave. Walking away had been a turning point, yes. I had done it for the right reasons, at least, I thought I had. To prioritize the people I loved. But deep down, I wasn't doing it for me.

I had never thrown away my dance clothes. They stayed tucked away in a bag Knox never knew about. Every so often, I'd wash them with the laundry, keep them clean, just in case. At least this time, I wasn't starting from scratch. All I needed was a new pair of shoes.

Through social media, I reconnected with Liora, an old associate from my past. We had never danced together, but we both knew the game. She was starting a business and needed some extra cash. She knew a couple of clubs out in Largo and Holiday, far enough from Tampa, far enough from my past. Places I could work without the weight of old faces and old memories.

We set a date to audition.

We sat in silence for a moment, the glow of the club lights bleeding through the windshield. It had been years since either of us danced, but here we were again.

"You ready?" Liora asked, glancing over at me, her nails tapping a slow rhythm against the steering wheel.

"Girl..." I exhaled, tightening my grip on my purse. "I'm just here to get what I need and get the hell out. You already know how grimy this game is."

She let out a low, bitter laugh. "Facts. Ain't nothing changed but the faces and the price of outfits."

"We older now. And so are the kids," I said, eyes locked on the front doors. "This ain't no comeback tour. I just need cushion money to move out, get this separation handled, and start fresh with the boys."

"Same," she said, adjusting her wig in the rearview mirror. "I need new high-grade equipment if I wanna scale this cleaning biz. It's cutthroat out here. I'm not about to be the weak link. This right here?" She nodded toward the club. "Just a pit stop. Quick in, quick out."

I nodded. "I'm proud of you, though. You really building something from scratch. That's real."

"Girl, don't start that sentimental shit before we even step inside," she laughed. Then her voice dropped, more serious. "Look, we ain't walking in here lost. We got a plan. This ain't a lifestyle, it's a launchpad. We do what we gotta do and bounce. Hell, maybe one of these fools'll sponsor the mission."

We both laughed, half joke, half hope. She grabbed her bag, and I grabbed mine. "Alright," she said, straightening her posture. "Let's get in, handle business, and remind them why we never had to try too hard."

I took a deep breath. "Clock in, stack up, and keep it movin'."

This time, I wasn't nervous. I wasn't that same wide-eyed girl stepping into a world she didn't understand. I just needed to get back into rhythm and figure out how this club ran.

The biggest difference? It wasn't fully nude. Topless only. Which meant they served alcohol, and I didn't have to sneak in my own drinks anymore. Customers could buy them for me.

The money was steady. I made $400 to $600 a shift, working just three nights a week. But the vibe? Completely different.

This club wasn't glamorous, it was gritty. Rough. No sparkle, no fantasy.

The dressing room was cramped, lockers barely holding together. The space was so small, only two girls could sit comfortably at once. The floor was a mess, makeup, wigs, weaves, curling irons, baby wipes everywhere. It smelled like stale smoke and cheap liquor.

Out front wasn't much better.

The chairs were worn down, sagging from years of use. There were three stages, one main one and two off to the side for guys who didn't want to be seen. One of the poles spun too fast; I never got the hang of it. I slipped a few times, but always managed to land it with grace.

The pace was wild. DJs flipped songs fast, names got called nonstop. It was hard to keep up.

And the dances?

There was no real privacy. Just rows of seats lined up like church pews, girl after girl grinding next to each other in a room full of wandering eyes.

Even the champagne rooms weren't luxurious, just a curtain, a mirror, and a bench. No ambiance. No seduction. Just business.

The tip-out structure wasn't too different from what I was used to, but now I had to tip the bar too. At least they didn't fine us for missing shifts. No pressure. I could work when I wanted, how I wanted.

The girls? They weren't Instagram pretty. They weren't pretending. They were real dancers: gritty, loud, bold. They weren't there for fun. They were there to *eat*.

I didn't get close to anyone. Except for Liora, and even then, we didn't always work the same nights. When I was alone? Those shifts hit different. Having someone in your corner makes it easier. But I'd learned how to survive the silence. Because this time, I wasn't naive. This time, I wasn't walking into a trap. I was walking in with my eyes wide open. And I was doing it on *my* terms.

Chapter 21

Second Chances in the Small Things

A fter almost two years of living with family in Land O' Lakes, I was finally approved for a three-bedroom, two-bath apartment in Tampa.

It wasn't in the area I wanted. It wasn't close to family, friends, or anything familiar or comforting. But at this point, it wasn't about what I wanted; it was about what we needed as a family. I never imagined that this apartment, this place I chose out of pure necessity, would become my cocoon. A place where I would break down, unravel everything I thought I knew, and slowly piece myself back together.

A metamorphosis.

Like a caterpillar becoming a butterfly, I didn't even recognize it at first. But deep inside, my soul was crying out. My life, my spirit, a part of me I hadn't known existed, began to wake up.

This apartment became the sanctuary I had longed for. But embracing it would take time. This is how God began to move on my behalf. I had to be separated. I had to be alone. I had to begin the real healing I'd been running from for years. Eventually, I came to understand something powerful:

The world outside was more broken than I had ever been.

The world had used me...abused me...bullied me...accused me...rejected me...deceived me...tried to destroy me. But still, I was standing. I was here. And the best was yet to come. I just didn't know it yet.

Even when my inner world felt dark and cold, there was a light on its way to rescue me. By all odds, I shouldn't have made it. By all statistics, I should have been another lost cause. I should have been dead. But the light of God found me.

He left the 99 to save the one.Me.

***

13 years after he was first sentenced to prison, Benny came home.

When Benny was released, he was placed on supervised release, a year-long period of post-incarceration monitoring. He had to report to a probation officer, take drug tests, and stick to a strict set of conditions.

Wes and I were the ones who picked him up that day.

ADDICTED TO PAIN

Our first stop? Publix, so he could buy flowers for his mother. Then we drove him back to the old neighborhood.

Seeing him again after all those years felt surreal. For both of us. Benny was quiet during the drive, his energy calm but heavy. I could tell he was deep in thought. He asked about Knox. I gave him the short version, just enough to catch him up. He didn't say much, but I knew he was processing a lot beneath the surface.

When we pulled up to his mother's house, the moment turned emotional.

There were tears, laughter, hugs, pictures. A full-circle moment. Walking into that house, just driving through the neighborhood, it stirred up memories I had long buried. If I felt that way, I could only imagine what it was like for him.

Not long after, I introduced Benny to a cousin of mine, someone from my father's side of the family. We had reconnected after being out of touch for over a decade, so I wasn't immediately open about everything I had been through. I figured we'd catch up, rebuild some trust, ease into it. But somewhere along the way, she and Benny hooked up.

It quickly turned into a relationship. And I wasn't thrilled.

Benny had just come home. He needed time to breathe, to heal, to reacclimate. She had just come out of her own toxic relationship. She needed space to figure herself out. But neither of them wanted to hear that.

Soon, things between Benny and me shifted. Not just because of our past. Not just because of Knox. But because now... he was dating my cousin Bella.

And it was weird.

BRANDY GRILLO

It was weird seeing her car outside his place. Weird watching them move in together.Weird witnessing them play house while our own bond faded into the background. It created distance. An unspoken tension.

And just like that, Benny felt farther away than he had before he came home. Benny wasted no time trying to rebuild his life.

He started studying to become an electrician and picked up steady work in construction. He built his credit from the ground up, eventually buying a brand-new car straight off the lot. From the outside, it looked like he was thriving, especially for someone who had just done serious time.

But the streets still had their grip on him.

He started small, dabbling in weed sales again. That soon escalated to cocaine, but the game didn't sit right with him. It wasn't long before he dropped it and went back to what he knew best: weed. No trap houses. No chaos. Just quiet meet-ups with a tight circle of trusted people.

A few months later, Kato came home, having served ten years. I was the one who picked him up from the state prison.

Seeing him walk free was emotional, but we had never shared the kind of bond I had with Benny. Kato was more of a mystery, always had been. He moved in with his brother, who ran an auto body shop. He was also on supervised release. But unlike Benny, Kato didn't adjust well to life on the outside.

He seemed... untethered.

The demons he'd wrestled with inside followed him back into the world. And before long, they started to win. Kato fell straight back into the streets. But Kato was never a hustler. He didn't have the

296

discipline, the control, or the game for it. He just had a pattern: wrong people, wrong places, wrong decisions.

Then the worst happened. He started using. At first, it was quiet. Easy to ignore. Then it became clear. Then it became dangerous. His life spiraled fast. He fell into a toxic relationship that turned violent. He owed money to people who don't forget. He was high more often than he was sober. His rage became his default, and his demons, the ones he could never quite outrun, took full control.

Eventually, Benny had to cut him off. And I did too. Within a year of his release, I wanted nothing to do with Kato. I had lost too much already, and I wasn't about to lose anything or anyone else.

In my own life, I finally saw the Nigerian doctor's office for what it was.

I had worked there for nearly six years, no PTO, no sick time, no benefits. No health insurance. No dental. Nothing. I was being underpaid, undervalued. But I told myself it was stable. After so many years of accepting the bare minimum, I had stopped asking the question: *What do I deserve?*

It wasn't until a coworker left for the same reasons I had silenced in myself that I really saw it. She told me about a nonprofit where her brother's wife worked, a place that actually valued its employees. They were hiring. She described the pay. The benefits. The respect. It sounded like a fantasy. But I updated my resume, sent it in anyway, and within weeks, I had an interview. Then an offer.

A $5 raise. PTO. Sick time. Full health coverage.

It was the security I had spent years convincing myself I didn't need. But the moment it was offered, I didn't hesitate. I put in my two weeks and walked away. It felt like I was finally closing a door that had been cracked open for far too long.

And the club? That was another door I needed to shut.

Dancing had been a temporary fix. A Band-Aid on bullet wounds. Something I convinced myself I could manage, that I could dip into and out of without it taking over. But it didn't take long for the lines to blur.

The manager started pressuring me to take more shifts, weeknight slots I couldn't commit to. That was the first red flag.

Liora, my closest friend in the industry, had already moved on. She had gotten what she came for: a business, a sugar daddy, and financial stability. She no longer had to walk into the club. Her exit left me more alone than I realized.

For a time, my cousin, Bella, filled that space. She'd drive me to work, sit at the bar, and keep watch when management let her stay. Her presence made it bearable, offered a thread of safety in a space where trust was thin and the air reeked of desperation.

But eventually, even she stopped coming. And I was left to navigate the nights alone.

One of the last times I danced, I met a guy. He was close to my age, which was rare. He tipped well, bought drinks for both me and Bella, and, against my better judgment, caught my attention.

I broke my own rules. I blurred the line. We hooked up. For all the years I had been sexually active, for the first time, I got burned. He gave me an STI.

The fallout was fast and suffocating. He started showing up more often, texting nonstop, even tracking me down on social media, sending friend requests I never accepted. No matter how clear I made it, he wouldn't let go. In his mind, I was his now.

And suddenly, the club wasn't just draining. It was dangerous.

Management began turning me away. "We've got enough girls for tonight," they'd say, even when I showed up early, ready. The message was clear: I wasn't wanted anymore.

One night, I sat alone in my car outside the club, hands on the wheel, the engine off. The neon lights from the parking lot spilled through the windshield, casting hard shadows across my face.

I stared at my reflection in the rearview mirror. And I didn't recognize the woman looking back at me.

What dreams had I once had? What kind of woman did I want to be? What kind of mother? What kind of example? Why was I still here? What was I chasing?

Staring at my reflection, I asked myself *what I want my life to look like five years from now. Ten. What kind of legacy did I want to leave?*

The life I had been living... wasn't going to get me there. I was caught in cycles of destruction. Hoping for transformation while making the same decisions over and over again. Expecting growth in the same soil I'd always bled in.

But I wanted more.

I wanted a marriage rooted in peace, not panic. An education. A degree with *my* name on it. I wanted to be an author. A better mother. A whole woman. I wanted a life that was simple, sacred, and filled with love. But the truth was hard: I had been selling myself short, and I was tired of it.

I had been living a double life, not just in what I did, but in who I allowed myself to be. The woman I showed the world in daylight wasn't the same one who moved through darkness. And yet... There was still something left inside of me.

A whisper, deep in my gut, too honest to ignore anymore: There is more for you than this. This is not your full potential. That night, I made a decision. That was the last night I ever danced in a club.

Chapter 22

When the Mirror Finally Spoke

J ustice had started speech therapy, a process that dragged on for two long, exhausting years.

By the time we moved into the apartment, Amadeus was starting high school. I should have been there for him more. I should've met his teachers, checked on his grades, made sure he had what he needed to survive those difficult years. But I wasn't.

I was barely home.

After spending so many years fighting my way out of one struggle after another, I didn't know how to just *be*. I only knew how to keep moving. So I filled every hour with something: work, friends, clubs, drugs, men. Anything that kept me from having to sit with myself.

Amadeus and I talked, but only on the surface. Our conversations rarely went deeper than food, chores, or what time he had to be home. He was quiet. Distant. Withdrawn. And in the moments I felt the most frustrated with my life, instead of trying to reach him, I controlled him. I yelled. I cursed. I took his Xbox away. I grounded him for things that didn't deserve punishment. The more he shut down, the more I lashed out.

Looking at him was like looking in a mirror I wasn't ready to face. He reminded me too much of my mother, and I couldn't stand it.

The resentment I had buried for years was layered like sediment, years of grief and comparison hardened into something brittle. My mother's way of mothering was always different from mine. And because it was the only example I had, I labeled her way the *right* way. The *good* way.

Which meant mine was the wrong way. The broken way. The *bad* way.

And every time she stepped in to help with Amadeus or Justice, out of love, out of loyalty, out of instinct, I didn't receive it as support. I received it as performance. As proof of my failure. A live-action demonstration of the kind of mother I *should* have been but wasn't.

Her love, which was sincere, I twisted into judgment.

Every act of help felt like criticism. Every gesture of care felt like a spotlight on what I lacked. And the more I internalized those lies, the angrier I became, at myself, at her, at everything.

I wish I didn't think that way. I wish I could've seen her intentions for what they were: love, support, sacrifice. But in those moments, all I could feel was the weight of my own disappointment, and I passed that weight onto the people around me, especially the ones who didn't deserve it. Amadeus and my mother got the worst of me.

One night, everything snapped. I told them, both of them, to leave. And this time, it wasn't an empty threat. It was real. I meant it. For years, I'd said it whenever things got heated: *This is my house. You don't like it? Leave.* But this time, I followed through.

"Why does it always have to be your way?" Amadeus asked, frustration bubbling. "Why can't we just talk about things without you shutting me down?"

"Because it *is* my way," I snapped. "You live under *my* roof. You pay no bills, buy no groceries, handle none of the stress, so what exactly are you questioning me for?"

"You're barely home. Nanie's the one taking care of everything..."

"What the fuck are you trying to say?" I cut him off. "That I don't do my part?"

"You see? This is what I mean. You don't even listen, you just start yelling."

"Fucking deal with it," I shot back. "This is me. You don't like it, don't come at me, throwing guilt in my face."

"I'm not throwing anything. I'm just telling you how I *feel*. But you don't care, do you? It's always about you."

"Don't start with that bullshit," I said, voice rising. "You live under my roof. You pay no bills, buy no groceries, so what are you even talking for?"

"So just because I don't pay rent, I don't get to speak? That's wild, Ma," he said, shaking his head.

"Brandy, he's not your enemy," my mother said softly from the side.

"Oh, now you're taking his side too?" I snapped. "Y'all trying to make me look like the bad guy?"

"No, she isn't, you're doing that to yourself!" Amadeus' voice cracked, angry in a way I rarely heard. "I'm here! I'm trying! But you curse me out like I'm some enemy. You don't even hear me!"

"Brandy, you're like a pit bull," my mother said. "No one can talk to you."

"I *hold everything together!*" I yelled. "Don't come at me sideways in my own house!"

"But that's the thing," Amadeus said. "It's *always* your house. Never ours. Never a place where I can breathe without stepping on your pride."

That was the final trigger.

"You know what? I'm done," I said, cold. "You want to question me? You want to make me out to be the villain while you live under my roof, eat my food, sleep in my house, and treat me like I'm the problem?"

"Ma, this is *exactly* why I don't come to you," he said, the words hitting hard. "Every conversation feels like a landmine. We're all just trying not to set you off. It's not fair. I haven't even seen you this whole weekend!"

"I don't want to hear another word," I snapped. "You don't like how I run things? Then get the hell out. Both of y'all!"

"What?! You're seriously kicking us out?" Amadeus' voice cracked with disbelief.

"Dead ass. I've said it before, and this time I mean it. This is my house. And I'm done being disrespected in it."

"Wow. This is *fucking crazy*. And you talk about Nano being the crazy one, but *look at you!*" he shouted, walking to his room. I heard the rustle of his backpack as he stuffed clothes inside.

"You've really taken this too far, Brandy," my mother said, barely above a whisper.

"Oh, go ahead. Be on his side. The both of you can go and be happy, *without me.*"

My mother muttered something under her breath and went to pack her things. I grabbed Justice from the living room, stormed into my room with him in hand, and slammed the door.

A moment later, I heard Amadeus outside the door. "Can I say bye to Justice?"

"No. Get the fuck out!"

Then came the sound of the front door slamming shut. I didn't cry right away. I stayed quiet. Still. Numb. But an hour later, Justice looked up at me, eyes wide, searching the space around us.

"Mommy, where's Brotha? Nanie... Nanie, where are you?"

And just like that, the tears came.

"They went outside, baby," I said softly, wiping my face.

"Is Brotha mad?" he asked.

Trying to keep my composure, I smiled weakly. "Yeah... he's a little upset right now. But it's not your fault, okay?"

Justice handed me his SpongeBob toy. "Here, Mommy. You can play with SpongeBob. He makes me happy."

"Thank you, baby," I whispered, hugging him close.

"Don't cry, Mommy. I give you hug."

Eventually, I called my mother. She answered, but her voice was cold.

"Hey... where did y'all go?"

"Does it matter?" she replied. "We're not in your house."

"I'm sorry, Ma. I shouldn't have let my emotions get the best of me like that... can y'all come home?"

"Not right now. We need time."

"Is Amadeus okay?"

"What do you think, Brandy? You kicked him out of his home."

"I know... it wasn't supposed to be like that. It just came out."

"No. You meant it."

"No, I didn't. I need y'all."

"No, you don't. Remember? You *handle everything.*"

"Ma, please..."

"No, Brandy. You did this. Not us. I gotta go."

When they came back later that night, Justice and I were already asleep. For the next few days, the house was heavy with silence. I tried talking, apologizing, and explaining. But nothing softened.

Amadeus wouldn't even look at me. He took it hard, being kicked out like that. Harder than I expected. And no amount of cleanup could undo what had already been said.

They only left for a few hours. But the damage? That stayed. Some words don't fade, no matter how much time passes. Some actions don't unwrite themselves.

The truth? I was still resentful that I needed my mom's help to raise my sons. Still angry that I wasn't free. Still bitter that after everything I had survived, everything I had clawed my way through, I was *still* stuck. Still carrying the weight of everyone else.

I looked around at my friends, watched them live in homes of their own, raise kids on their own, breathe in ways I couldn't, and something ugly rose inside me. I told myself I just wanted space. But what I really wanted... Was *freedom*. Even if I didn't know what that meant.

***

At work, I was the fun one, lighthearted, energetic, the person who could lift a room's mood just by being in it. But at home, I was bitter, impatient, and always on edge. I chalked it up to being tired, exhausted from juggling work, bills, motherhood, and emotional weight. But deep down, I was running from something more than stress. I was becoming my father.

I had his temper, quick, sharp, unforgiving. I was defensive, reactive, always ready for a fight, even when no one was coming for me. My mother noticed the change before I did. She started calling me a pitbull because of how I barked and snapped at the people closest to me. The truth was, I wasn't fighting for anything meaningful. I was just fighting to survive. Fighting to feel seen. Fighting to keep myself from falling apart.

It was hurting me. And it was hurting the people I loved.

Soon, my body started to reflect the chaos inside me. I broke out in hives, red, burning, itchy patches that spread across my arms, my back, my stomach. The doctors all said the same thing: stress. My body was begging me to slow down, to take care of myself, to acknowledge that I wasn't okay. But I ignored it. I kept going, kept numbing myself with drugs, alcohol, and meaningless sex. I convinced myself I wasn't hurting anyone else. That if I self-destructed quietly enough, it wouldn't touch my kids or my family.

But that wasn't true. I was damaging everything around me.

And yet, in the midst of all that, Justice was my miracle. Not because he saved me or changed everything overnight, but because, with him, I got a second chance at motherhood. When I had Amadeus, I was still a child myself. I was lost, overwhelmed, and broken in more ways than I could admit. With Justice, I wasn't perfect, but I had grown. I had more patience. More awareness. More intention.

I worked. I cooked. I tried to be present. I made his baby food from scratch, watched what he ate, paid attention to his cues. I didn't want my mother to raise him the way she had to raise Amadeus, not because she didn't do a good job, but because I wanted to do it right this time. I wanted to be his mother in a way I hadn't been before.

Justice was a bright, joyful, imaginative child. He built entire worlds with his toys and acted them out with conviction. He loved music and dancing. He struggled with speech early on, but that didn't stop him from making his presence known. Even before he had all the words, he knew how to take up space.

He never asked about his father, never cried for him. Maybe he was too young to understand that Knox wasn't coming back. I kept a few old pictures of me and Knox from when we were kids, images I showed Justice from time to time so he could have a sense of who his father was. Knox would write letters from prison, usually around birthdays or holidays. I read them aloud to Justice. I sent back photos, trying to keep the connection just alive enough without letting it take up too much space in our lives.

But even as I did that, I knew the questions would come one day. And I wasn't sure if I'd be ready to answer them.

Chapter 23

My Son, My Mirror

When Amadeus turned fifteen, he started asking questions. Not the kind you can dodge with half-truths or distractions, but the kind that lands heavy in the room and settles in your chest.

"Why isn't my father in my life?" "Why doesn't he talk to me?" "Why doesn't he want me?"

These were the questions I had always known would come, the ones I had rehearsed answers for in my mind for years, but when they finally arrived, they knocked the wind out of me anyway. I had spent so long shielding him from the truth, hoping to protect him from the shame I had carried. I told myself I was defending him. In reality, I was defending myself.

The truth was, I had always claimed Mateo as Amadeus' father. Deep down, I believed it. My mother believed it. But no one else did. They believed his stepbrother, Asael, was the father, and maybe that lie gained so much traction because of the shame I carried about what happened between us. Maybe it was easier for people to cling to the mess than believe the quiet truth I held in my heart.

And maybe, just maybe, Amadeus didn't have a father in his life because of what I had done. That's the part that haunted me. If I had made different choices, maybe Mateo would've stuck around. Maybe Amadeus would've had someone to look up to. I wondered if, once he knew the truth, it would fuel more anger towards me.

But I knew the silence between us couldn't last forever. I couldn't risk him hearing it from someone else. I had to tell him myself, no matter how badly it hurt.

So one day, I sat him down. My heart was racing. I could feel the blood pulsing in my neck. I looked him in the eyes and said, "There's something I need to tell you. It's about your father, and what really happened."

He looked at me with confusion, but he didn't interrupt. He just waited. And I told him everything. The stepbrother, Asael. The betrayal. The shame I had buried for so long, I almost forgot what it felt like to speak it out loud. As the words came out, I felt like I was unraveling in front of him, layer by layer, exposing the version of myself I never wanted him to see.

He didn't say much. Just sat there, taking it all in. But the hurt in his eyes cut through me. Watching my truth land on his shoulders, watching him carry what I had carried for so long, was unbearable. I wanted to take it all back. But I knew I couldn't. He deserved to know.

Eventually, he asked, "Why didn't you tell me sooner?" His voice was quiet, but steady.

I swallowed hard. "Because I was scared," I said. "If you heard it from your father, he would've told you I was a whore. That I slept with his stepbrother. And I thought... if you believed that story, you'd hate me. I didn't want to lose you. But I've realized that not telling you was hurting us more. I want us to move forward, and we can't do that if the past is still a secret."

He nodded slowly. Took a deep breath. "It's a lot to take in," he said. "But I'm glad you told me."

And something shifted. The air between us didn't clear, but it changed. Lighter, maybe. Honest. For sixteen years, I had carried this weight alone. And now it was out. The truth had hurt, but it had also done something sacred. It cracked open the space between us and made room for something new. I didn't expect forgiveness. I didn't expect everything to be perfect. But for the first time, I felt like we had a chance at rebuilding something real, something rooted in truth.

A year later, when Amadeus turned sixteen, I finally did the DNA test. After sixteen years of whispers, rumors, and uncertainty, I wanted to silence all the outside voices. I needed to know for sure.

And just like I had always believed, the results confirmed it: Mateo was his father. Not Asael. Not the lie that had followed us like a shadow. Mateo.

I wish I could say that knowing the truth fixed everything. That it healed every wound. That all the anger and confusion just... dissolved. But it didn't. And I didn't expect it to.

Still, it was a beginning. A fresh page. A moment of truth I could finally stand on without shame or apology. No more lies. No more doubt. No more pretending.

No one could deny it anymore. No one could twist it. No one could question who Amadeus belonged to.

But even with that confirmation in hand, I still blamed myself. For all of it. For the silence. For the shame. For not protecting him better. For the time lost. For the truth that came too late.

That guilt doesn't disappear with paperwork. But at least now, I could start facing it. Every hardship. Every consequence. Every wrong turn.

I bore the burden, not just for my own choices, but for all the pain that followed. I carried it like it was mine alone, like somehow if I held it tightly enough, no one else would have to suffer.

It took time for me to realize that while I had made mistakes, not all of the suffering was mine to own. Some burdens weren't mine to carry. Some pain had been placed on me by others, and I had absorbed it as if it were my own.

Over the course of Amadeus' life, I've only spoken to his father a handful of times. None of those conversations ever led to closure. They didn't bring understanding. They didn't bring healing.

We don't speak now. He has no real relationship with our son.

And Amadeus is still figuring out what that means for him, as a young man, as a person. Still trying to navigate what it feels like to grow up with a father who was never really there. No birthday calls. No guidance. No connection to that side of his family. Just silence.

That absence, that void, is something only he can process. In his own time. In his own way.

But for me, as painful as this journey was, it marked the beginning of something else: the beginning of *my* healing.

I had to learn how to forgive myself. I had to seek forgiveness from those I had hurt. I had to confront the past if I was ever going to build the future I wanted, for myself, for my sons, for the woman I was trying to become.

It was a long road. And not a clean one. There were setbacks. There were moments when I doubted whether healing was even possible for someone like me. But step by step, I moved closer to the version of myself I could finally live with.

A mother who could offer her sons more than survival: love, truth, stability. A woman who no longer lived in the shadow of her shame. A soul who found peace, through faith, through growth, through the relentless pursuit of becoming whole again.

And this time, my voice wasn't drowned out by the noise of my past. It was mine. And it was stronger than ever.

In his last year of high school, something between me and Amadeus began to shift. Not all at once. Not dramatically. But slowly, in small, almost imperceptible increments, like the soft light of dawn pushing through after a long, dark night.

Until then, there had been no depth. No real connection. We lived under the same roof, but we were strangers in our own house. He stayed in his room, lost in his Xbox games. I buried myself in distractions, running from my own demons. We were physically close, but emotionally... We were galaxies apart.

But something began to change. A conversation here. A shared laugh there. Tiny moments, building on each other. It wasn't magic. It was work. Quiet, unglamorous work. Showing up when it mattered. Choosing patience over pride. Choosing presence over performance. And in those small, quiet moments, I began to feel something I hadn't felt in a long time: Hope.

Amadeus started finding his voice.

He stopped accepting things in silence. He stopped shrinking. Instead, he began to step forward, carefully, cautiously, testing the weight of his words to see if they would hold. It was slow, like a muscle being stretched after years of stiffness. But it was happening.

He got his first job in his senior year, working fast food. And suddenly, he was out in the world, interacting with people outside the walls of our home, outside the games, outside the emotional isolation he had grown so used to. I watched him begin to navigate life on his own terms.

And I realized something that hit me harder than I was ready for: He had been carrying depression. Real depression. And I hadn't seen it.

Or maybe I had. Maybe I caught glimpses of it and chose not to look too closely because I didn't know how to handle it. I didn't know what to say. I didn't know how to help. We didn't know how to talk to each other. Not really. So we relied on my mother to stand in the middle, our translator, our bridge. She would help us find each other's hearts when our own words failed. Without her, our conversations might have stayed fractured, incomplete.

But then, we found another way.

I started writing him letters. And he wrote back. And there, on paper, in ink, we discovered a language we could both speak. Vulnerability. Honesty. No yelling. No walls. No confusion. Just words. Just the truth.

For the first time, I wasn't responding just to be heard. I was listening. Really listening. Not just to what he was saying, but to what he *wasn't* saying. The pauses. The pain between the lines. The years of quiet, stored emotion, tucked into the margins of every reply.

It wasn't a miracle moment. It wasn't some dramatic breakthrough you see in movies. But it was *something*. A bridge. A beginning. A slow unraveling of the distance that had settled between us for far too long.

Chapter 24

A Night to Remember

A night in late June.
2 a.m.

I was sitting in the back of a patrol car, wrists aching from the tightness of the handcuffs, my mind spiraling with everything I was about to lose. I had only been a few blocks from home. Tired. A little buzzed. Telling myself I was okay to drive. But two officers pulled me over for driving too slowly and hesitating at a green light. They saw what I was still pretending not to admit.

The sobriety tests felt like a dream I couldn't control: stand on one leg, walk in a straight line, follow the pen with your eyes. I told myself I did fine. But when they asked for a breathalyzer, I refused. I already knew what it would say. And in that moment, everything shifted.

"Put your hands behind your back."

I'll never forget the sound of the handcuffs clicking shut. That cold snap of metal around my wrists. That moment when it all became real, I wasn't going home.

This wasn't my first run-in with the law, but it was my first DUI. My record wasn't spotless, but I had never seen myself as a criminal. I was a mother. I was in school. I had a job. But none of that mattered now. As I sat there, locked in the back of that cruiser, fear settled into my bones. Guilt. Regret. Shame. Work. My sons. My car. School. My mom.

Everything felt like it was slipping through my fingers.

And the truth was, this wasn't just about drinking. It wasn't about one bad choice. It was about everything I hadn't dealt with. Everything I was still trying to outrun. I wasn't just intoxicated by alcohol. I was numbed by pain, by grief, by all the parts of my past I refused to sit with.

We pulled up to the jail, and the energy changed. The air felt different, heavy, hopeless. Inside, the officers, especially the women, wore disdain like a badge. They searched me like I wasn't human. Their hands were rough, their words sharper. And when they saw my hair, my locks threaded with bright yarn and beads, they mocked me.

One by one, they removed them. Not just the pieces of thread, but pieces of me. Pieces of my expression. My culture. My identity.

I cried. But I didn't speak. I knew better than to expect kindness. Still, I had hoped for some shred of dignity. I got none.

Fingerprinting. Mugshots. Cold stares. I moved like a ghost through the system, silent, watching myself from somewhere outside my own body. Eventually, I found a hard red chair in the corner of the holding area and curled into it, trying to disappear. The room was chaotic, women shouting, officers yelling back, loud clattering and movement, but all I could hear was the sound of my own heart pounding in my ears.

I kept thinking, *I just want to go home. I need to be with my sons.*

At 5:04 a.m., they handed me back my things. My phone lit up the second it hit my hand. Amadeus was calling. My baby. He didn't know where I was.

I pressed to answer. But before I could, the officer snatched the phone away and shut it off. "No calls until 7 a.m." It had already been two hours. Now I had to wait two more before I could even let my son know I was alive.

When 7 finally came, I stepped up to the jail's phone system, typed in the code they gave me. It didn't work. I tried again. And again. No one helped. No one cared. My son's voice, the one thing I needed in that moment, was kept just out of reach.

Frustration burned in my chest, hot and pressing, the kind of heat that doesn't ask for permission. It just settles and simmers. The kind that makes your eyes sting long before the tears fall.

Then a woman, another inmate, offered me her code. She didn't ask for anything in return. She just saw me drowning and threw a rope.

I hesitated. It's strange how shame can make you hesitate even when your world is on fire. But I knew who I had to call.

My mother.

She picked up immediately. Her voice cracked with panic. I don't remember what I said first, only that I needed her to come. I needed her to bail me out before 10 a.m., before they put me in the orange jumpsuit. That felt like the final line. The point of no return.

I had been awake for over 24 hours. My body was running on adrenaline and regret. I needed fresh air. A soft surface. A hot shower. Something, anything, that didn't smell like bleach and despair.

At exactly 10 a.m., I walked out of that building.

I looked like what I had been through: eyes swollen, lips dry, my body still wearing the same clothes from the night before. I could feel the night clinging to me like smoke. I was completely drained, physically, mentally, and emotionally. There was nothing left in me except the echo of everything I had just endured.

In the car, my mother stayed composed, but her voice held that familiar weight. The one she used when love and disappointment were battling in her chest. She told me to call my supervisor.

I didn't want to. I couldn't even face my reflection in the rearview mirror. How was I supposed to explain myself to someone else?

But she was right. She always was.

I opened my phone. Missed calls. Texts. Voicemails. The screen flooded with concern from coworkers, family, people I barely talked to regularly. Somehow, they all knew something was wrong. My supervisor had already reached out. We weren't close, but when I finally called her, she answered with relief in her voice.

"Don't be hard on yourself," she said.

If only she knew.

The self-loathing had already wrapped itself around me tightly. It was in my throat, in my lungs. I was suffocating under the weight of my own choices.

When we got home, I didn't care about anything except finding my sons. Amadeus hadn't gone to school. Because of me.

When I found him, the tears I'd been holding back finally spilled over. I was unraveling.

"I'm so sorry," I said. My voice cracked under the pressure of everything I hadn't said before. I expected anger. Distance. The cold wall of teenage resentment. But instead, he met me with grace.

No lectures. No accusations. Just presence. He gave me something I hadn't given myself in years: Understanding. Compassion. Love.

And it wrecked me.

It was more than I deserved. Which made it harder to receive.

I spent the rest of the day in bed. I didn't eat. I didn't shower. I didn't speak. I lay there, curled into myself, replaying the night on a loop. The flashing lights. The metal cuffs. The sharp tone of the officers. The hard red chair. The phone was snatched from my hand the second my son tried to call.

The shame didn't just live in my memory... it lived in my body. I felt it in my joints, in my chest, in the pit of my stomach. And the worst part? I had seen this story before. I had watched my father make bad decisions. I had watched him burn down every good thing in his life.

And now, I was standing in the smoke of my own fire. No, I wasn't walking the same path. But I was close enough. Close enough to feel the cycle tightening around me. Close enough to recognize the

323

patterns. Close enough to know that if I didn't wake up, if I didn't change, I would end up exactly where he did.

This wasn't just a bad night. It was a mirror. A reckoning. A moment that demanded truth. And the truth was this: I had two choices: Keep falling. Or finally...*finally*...rise.

***

My case dragged on for over a year. It drained not just my savings, but something deeper, my energy, my resolve, my will to keep pushing. Every month brought new paperwork, new fees, and another reminder of how far I'd fallen. And yet, even with all of that, I knew I was still one of the lucky ones. It could have been worse.

Because I refused the breathalyzer that night, I lost my license for the first three months. After that, I had to apply for a hardship license, a slow and expensive process that reminded me that freedom, even the smallest kind, came at a cost. I paid three hundred dollars out of pocket for a three-day DUI school. I completed nearly a hundred hours of community service. I found a lawyer I could barely afford and prayed she was good enough.

When my court date finally came, the sentence was official: one year of probation. That meant monthly check-ins, monthly fees, no room for error. They installed a breathalyzer in my car, an "ignition interlock device," they called it. But to me, it felt like a collar. I had to blow into it for ten seconds, three times, every time I wanted to go anywhere. If I failed, the car wouldn't start. And of course, there were more fees: an installation fee, a monthly fee, a maintenance fee. Every breath came with a price tag.

I attended mandated therapy classes. I paid court costs and probation fees. I sat through lectures where I was just another face in a crowd of people who'd made mistakes. And I told myself I deserved it. All of it. Because this wasn't just about a DUI. This was about the mess I had become.

The total financial cost neared ten thousand dollars. But that wasn't the part that broke me. The emotional toll was something no spreadsheet could tally. I was unraveling. Pride, ambition, confidence, all of it had disappeared. I barely recognized the woman I used to be. What remained was a hollowed version of her. A woman who smiled at work and cried at red lights. A woman who couldn't stop craving the very things that had wrecked her.

Even with probation hanging over me, I still wanted to drink. Still wanted cocaine. Still wanted to disappear into the numbness that had become my escape. The court saw a woman who needed consequences. But what I needed was healing.

My life had become a loop I didn't know how to exit. I was functioning, but just barely. I moved through my days like a zombie, dragging the weight of every bad decision behind me. I sought comfort in lust, lost myself in substances, and surrounded myself with people who were just as broken, men and women with court dates, hustles, addictions, and big plans to change that never made it past the first step. We all talked about getting out. But no one moved. We stayed trapped in the same conversations, the same cycles, the same smoke-filled rooms filled with temporary highs and permanent damage. We were dreamers in prison cells we had built ourselves.

And then, without warning or fanfare, I hit my breaking point.

It wasn't one dramatic moment. It didn't come with flashing lights or tears or a big revelation. It came quietly, like a whisper inside my chest. I was tired. Not just sleepy, not just overworked. *Tired.* Soul tired. I was tired of the losses, the weight, the shame that wrapped around my spine and pulled me downward every morning.

Something stirred inside me. A faint memory. A feeling I hadn't touched in years. I thought of my younger self: the girl in the private school uniform reciting Bible verses in chapel. I remembered hearing about a loving God, an amazing God, one who could take broken things and make them whole again. One who saw pain and offered peace. But I had stopped looking for Him a long time ago.

I hadn't stepped inside a church in years. I didn't pray. I didn't open a Bible. My faith lived in fragments, verses I had memorized as a child, now floating aimlessly through the back of my mind. *For God so loved the world... The earth is the Lord's, and everything in it...*

I believed in God. I never stopped believing. But belief is not the same thing as *seeking*. And I was still lost.

***

During this time, while I was still unraveling, still piecing myself together. Wes and I were still in each other's lives.

We had tried just about every hustle we could think of. Social media marketing schemes. Facebook ads. Buying and reselling on Amazon. None of it ever really stuck. None of it ever made us more than a few quick dollars. I wasn't looking for an empire. I was just trying to keep my head above water. Wes, though, was still chasing the fantasy. Wealth. Luxury. Power. He had a mind for business, that much was true. He could hype up just about any idea, turn it into a pitch that sounded like gold. But his mental health, especially his depression, always pulled him back down. It was like he was building dreams in a storm he refused to admit he was standing in.

He never sought help. Not the kind that required vulnerability, anyway.

Still, we talked weekly. We saw each other at least once a month. Our friendship, on the surface, hadn't changed: movie nights, long phone calls, last-minute meetups to talk about some "next big thing." But underneath, the truth lingered: our relationship had become superficial. We were holding onto something that looked like friendship, but felt more like nostalgia.

I clung to it, I think, because of how long it had existed. Because of the time invested. Because it was familiar, even if it wasn't safe. Wes had been around through some of my hardest moments. He wasn't always the cause, but more often than not, he was somewhere nearby when the damage happened.

And deep down, I knew he carried guilt.

He never said it out loud, but I could see it in the way he moved around me. Always trying to help. Always trying to make things right. But more often than not, his help created more chaos than clarity. Most of the worst things that had happened to me could be traced back, in one way or another, to my connection with him, or with Knox. Or with Benny.

Like the time my car broke down, right when I was barely keeping up with DUI payments. The repairs cost over a thousand dollars. I didn't have it. I was barely making rent, barely feeding my kids. Wes stepped in, said he had a guy who could fix it for less. I trusted him.

I got screwed over. Again.

Just like when I let his guy install my car's sound system, because Wes vouched for him, said he was solid. That time, too, turned into a mess. Expensive, stressful, damaging. And every time something like that happened, Wes would apologize, not directly, but with his actions. He'd try to fix the problem he helped create, and in the process, make it worse. I could see he felt bad. I knew that. But knowing someone feels bad doesn't undo the pain they cause.

My mother saw it. So did Amara. My cousin, Bella. They had all grown tired of the pattern.

"He manipulates you," they'd say. "He's not a real friend. He only shows up when it benefits him."

No one in my circle trusted him. They saw the pride, the arrogance, the constant need to make every situation about him, his struggle, his genius, his plans, his pain.

I didn't *want* to see it.

Because if I saw it, I'd have to admit that someone I had called a friend for years, someone I had defended, forgiven, trusted, wasn't good for me. And I wasn't ready to let go. Not yet.

I had spent years defending my friendship with Wes. To my mother. To Amara. To anyone who raised an eyebrow or gave me that knowing look. I always had a reason. I'd tell them he'd been through a lot. That he was misunderstood. That we had history. That he wasn't perfect, but he had been there for me in his own way. I'd say, *"He's just trying to figure it out like the rest of us."*

But the truth was, every time I talked to him, every time I was around him, I changed. Subtly, almost invisibly. But I did.

I started sounding like him. I adopted his tone, his cynicism, the way he'd mock people who cared too much or tried too hard. I found myself speaking with his rhythm, his lingo, even his sense of superiority. I mirrored his frustration with the world, his belief that everyone else was playing a rigged game, and we were the only ones smart enough to see it. I acted like him, too, rationalizing bad choices, minimizing consequences, leaning into the image of someone who was above the rules. Someone untouchable.

And I didn't even realize I was doing it. It crept in. Quiet. Familiar.

Then one day, in the middle of a conversation that was probably about money or dreams or some scheme that would never happen, Wes said something that stopped me in my tracks.

"You need to go to church and get rid of all the bad juju."

I nearly laughed out loud. Wes? Church? This was the same man who, as far as I knew, never once set foot inside a church. The same man who talked about energy and manifestation, but never God. The same man who refused help for his own depression and mocked people who believed in anything they couldn't control. Now he was telling *me* to go to church?

But his words lingered. I brushed them off at first. Smiled. Changed the subject. But later that night, they came back. And again the next day. And the one after that.

"Go to church."

It echoed, not in a pushy way, not in guilt, but like a soft knock on a door I'd forgotten was there. And then I started to wonder, *what if he was right?*

What if the answer I'd been searching for all along hadn't been buried in some expensive recovery program, or in the next man, or in the bottle, or in the white line on the table? What if everything I thought I needed, peace, clarity, purpose, wasn't something I had to hustle for, seduce for, numb myself to get?

What if it was already there? Waiting.

I didn't know how to find God. I didn't know how to start. I hadn't prayed with sincerity in years. All I knew about God came from a few childhood memories, reciting verses in private school, listening to worship songs during brief seasons when I had tried to "get my life together." I believed in God, but it had been a passive belief. A background presence. A distant maybe.

Belief isn't the same thing as seeking. And I was still lost. But now, I realize something I didn't see back then: God was calling me.

Using the most unlikely person. Someone who had no business being a messenger. Someone who didn't even believe in the message. But that's how God works sometimes. He sends truth through cracked vessels, through unexpected mouths, through the noise of our broken lives.

God was calling me home. And this time, I heard Him.

There were plenty of churches in the Tampa Bay area, but I knew, somewhere deep in my spirit, that I was called to Crossover Church.

I remembered it from childhood. Back when we lived on Clifton Street, not far from Lowry Park Zoo. I hadn't gone often, maybe a handful of times, but it had left a mark on me. It felt different. Urban. Honest. Raw. The kind of church that met people where they were, instead of asking them to pretend they were someone else. They embraced rap and beatboxing. Graffiti. Youth culture. Sports. It was alive in a way most churches weren't. It spoke to the streets and the struggle and the sacred, all in the same breath.

Still, even after Wes said those words, go to church, it took months for me to walk through those doors. I wasn't ready. Or maybe I was just afraid of what would meet me on the other side.

The invitation finally came from someone I trusted. Liora. An old friend from high school, one of the women I had been with the night of my DUI. She carried guilt for not stopping me that night, for not taking my keys, for letting me say I'm fine and drive off into destruction. But I never blamed her. I was grown. I had made the choice. We had hugged goodbye, said we'd text when we got home. She made it home. I didn't.

That first Sunday in October 2019, she picked me up and took me to church. I don't remember everything about the drive, just that I was quiet. My mind was spinning. My chest was tight. I had spent so much of my life calling the shots, running the show, making the rules. But look where it had gotten me. I finally had to admit the truth: I had no idea what I was doing.

I needed a new leader. Someone who could guide me. Someone who could help me help myself. I needed to find the best version of me, even though I didn't know who she was. But I believed she was in there. Somewhere beneath the shame and the survival and the hardened habits, she was still alive. Still trying to breathe. And I was willing to meet her.

That day, I laid down my pride. I began a quiet, trembling quest to cast out the bad juju, to strip away the lies, to find my identity, not in hustle or pain, but in God. The God I had barely spoken to in years. The One who, I hoped, was nothing like my earthly father. I needed Him to be different. Better. Safe.

But I had questions: Would He accept me, with all this baggage? Would He even want to? Would He have time for someone like me? Would it even matter?

Doubt clouded my mind as we drove. Every version of myself, mother, addict, fighter, hustler, daughter, sinner, sat beside me in that car. I felt like I was carrying them all on my back. But I had no other options. Everything else I had tried had failed. Money. Drugs. Sex. Rage. Shame. Escape.

They had all left me empty. I wasn't living, I was floating. Hollow. A zombie. Addicted to pain. Holding on to dead things. Lustful without love. Busy without purpose. Angry and tired and numb.

I had spent years walking the wide road, chasing money, dodging bullets, hiding behind masks. Living in paranoia. Sleeping next to an arsenal. Looking over my shoulder. Battling addiction. Waiting for the next betrayal. The next hit. The next heartbreak.

I had been trapped in a grave, trying to decorate it with distractions. But pain doesn't leave when you ignore it. It only grows.

I didn't fully understand what God was offering me; I only knew I needed a way out. Life as I knew it wasn't working. I was exhausted, empty, and desperate for something real. The narrow road isn't easy, but it leads to life, real life, not the illusion of it. I clung to the words in Revelation 21:4: *"He will wipe every tear from their eyes. There will be no more death, or mourning, or crying, or pain."* That was the first promise I held onto. After experiencing hell, the choice became clear: I wanted heaven.

But there is no magic potion. No one-time event that fixes everything. Transformation takes effort, intention, and daily commitment. Every single day is a battle. Romans 12:2 became my anchor: *"Do not conform to the pattern of this world, but be transformed by the renewing of your mind…"* Before anything could change, I had to make a decision. I had to claim Jesus as my Lord and Savior.

A quote by Arthur Gordon Webster stayed with me: *"Nothing is easier than saying words. Nothing is harder than living them, day after day. What you promised today must be renewed tomorrow, and re-decided tomorrow, and each day after that…"* That became my reality.

In October 2019, I walked back into church. I didn't expect anything miraculous. I wasn't hoping for a breakthrough. I was just curious, and that curiosity, paired with consistency, became the soil where change could finally take root. God had always been with me. I just hadn't been looking.

When I accepted Liora's invitation to visit her church, I didn't know how much love God was about to restore me with. I had no expectations, just a heavy heart and a numb spirit. I was reaping the sins of my father, carrying the burdens of my mother, and haunted by the ghosts of my past.

The truth? The dead things weren't around me. They were inside me. And they were killing me.

I didn't need another job or another plan. I needed a different kind of doctor. I needed amazing grace to save a wretch like me.

I can't tell you what sermon was preached that first Sunday back. But I remember they were offering something called a 3D Growth Track, a class to help people discover their spiritual gifts, understand God's purpose for their lives, and get connected to the church community. At the end of it, you could begin serving in ministry.

I signed up immediately.

I had no other plans. No other hopes. No backup strategy. This was a gamble. Either God would meet me there... or I'd go back to the life I knew was destroying me.

I didn't expect to hear from God. I didn't expect to feel Him. But something about that building, the smiles, the warmth, the peace in people's eyes, stirred something in me. For the first time in a long time, I didn't just want hope. I needed it.

At first, I just showed up. Sat quietly. Observed. But slowly, I began to lean in. I got planted in the church. I joined small groups. I went to Bible studies. I started talking to other women, listening to their stories, and realizing I wasn't alone. My heart of stone began to soften. I was healing in ways I didn't think were possible.

It wasn't about religion. It was about relationship.

It was during one of those small group sessions that I had a break-through. We were discussing forgiveness, how holding on to pain keeps us bound, and how letting go isn't about excusing the offense, but about setting yourself free. I had carried so much: anger, resentment, bitterness. That day, as I shared my truth, something cracked open. And through the tears, I felt something unfamiliar, relief.

For the first time, I realized that my past wasn't just following me. It was controlling me. And I didn't want to be controlled by pain anymore.

In the months that followed, I started seeing God's hand in my life, subtle at first, then undeniable. Doors opened that I couldn't have forced open on my own. Relationships began to mend. Opportunities I never imagined were suddenly in front of me. The more I surrendered, the more I experienced His grace.

Chapter 25

When God Interrupted My Destruction

I didn't start this journey with faith. I didn't even own a Bible. I knew no worship songs. I didn't know any Christian artists. I only knew the few verses people quote growing up, mostly out of context. The only familiar faces at church were the pastor from my childhood and the friend who invited me. I had no prayer life. No spiritual habits. Nothing.

And honestly? I had no intention of knowing God.

I believed in Him, I always had. But He existed for other people, not for me. I didn't curse Him. I didn't blame Him. I just kept my distance. I was trying to get grounded in His Word while still living in sin. I had accepted Jesus into my heart, and I *wanted* to do better.

But the moment I stepped into that church, the fight for my soul began. I knew how to fight. Life had taught me that. But this was different. This battle was internal.

I found myself slipping. Relapsing. Struggling between the person I wanted to become and the person I had always been. Some Sundays, I went to church hungover, still reeking of liquor from the night before.

One Saturday, I drank too much, again. The next morning, I was supposed to attend a wedding and a growth track class at church. But I woke up to a notification that I'd violated my DUI case. The breathalyzer in my car had detected alcohol from the night before.

I panicked. That one mistake cost me another $500 just to have my lawyer show up for me in court. I sat there that day, terrified I'd be thrown in jail.

But God showed up. The judge pardoned me. Let me off the hook.

That wasn't the only moment grace met me in my mess. I had several close calls, moments when I knew I was walking a fine line between redemption and destruction.

I wanted to live right. I really did. But addiction had its claws in me. And the more I tried to break free, the tighter it held on. Because the enemy doesn't come for you when you're deep in sin. He comes for you when you try to walk away from it.

Every stumble was followed by shame. I'd get high on cocaine, and the next morning I'd cry in disgust. I couldn't look anyone in the eye. I didn't want to eat, didn't want to talk, didn't want to *feel*. I'd tell myself, *That was the last time.* But by Friday night, my addiction would whisper: *You deserve this.*

And I'd fall...again.

My cousin Bella, who was dating Benny at the time, tried to call me out with love.

"Why do you pay to get high just to sit in regret the next day? That makes no sense."

I hated hearing it. I'd get defensive. Push her away. Accuse her of using my pain against me. But deep down? I knew she was right. And I wasn't ready to hear the truth.

Because when you're addicted, the truth feels like an attack. Even love feels like judgment. Even help feels like control.

Bella was tired. Tired of watching me self-destruct. Tired of seeing me spin in circles, promising change, only to end up in the same broken place.

And I wish I could say her words snapped me out of it. I wish I could tell you that was my turning point. But healing isn't like that. It's not a lightning bolt. It's a slow, stumbling, painful crawl.

For me, it looked like being double-minded, one foot in church, the other still dancing with my demons. I wanted to be godly. I wanted to be whole. But the addiction still called. The pain still whispered. The guilt still ruled my mornings.

And then there was Amara. We hadn't spoken in months. Our first real disagreement had left us both bruised, quietly nursing wounds we didn't know how to name. The silence between us wasn't just distance. It was grief.

What she didn't know was that, in those months, I'd caught a DUI case. One of the hardest things I've ever gone through, and I went through it alone.

When her name lit up my phone screen, I stared at it for a long time. Then I opened the message.

AMARA: Hey... you crossed my mind today. Hope you're okay.

I wasn't okay. But hearing from her made me feel a little less alone.

We met up a few days later. The conversation started slowly, like we were both stepping through broken glass, careful not to cut each other again. But once I opened up, the flood came.

"I got a DUI," I confessed, barely able to meet her eyes. "It's been months, and I've just been trying to keep my head above water. I go to church, yeah... but I'm still getting high, still drinking on the weekends. Then I show up on Sunday, pretending like I've got it all together. I feel like I'm living two lives."

She didn't flinch. Didn't judge. Just looked at me, present, steady. "I'm not here to shame you," she said softly. "I know what you've been through. But I also know who you are. And you are not the version of yourself you've been listening to."

I looked away. Swallowed hard.

"You've got to stop waking up every day carrying that old identity," she continued. "You're not just a dancer. You're not an addict. You're not a bad mother. Those are lies. Lies you've believed because they've been louder than the truth."

Her voice was gentle, but every word hit like truth. "You're still here, Brandy. After everything, you're still standing. That means something. Don't let what broke you become who you are. And stop beating yourself up for surviving the only way you knew how."

Tears welled in my eyes. "It's hard, Amara. That voice, it doesn't stop. It starts the second I open my eyes."

"Then speak back to it," she said. "Every morning. Remind yourself of the truth. Who you are now. Not who you were. Because God isn't done with you yet."

That line lingered long after our conversation ended. **God isn't done with you yet.**

I never knew God wanted to talk to me now, in the mess. I didn't know the Bible wasn't just a rule book. It was a love letter. A message for the lost. For the broken. For the forgotten. For me.

And I couldn't help but wonder: *How many of us are living like I was, lost, without even realizing it?*

I didn't think anything was missing spiritually. I had a body. I had desires. I had needs. I just focused on satisfying them. I thought the "spiritual life" was something you lived after death, not something meant for now.

The world taught me to chase my heart's desires. No one warned me that the heart can lie. That it can wrap you in what *feels* right while dragging you deeper into destruction. The heart isn't just a muscle. It's the engine of every choice we make.

But God's heart? His is different. His is lowly. Gentle.

And that was the hardest part for me to believe. I could see God as powerful. As Creator. As Redeemer. As a miracle worker. But *Father*? That one I couldn't accept.

Because if He were a father, what kind was He? Was He like mine, here today, gone tomorrow? Was He inconsistent, providing only when it suited Him? Did His love come with conditions? Was He just another person who'd change up on me?

Speaking from my inner child, I was afraid. Afraid to be hurt by love again. Afraid that closeness would come with pain. But it was pain that brought me to God. Not peace. Not joy. Not some spiritual awakening.

Pain.

I had tried to fight this on my own, and lost. And for the first time, I realized: I wasn't enough. I couldn't win this battle with my own strength.

Sitting in the back of that police car wasn't the first time I'd reached the bottom... But it would be the last time I stayed there.

Because the truth? I had been addicted to pain since childhood. Feeding addictions. Starving my spirit. Running on fumes until I collapsed. And when I finally looked in the mirror...

I didn't just see myself. I saw him. My father.

Because when you let one demon in, they never come alone. They bring others.

And that day, I saw two faces in the glass. One was mine. And one belonged to the demons I had carried for far too long.

Chapter 26

The Father I Couldn't Save

2020 was supposed to be the year everything finally turned, the year I would find some steady footing after all the stumbling. Then the world shut down. People were dying, masks hid our faces, and even breathing near another human felt risky. It wasn't just *my* life that changed overnight; it was everyone's. And yet, in the hush of lockdown, the loudest sound in my world was still the unfinished argument between me and my father.

We hadn't spoken for about a year, caught in the same loop we'd spun since I was a child: I reached for something that didn't exist, and he let me grasp at empty air. I wanted a father so badly I kept accepting scraps, phone calls laced with blame, half-hearted apologies that turned into fresh wounds, the hollow promise that next time would be different. I held on longer than I should have because a part of me still believed in "maybe."

But the old refrain, *You know how your father is*, wasn't enough anymore. He needed to *acknowledge* what he'd done. And now that I was grown, I was determined to make him.

So I confronted him: about the nights I hid under blankets while he raged, about the bruises my mother explained away, about the fear that soaked our house like humidity you never quite dry out. I had confronted him before, more than once, but fury had always driven the car. I hadn't yet learned what a counselor would later tell me: *Speak the truth in love, not rage.* Back then, rage was all I had, and I believed anger was armor.

I thought he couldn't hurt me anymore, until he denied it.

Hearing him dismiss the abuse cut through me like a clean blade, replacing something soft with something cold and metallic. In that moment, I realized he had gotten away with hurting my mother, partly because I never spoke up. I was a child, afraid that if I told, I'd lose the father I kept chasing. That silence made me complicit, though I didn't have words for it yet. I only felt the shame of protecting toxicity because it shared my blood.

So I kept confronting him, every phone call a courtroom. I imagined one perfect future scene: he would break down, I would break down, we'd cry together, and somehow the tears would cement us back into a family. A neat ending, cue the credits, where truth un-locked love and we finally started over.

But some stories don't sign off that way.

To this day, my father has never admitted the bruises, the fear, the damage. Since my mother packed us up and left, our relationship has never returned to whatever fragile good it once held. I still miss him, in that strange way you miss a phantom limb, you remember the feeling, but when you reach, there's nothing there.

I never became Daddy's girl again. The safety I once felt around my father was gone. By this point, the imposter, the monster, was too easy to recognize. His face hadn't changed, but everything behind it had. Or maybe it had always been there, and I was just old enough now to see it. His demons and I had grown up together. They knew me well. Knew exactly how to find the soft spots and press down hard.

As a child, he never called me names. Never raised a hand. He wasn't tender, but he wasn't cruel, at least not to me. I was protected by innocence, maybe by age. But as I grew older, as I grew bolder, the invisible shield began to crack. The words changed. The tone shifted. I started to face the same kind of verbal abuse my mother had endured for years.

My father's words had a blade to them. They didn't just hurt, they humiliated, confused, collapsed you. His voice could wrap itself around your mind like smoke, making you second-guess your own worth. I hated the way my body responded to him, how my chest would tighten, how my stomach would churn, how my heart would race just at the sound of his voice. I hated that he still had that kind of power.

And when he was angry, I wasn't his daughter anymore. I became a bitch. Sometimes a stupid bitch. Sometimes worse.

"Go fuck yourself.""You fucking bitch...you're just like your mother.""Go to hell.""You're full of shit.""I don't give a rat's ass who the fuck you think you are. You're just like your mother, who uses me for my money. I don't need you."

His insults didn't come alone; they came with records. He'd throw in my face everything he'd done for me. What he paid for. What he remembered. What he resented. He'd reach back five, ten, fifteen years and pile it all at my feet like proof that I owed him something, like love had to be earned and was never freely given.

And yet...Somehow, I used it for revenge.

My body had been conditioned to respond to him with fear and fury. For years, that fear kept me small, compliant, silent. But eventually, the fury took over. It hardened. Sharpened. I stopped shrinking. I started speaking. I didn't care if it made things worse, because for the first time, I felt like I wasn't just surviving. I was fighting back.

That rage gave me something I hadn't had in a long time: a sense of identity. Not one I'm proud of, but one that kept me alive. That unforgiveness in my heart gave me fuel. That resentment gave me voice. When he lashed out, I lashed back harder.

I was never a fighter by nature. But life made me one. And sometimes, when you're raised in chaos, fighting feels like home.

I stood in the doorway of the home I grew up in and felt my chest cave in.

The living room lamp threw a weak yellow circle over everything that was broken: splintered doorframe, overturned drawers, the floors were caving in within certain spots, the linoleum floor was now a urine yellow color, and cigarettes with beer cans were piled on the small table he used in the living room. But it was my father, slumped on the edge of the couch, who looked the most ransacked. Purple bruises ringed both forearms, fingerprints blooming there like rotten fruit. A gash split the delicate skin beside his cheekbone; the dried blood had already cracked. He smelled of sweat and old fear. His clothes hung loose, as though he'd shrunk overnight.

For a long moment, neither of us spoke. We just stared, measuring the distance between who we'd been to each other and who we were right now. Then the anger that had always lived just beneath his ribs flared to life.

"Your cousin, Cayden," he rasped, pointing a shaking hand toward nothing in particular, "did this to me."

I said nothing because I didn't have language yet for the collision of compassion and fury. Part of me wanted to throttle Cayden for daring to put his hands on my father. Part of me wanted to remind my father that violence has a way of circling back. Mostly, I wanted to leave the whole scene and pretend it wasn't mine to clean up.

But it was. He was.

So I knelt in front of him, the way I might kneel beside a stranger on the street, and inspected the cut. I asked if anything felt broken. He said his pride. I almost laughed, not because it was funny, but because grief sometimes disguises itself as a laugh trapped behind your teeth.

"I'm taking you home with me," I said.

He didn't argue. Maybe the pain dulled his pride, maybe the loneliness did. I gathered what little he needed: medication bottles, a wrinkled grocery bag of clothes, his case of natural ice beer from the fridge, and we left the house the way paramedics carry survivors out of fires: gently, quickly, half amazed they're still breathing.

Bringing him into my space was like inviting a storm into a glass house. For the first forty-eight hours, I moved on instinct: scrubbed the wound, filled prescriptions, set alarms for antibiotics, got the couch as comfy as possible, opened windows, and Amadeus helped me with getting him a bath. The smell that came from him was horrendous. I had no idea the last time he bathed, since the bathroom was torn up due to his saying he was remodeling it years ago. Mostly, he slept. When he woke, he'd shuffle through the hallway cursing under his breath, railing against Cayden, against the police who "did nothing," against a world that kept proving it owed him nothing.

I kept the TV low and the prayers loud. At night, after everyone was down, I'd sit in my prayer closet, Bible open, journal nearby, trying to make sense of a God who would let my father be brutalized and still ask me to forgive what felt unforgivable.

And yet forgiveness kept tapping on the door.

Not the tidy, ribbon-wrapped forgiveness the church sometimes advertises. This was a rough, splintered thing that said: *You are free to acknowledge every wound **and** still choose to lay the weapon down.*

One morning, while I changed the bandage on his cheek, he winced and muttered, "I don't know why you're doing all this."

Because I love you, I wanted to say. Instead, what came out was, "Someone has to." It sounded colder than I meant, but he nodded, as if he understood that love, in our family, often arrived dressed as obligation.

By the end of the second week, he was stronger, restless. The bruises yellowed, the cut scabbed. We repeated the same dance: he snapped,

I breathed; he reminisced, I listened; he blamed, I deflected. One afternoon, he accused me of siding with my mother, old script, familiar lines. For once, I didn't bite. I folded the dish towel, looked him in the eye, and said quietly, "I'm on the side of healing. If you want to live there, too, you're welcome."

He didn't respond. But something in his shoulders loosened, just a fraction. It was the closest we'd come to peace in years.

A few days later, he packed his bag and said he felt ready to return to his apartment. I drove him back, neither of us mentioning Cayden or the gun or the nightmares that still jerked him awake. Before I left, I kissed him on his forehead and told him I would have one of my guy friends, Benny, come look at his door to see if it could be fixed.

"Thank you," he said, voice almost shy. "For everything. I love you, sweetheart. That son of bitch is going to get what is coming to him. I'll shoot his ass next time he comes. I just need a gun. "

I nodded. He could not have a gun; I wasn't going to tell him that.

It wasn't an apology. It wasn't a confession. But it was a beginning, and beginnings, I was learning, are seeds. You plant them, water them with steady grace, and trust God to bring the growth.

I walked to the car, breathing in the humid Tampa air, tasting salt and possibility. Somewhere deep inside, the girl who once shook at her father's voice realized she no longer did. And in that quiet victory, the first green shoot of forgiveness pushed through the soil.

I hated the thought of leaving him in that place. I hated knowing that if someone wanted to hurt him again, there was nothing to stop them. My father was a lot of things, but he wasn't invincible. He wasn't in the best physical shape, and his mind? His mind was running wild with paranoia.

He was nervous. He wanted a gun.

I knew that look in his eyes. That desperation, that need to reclaim control, to arm himself before the streets could take another swing at him. He was a felon, but that never mattered in the streets. If he wanted a gun, he could get one.

And that terrified me.

I prayed he wouldn't. I prayed for his protection at night, in the daylight, in his coming and going. I prayed that God would deliver us both from this cycle of pain and fear. Because if He didn't... I didn't know how this would end.

From that day forward, I committed myself to getting him help. He needed to get sober. He needed to be in a safe environment. He needed something better than the life he was barely surviving in.

My prayer was simple: that once he was sober, he would finally want to help himself.

I started researching local rehab facilities. There were plenty, but they all came with a price tag. A price tag that neither of us could afford. That's when I turned to Medicare and Medicaid, since he was on disability, I hoped they could point me in the right direction.

What a process.

It took me a month to find a facility that would accept him through his insurance. A place in Clearwater was willing to take him in, but only if he was willing to commit. That was the tricky part.

I organized an intervention at my home. It wasn't just me and him, this time, I brought everyone. Amara. My two sons. My mother. I needed him to see that we weren't just people in his life, we were people who loved him, who wanted him to live, who wanted him to be free.

But interventions never go the way you hope they will.

The moment rehab was mentioned, he shut down. He refused the rehab center known as DAACO outright; something about an experience with them had left a bad taste in his mouth. But after hours of going back and forth, he finally agreed to let me drive him to the Clearwater facility.

I had him stay with me that weekend so we could go first thing in the morning. I thought I had won. But over the next year, I would learn the hardest lesson of all: You can't save someone who doesn't want to be saved.

COVID shut the world down, and my father shut down with it.

I took him to several facilities. He refused every single one. He had every right to make his own decisions. And I hated that.

I couldn't understand it. I couldn't understand how no one could help me or him. I took him to his PC several times. They saw the bruises, how he was deteriorating, how he wasn't taking showers anymore, how bad it was. But because "he was in his own mind" and told them he didn't want to be cared for, they couldn't do anything for him. I wanted them to force him to go, but it was like the entire medical community was against me.

I kept thinking, *How could they believe he chose this? How could he want to live like this?*

His body odor from not showering made my stomach turn. He barely ate. His health was declining right in front of me. The home he lived in was practically caving in around him.

And yet, he refused help.

He would cry about wanting to be safe, about wanting to leave this life behind... but when I gave him the way out, he turned his back on it.

I never knew which version of him I was going to get. Would I be speaking to the independent, self-righteous, I-don't-need-anyone version of him? Or would it be the irrational, needy, victim version of him?

I would just sit there and listen, waiting for him to break through. Those moments, those brief, flickering glimpses of the man I once knew, were what I held onto. No matter how much the monster raged, no matter how much he pushed me away, I held onto the pieces of him that still existed beneath the wreckage.

And every single day, I had to ask God to help me. To posture my heart. To remind me that love isn't about fixing someone, it's about being there, even when they don't know how to accept it.

Life was relentless.

I was working full-time, paying bills, trying to live according to God's word, managing my personal life, raising my kids, and some-how, in the midst of it all, dealing with my father and his reckless, self-destructive lifestyle. It felt like a tug-of-war, and I couldn't tell if I was winning or losing.

But I kept showing up.

I wanted to see if God would really show up for me the way I needed Him to. But as I would come to learn, God's ways are not our ways. I prayed for God to change him. "My father is the one who needs help, not me."

But God wasn't just working on him; He was working on me. He kept showing me who I was in all of this, holding up a mirror to the parts of myself I had ignored. I wanted God to soften his heart, but it was mine that He was shaping first.

And slowly, my heart began to thaw.

I had lived with it numb and cold for so long, keeping myself at a safe distance from my own emotions, from my own pain. But God wouldn't let me stay that way.

He kept telling me it was time to face what I had spent my entire life running from. It was time to heal my inner child. It was time to let go of the fear. And, most of all, it was time to forgive.

I fought Him on it. "I don't know how to forgive him." "I don't even know if I want to forgive him."

But God wasn't asking me to feel ready. He was asking me to choose differently.

And honestly? It felt impossible. I felt like a maniac, a mess of emotions constantly colliding inside me. I was unraveling, and yet God kept telling me to be still. To trust Him.

But this wasn't just about my father. This was a spiritual battle. And deep down, I knew I could keep pushing forward and eventually get my father into rehab, force him into a better situation, and make him get the help he needed.

But that wasn't the real mission.

God wasn't asking me to fix my father. He was asking me to love him. To extend grace to him. To see him the way He sees him.

And that meant doing the hardest thing I had ever done.

It meant putting him above my pain. It meant putting the man who had hurt me before my own hurt. It meant forgiving him, really forgiving him, not just in words, but in action.

And that? That was the real test.

Anytime we argued, I would *shrink* the way I had when I was a little girl.

My voice would crack. My heart would pound like a rock drummer. My breath would turn shallow, like I had run a marathon while standing still. Tears would sting my eyes, falling without my permission. The words coming out of his mouth didn't even have to match the emotions overwhelming me. It wasn't about *this* argument, *this* moment, it was about *every* moment before it. *Every* hurt. *Every* memory. *Every* fear.

I would spiral.

A part of me, the little girl in me, would feel *hopeless*. But the other part, the woman I had become, would feel *furious*. And together, they would create *a storm of other emotions*.

My mind and spirit could know *logically* that I was safe, that I was an adult, that I wasn't a helpless child anymore, didn't matter if I was in my car on the way to see him, sitting next to him, or just answering the phone when he called. *Fear ruled me.* It changed the way I moved, the way I spoke, the way I reacted.

And I *hated it*. I *refused* to keep living like this.

So, I did the only thing I could think to do. I prayed. I remember whispering through tears, "God, please change him so I can love him." I said it more than once. I said it, hoping the heavens would bend and make my father into someone I could finally embrace without resentment. I was exhausted from the bitterness, tired of holding back love just because I didn't know what to do with the pain.

But the answer didn't come right away. For weeks, I sat in silence, journaling, crying, trying to hear something from God that didn't sound like my own disappointment echoing back at me. It wasn't until I started writing about my father, about all the ways he broke us, that

God began to reveal something I wasn't ready for: it wasn't just him. It was me, too.

That realization hurt. How could God expect me to change when I wasn't the one who caused the damage? How could He ask me to forgive someone who never even said sorry?

I wrote those questions down. I prayed them out loud. And in the quiet, I felt a response, not an audible voice, but a deep knowing in my spirit. It was as if God was saying, *"Yes, he hurt you. Yes, it wasn't fair. But you holding onto this is hurting you more than it's hurting him."* Then I sensed Him remind me, *"Even My Son offered forgiveness to those who didn't know what they were doing."* That truth cut deep. I realized I was trauma responding. I didn't want to hear any of it. I didn't want forgiveness, I wanted justice. I wanted transformation, but only on my terms. I kept praying, "God, please... change him. Make him softer. Make him see what he's done." But God, ever patient, kept turning the mirror back toward me, not in judgment, but in invitation. And then it hit me: my debt was even greater than my father's... and yet, He forgave me.

What if the healing didn't start in his apology, but in my release?

I wrestled with that. How do you release something that shaped your whole identity? How do you forgive someone who never even admitted the truth?

That's when I began to understand that forgiveness is unconditional. It doesn't excuse the offense or downplay its seriousness. It's not about letting someone off the hook; it's about freeing yourself from the burden. It's about laying down a weight you were never meant to carry. I realized then: forgiveness wasn't for him. It was for me.

And I began to pray differently.

Instead of begging God to change my father, I started asking Him to soften my heart. I asked for peace. For clarity. For the courage to set myself free from the identity that was wrapped in pain. I no longer wanted to be the angry daughter, the bitter little girl, the grown woman still chained to childhood hurt.

God began showing me that I was reacting from wounds rather than authority. He reminded me that I wasn't just a daughter, I was His daughter. That meant I had power, not just pain.

So I opened my Bible and searched for every verse I could find on fear, strength, and forgiveness. I didn't want platitudes, I wanted truth. I wanted words that felt like armor. And I found them. They were there all along.

Verses that reminded me I was not alone. That I was covered. That I was seen and chosen, even in the middle of my mess. I read them out loud. I let them wash over me. And slowly, something in me began to shift.

I wrote them on my bathroom mirror so I would see them every morning when I woke up and every night before I went to bed. I spoke them out loud over my life. At first, I read them with hesitation, as if I was testing their strength. Then I started saying them bolder, clearing my throat, standing taller, letting my voice own them. Because this was my life, not just words on a page.

I highlighted them in the Bible I had received from church, folding the pages so I could return to them easily. I wrote them down in a small notebook that I carried with me everywhere. Fear follows you wherever you go. And until I had fully internalized God's word, I needed it within reach at all times. Any time I felt fear creeping in, on the way to see my father, during a conversation with him, even just thinking about the past, I read those scriptures. I spoke to them. I clung to them. It happened more times than I could count. Fear had infested every part of my life. So I had to fight back just as often.

I started seeking out sermons and Bible-based lessons on fear. Amara helped me to start listening to a pastor online she vouched for. Instead of drowning my mind in music that numbed me, I filled my ears with truth. I prayed before any interaction with my father. I asked God to be with me, to guide my words, to keep my heart steady, to remind me who I was. This was the start of allowing light to enter the darkness.

But scripture alone wasn't enough. I had to recognize how fear was controlling me. I had to face my triggers. Because how can you fight something if you don't even know where it's attacking you? So I journaled about my emotions. I wrote about my triggers. I wrote out my prayers to God when I couldn't speak them. Because sometimes, fear grips you so tightly that words get stuck in your throat. But writing them down? That was powerful. It was like handing my burdens to God, one page at a time.

And the beautiful thing about God? He meets you exactly where you are. I didn't know how to pray like the people at church. I didn't know how to speak in tongues, how to sound like a seasoned prayer warrior, how to articulate faith in a polished way. But that didn't stop me. Because I knew God knew me more than I knew myself. He had ordained these days before I ever walked into them. And every relationship, including the one with God, requires honesty. So I came to Him exactly as I was. And that was enough.

Fear is still present in my life, but I no longer let it consume me or have power over my mind, choices, or heart. I've learned to do it afraid. I am confident that the God I serve is fearless, and if He asks me to do something, I won't let fear hold me back. God doesn't give us anything we can't handle. Once His word is planted in your spirit, your mind begins to renew. You walk, talk, and behave differently.

It took time to get into a rhythm with God, and I can't express enough how patient He was with me through it all. Even when I felt impatient with myself, even when I questioned if I was capable, He was always by my side. I saw His presence even in the hardest moments, especially when it came to facing my father. Psalm 16:8 (ESV) says, "I will bless the Lord who counsels me, even at night when my thoughts trouble me. I always let the Lord guide me. Because He is at my right hand, I will not be shaken." The enemy wanted me to stay bound to fear, to believe that God was absent in my troubles. But God was never absent, not when I was a child, not when I was a teenager, not in my darkest days, and not now.

The more I replaced the enemy's lies with God's truth, the more I felt free.

Chapter 27

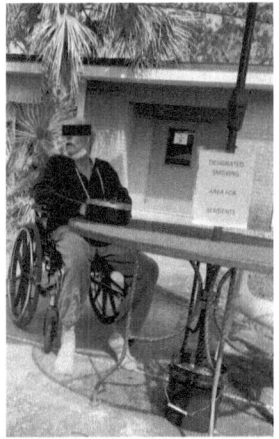

The Gift of Presence

H elping my father was the hardest assignment God had ever given me, and it didn't end the way I expected.

We had stopped speaking again for the same reasons as always: broken trust, old patterns, unrepaired wounds. Several months had passed with no communication when I got the call: he was in the hospital after suffering a stroke. A year after being robbed, now this. Two strokes back to back, leaving him even more fragile and alone.

I didn't know what to feel. Part of me wanted to retreat, to let the silence continue. Another part of me felt responsible, conflicted, unsure of what role I was supposed to play. Was I supposed to go back into his life again? Or was this the moment to finally let go?

I called my spiritual sister, hoping she'd give me clarity. And she did.

"What has God told you to do?" she asked, calmly but directly. "What is your assignment here?"

Her words cut through the fog of doubt. I wasn't that scared little girl anymore. I was a woman of God. And I was on assignment. Not to rescue. Not to fix. But to be obedient.

So I went to the hospital. He was sitting in the chair next to his bed, mumbling to himself, eyes cloudy and confused. When he saw me, he squinted hard, trying to make sense of who I was.

"Are you a nurse?" he asked. "Man, I got some bad eyesight. I need to use the restroom, but this damn gown keeps getting caught when I walk."

I smiled softly. "Daddy, it's me... Brandy."

He froze. Then tears welled up in his eyes. He wiped them quickly, almost in disbelief, and reached out his hand.

"Oh, sweetheart... is that you? Really you? I didn't think I'd ever see you again."

I stepped into his embrace, careful of his frail body. "Yes, it's me. You look a mess, though. They taking good care of you?"

He chuckled through his tears. "Yeah... I got some pretty nurses on this shift. Boy, if I was younger, you should see the hips and booty on my morning one. What's her name again? Think it was Shawna." He burst into laughter, then cried again. "I'm so happy to see you, baby. Come here." He wouldn't let go of my hand. And I didn't make him.

I stayed for about an hour. Just talking. Listening. Sitting in the space between pain and reconciliation. And before I left, I did something I'd never done before.

"Daddy... can I pray for you?"

He nodded, eyes glistening. "Yes, baby. I need all the help I can get round here."

I leaned over him, closed my eyes, and prayed to Jesus. Not a polished prayer. Not a performance. Just a daughter pleading for strength, for him and for me.

His strokes gave me an opening I never saw coming. A chance to walk back in, not from obligation or guilt, but with clarity. I wasn't there to carry him. I was there to carry out what God asked of me, with love, but with limits.

I took over his healthcare, managing doctor appointments and pushing DCF Adult Protective Services to step in. I tried again to get him help. But he resisted. Always. Pride and paranoia danced circles around him, and no matter what I did, he pushed back.

It was a draining cycle, one that tested every shred of patience and faith I had. And yet... somewhere in the middle of all that exhaustion, God did something unexpected.

He gave me a broken heart.

Not the kind that leaves you bitter, but the kind that cracks you open. That lets the light in. That reminds you what compassion feels like, not just for others, but for yourself.

It sounds strange to say that, but I mean it in the best way. A broken heart isn't always a bad thing. It can be the very thing that allows compassion to take root. Jesus had a broken heart; that's why He was able to serve people with grace instead of judgment. He saw their brokenness and loved them anyway. He died from a broken heart, and in this situation, my broken heart allowed me to see my father not as the monster I had known for so many years, but as a man who needed grace just as much as I did.

That broken heart is what made way for real forgiveness.

Another hard truth I had to face was that God had forgiven me for things far worse than what I was holding against my father. His mercy toward me was deeper than I could comprehend. I thought about Jesus in the Garden of Gethsemane, sweating blood from the weight of what He was about to endure. I thought about the pain He faced on the cross, the suffering He willingly took on so that I could be redeemed. If He could forgive me for all I had done, if He could love me even when I was an enemy of God, who was I to withhold forgiveness from my father?

It's astonishing how two people can live through the same events and yet walk away with completely different stories. In my father's version of our shared history, I'm the villain. The enemy. The one who turned against him. He can't or won't see the love, labor, and heartache that were poured into trying to save him. All he sees is betrayal.

After two relentless years, I finally got him into a safe and stable home.

During that time, he had been robbed repeatedly. Squatters had taken over his backyard, using and stealing from him while he lived in fear and squalor. The house was in ruins. His body was deteriorating. His mind was slipping. Something had to give.

With help from Benny, Amadeus, and my cousin, we removed the squatters and secured what was left of the property. But it was clear, he couldn't care for himself anymore. Not mentally. Not physically. Not emotionally. And certainly not in that house.

So I made a hard decision. I put the property in my name and found him an apartment through a connection my cousin, Bella, had with a local landlord. I paid the deposit. First month's rent. Furnished it with donated items. We filled it with love, pieces from Amara, Bella's mom, and others who wanted to help. Amadeus and I moved in a couch during a rainstorm.

I built that home for him out of hope. Out of duty. Out of love.

But within a month, I got the call.

"Hi, is this Brandy?"

"Hey, Laura, yes, what's going on?"

"This is about the unit you rented for your father. We haven't received the monthly rent."

"What? Are you saying he didn't pay?"

"No, ma'am. He didn't. And we've already passed the grace period. If it's not paid by the end of today, we'll have to move forward with eviction."

My mouth dropped open.

"Wait... I just moved him in. I paid everything up front. How could this be happening?"

She hesitated, then added, "Brandy... he's not in the unit either. We went by yesterday. It's abandoned. And we need to know what you're planning to do with the furniture inside."

I froze.

"What? So rent's unpaid *and* he's gone?"

"Yes. And since your name is on the lease, the landlord will likely charge..."

I cut her off, "Laura, I need to call you back."

I hung up and immediately called Bella.

"You will not *fucking believe this shit*," I snapped, breathless.

"Yo, cuzzo, what's going on?"

"He f*cking left, Bella. He LEFT the unit! I spent all this time and money. Amadeus and I moved that couch in the damn rain. Drove all the way to Pasco to get donations. Amara, your mom, everybody helped. And now he's just...*gone*."

"Wait... calm down. He left? Where the hell would he go? He can't walk or drive."

"I don't know! Laura's talkin' about charging me..."

"Man, *fuck that bum-ass landlord. He's a slumlord. He's not doing shit*. Yo... you think he went back to the house?"

I paused.

The house. Could he really have gone back? He had *cried* when I gave him the keys to the apartment. Said, "Free me from that hell house on La Salle Street." That's what he'd called it...not just my childhood home, but his. A hell house. And now he's gone? No rent paid. No goodbye. Just vanished.

"I wanna check," I said, my voice tight. "But I don't want to go alone. Can you come with me?"

"Yeah. Give me a few minutes. Start heading this way."

We pulled up to the property. My stomach turned. And there he was. Sitting in the living room like nothing had happened. Watching TV.

Like he never left.

That was it. I called the cops to have him escorted off the property and back to his residence at the apartment. They told me I'd have to go to civil court to fix it, since both of our names were still showing up in public records. Even though the property had legally been transferred into my name, his name was still showing on the tax records because those take time to update. This kind of thing is called a title discrepancy, and it can make it unclear who officially owns the property.

I cut him off again after that.

***

Knox had been locked up for almost eight years. About six months before he was set to get out, we started talking again. I even took the boys to see him. Somewhere in those phone calls and letters, I told him about my dad, everything.

One day, the recorded voice came on the line: *You are receiving a call from Isandro Reyes, an inmate at a federal correctional institution. This call is being recorded and monitored. To accept this call, press 5.*

I pressed 5. "Hello?" "Hey, B." "Hey, Knox." "How's it going?" I let out a long sigh. "A lot's going on with my father. I'm trying to get him help, but every time it comes, he refuses it. I don't even know where to start." "Talk to me." "He's been robbed. Squatters have moved in, trying to take over. The house is unlivable, no front door, just a piece of wood leaning there. The window in the living room is gone. His health is slipping fast. It's real bad." "Damn. Sorry to hear that. But you know your pops is a champ, he's gonna bounce back." "I don't know about this time. I'm exhausted." "I get it. Keep your head up. He's your pops, you gotta do what you can. What about the house? You ever think of doing something with it?" "I've got plans, but he's in the way. I can't do anything if he's living there." "Sounds like you got a lot on your plate. Listen, I don't know if you've heard, but I'm gonna be home soon. Could you bring the boys to see me? I'm more local now." "Where you at? Coleman?" "Yeah." "I'll talk to Amadeus. If he's good with bringing Justice, we'll come. You ready to be out?" "Yeah. Little nervous, but ready." "Nervous? That's a first." "There's a lot you don't know. But I'm not going back. I've got my son, and he deserves his papi."

Five minutes left. "Alright, B, I won't hold you up. Don't get too stressed about your pops. He's a survivor. Y'all will get through this. I'll be home soon, I'll help however I can." "Aight, bet."

A few weeks later, I made the two-hour drive each way to take Amadeus and Justice to visit him in Coleman Federal Prison. The road there felt endless, flat highways, sun glaring on the windshield, silence broken only by the hum of the tires. I stayed in the car when we arrived, watching through the glass as they walked toward the building.

"Baby, you're going with your brother to see your dad, okay? Listen to him. I'll be right here when you're done, and then we'll get food." "McDonald's?" Justice asked. "Yes, McDonald's." "Aight, Mom. We'll see you soon."

Amadeus kissed my forehead, hugged me, then took his brother's small hand and led him toward the metal doors. I watched them walk away, one tall, one small, both with the same stride, and felt tears sting my eyes.

In the visiting room, I knew Justice would see his father not as I'd known him, but as an image behind rules, behind a table, behind time lost. I imagined the sound of the guard's keys, the hard plastic chairs, the awkward pauses when you don't know whether to hug or just smile.

When they came back out, they were hand in hand again. Amadeus told me Justice had been happy to see his dad, that he didn't cry when it was time to leave. No tantrums, no visible sadness. Just quiet bravery.

Months later, after Knox was released from prison, he called again, this time, about my father. He had gone by the house to check on my dad and told me my dad's health had worsened. Against every instinct screaming *don't do it,* I took him in again, moving him into my apartment so I could sell the house. I figured the DCF apartment I'd been working on for him would come through at the same time.

But it didn't. What was supposed to be a few days turned into a month. And, as I should have known, it ended the only way it ever could, with more damage.

One day, I came home from work to find out he had been verbally abusing my mother. Amadeus stepped in to defend her, and things escalated. That was the last straw. That was the last time my father ever stayed under my roof.

In the end, I had to choose. Let him stay at the property, knowing it would eventually kill him. Or sell it and force a change that might just save his life.

I chose the latter.

It felt like a betrayal of my childhood, a surrender of everything that had once felt like home. But sometimes, saving someone means letting go of the thing they're clinging to most. And sometimes, even that isn't enough.

When I sold the property, it didn't feel like a victory. It felt like a deep, personal loss.

The real estate agent handed me a bottle of champagne, smiling like it was a reason to celebrate. I never opened it. How could I? I wasn't just selling a house, I was letting go of something sacred.

That moment brought the weight of my abuela's passing crashing down.

I hadn't truly mourned her when she died. But selling the home where so many memories lived... made her absence feel final.

My connection to that house ran deep. I had dreams for it. Real plans. I wanted to tear it down and build a little casita in the backyard for him. The neighborhood was on the rise. Property values were climbing. I saw the potential.

But I couldn't afford the demolition. I couldn't afford the re-build. I looked for help grants, assistance, anything, but nothing came through. Then the taxes hit. When the property was under his name, they were around $200 a year. Once I took it over, they jumped to nearly $3,000.

It became impossible to maintain.

And when he moved back into the house without telling anyone? That sealed everything. I couldn't build. I couldn't move forward. My hands were tied. The future I had imagined for that home was gone. And with it, another piece of her

Helping my father has been one of the most emotionally taxing assignments of my life. A journey filled with obstacles, heartbreak, and hard-earned clarity.

After nearly a year of persistent collaboration with the Department of Children and Families (DCF) Adult Protective Services, I finally secured housing for him. An apartment that met his very specific needs. It wasn't easy. His criminal record made him ineligible for most housing, senior facilities, mobile homes, and even low-income options were off the table.

I worked every angle. Coordinated with every agency I could. And in the end? He refused the help.

Every. Single. Time.

That was the cycle. Me: showing up, fighting, hoping.Him: retreating into fear, pride, and dysfunction.

Still, I kept trying. Because sometimes love doesn't look like staying, it looks like *still trying*, even after they've given up on themselves.

In my determination to shelter my father, I began paying for hotel stays out of pocket, hoping the temporary arrangements would lead to something more stable. But no matter how many opportunities I presented, he refused them. Eventually, his case was closed due to non-compliance, and things reached a breaking point when he showed up at my door, disheveled and deteriorating. In desperation, I reached out to the DCF agent who had helped us in the past. This time, he agreed to receive help, but only momentarily. He never pursued rehab and offered only fleeting gratitude. That's when I knew I had done all I could. I had extended myself fully, and the weight of his choices was no longer mine to carry.

Letting go of that responsibility wasn't easy. Somewhere deep inside, I still held onto the fantasy of saving him, of restoring the bond we had when I was a little girl and he was my hero. I convinced myself that if I just tried hard enough, he'd finally get the help he needed. That we'd heal. That we'd reconnect. But reality had other plans, and when the outcome proved darker than I'd dared to imagine, I spiraled into depression.

I was caught in a web of emotions, heartbroken and at peace, torn and somehow free, all at once. Part of me wondered if I had given up too soon, if there was something else I could have done. But another part of me knew the truth: I had done everything in my power. I pulled him out of an environment that was eating away at him. I gave him shelter when no one else would. I tried to preserve both his dignity and his life. In many ways, I had saved him, but neither of us ever acknowledged the magnitude of that. People often talk about the stories we tell ourselves, the ones where we become the hero, where everything ends in restoration. But when reality takes a different path, it's hard to see the worth in the journey we've actually lived.

All that remained were fragments, memories warped by disappointment and grief. And that grief spilled into my faith. How was I supposed to trust a heavenly Father when my earthly one had left so many wounds? I knew my dad loved me in his own way, but that love was unpredictable, sometimes tender, sometimes conditional, often painful. It made it hard to believe in a God whose love was supposed to be steady, safe, and unconditional. My understanding of love had been shaped by a man who meant well but could never fully show up.

So I had to relearn what love really looked like. I had to study God's heart, not through sermons, but through relationship. Because you can't trust someone you don't truly know. The deeper I went, the more I realized that the anger I carried wasn't just about my dad, it was directed at God too. And when I finally admitted that, when I brought it to Him in prayer, He didn't flinch. He didn't turn away. He met me with gentleness, already knowing, waiting.

The anger I carried wasn't just rooted in pain. It was rooted in belief. A quiet conviction that God owed me something. A better beginning. A better father.

And beneath that belief, if I was honest, there was jealousy. Not the obvious kind. The kind that whispered, *He could've chosen differently for me... and didn't.* If God is all-powerful, why didn't He give me a steady father? Who wasn't ruled by anger? Who didn't disappear when I needed protection, guidance, or someone to tell me I mattered?

I couldn't help but think, if I had that kind of father, maybe my life would've looked completely different.

Through the *Southside Rabbi* podcast, I came across Dane Ortlund's book *Gentle and Lowly*, and it changed everything. The book unpacks Christ's heart for sinners and sufferers like me. In the very first chapter, Ortlund writes: *"Jesus is not trigger-happy. Not harsh, reactionary, or easily exasperated. He is the most understanding person in the universe. The posture most natural to him is not a pointed finger but open arms."*

That sentence cracked something open in me. I had spent most of my life imagining God as distant and disappointed, just another father waiting for me to mess up. But Ortlund gave language to a truth my heart had forgotten: God wasn't punishing me. He was welcoming me home.

I realized my view of God had been shaped more by my wounds than by His Word. I read Scripture through the filter of my pain, like reading an email in anger, assuming the worst tone possible. I misunderstood His character because I had only known one version of fatherhood. But just because I had one perspective didn't mean it was true.

Learning the heart of Jesus required me to unlearn the fear I had long called love.

John Welwood once said, *"The most powerful agent of growth and transformation is something much more basic than any technique: a change of heart."* And that's what began to happen. Slowly, steadily, I let Jesus change my heart.

I started facing the tomb I'd been too afraid to name, the tomb of fear.

This wasn't just fear of conflict. It was a soul-deep fear, built over years of instability, volatility, and silence. But buried beside fear was another grave: unforgiveness. I had carried both like chains. Forgiving my father wasn't some soft, passive thing. It was a war between my will and God's. But in that battle, I found freedom.

Letting go didn't mean excusing his choices. It meant releasing my need for him to understand, apologize, or change. It meant releasing *me*. I laid down the right to stay angry and picked up the right to be free.

That freedom showed up in surprising places.

I stopped seeing him as *my father* and started seeing him as *a man*. A man with wounds. A man with choices. A man with a story. And in that shift, I no longer felt the need to fix what only Jesus could redeem.

I don't live in that prison anymore. I'm not just a survivor, I'm a woman who has been remade. The graves I once lived in, fear and unforgiveness, have become gardens. Places where something new has grown. Places where Jesus' presence lives. In those gardens, I've found peace, authority, love.

And every day, I choose to rise and walk in that freedom.

Forgiveness, I've learned, isn't about forgetting. That's not how the soul works. We carry memories. We carry pain. But forgiveness means that memory no longer stings. I can remember what happened without flinching. I can tell the truth without trembling.

Forgiveness is not about justice. It's about grace. It's letting go of my right to get even. It's remembering how much I've been forgiven, and letting that shape how I treat those who hurt me.

Sometimes forgiveness is a one-time decision. Other times, it's daily. Hourly. It's saying *I release this* over and over until bitterness loses its grip. Until the urge for revenge dissolves. Until I can pray for his healing, not out of obligation, but because I mean it.

Reconciliation is different. That requires change. That requires safety and effort from both sides. But forgiveness? That's mine to give. And giving it has been the greatest gift I've ever received.

Side B

The Gardens

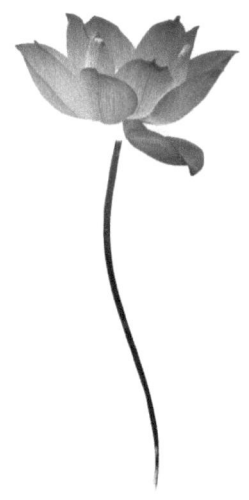

Chapter 28

When the Past Meets the Promise

I t had been a few months since I'd started walking with Jesus. There was so much in me that needed healing, but one area kept rising to the surface during my quiet time with Him: my desire for sex.

Sex had never been sacred to me. I had no real understanding of its beauty or purpose. I'd only ever known it as something distorted. Everywhere I turned, it was vulgar, transactional, or perverse. For me, it was never about connection. It was a weapon. A pleasure hit. A survival tool. A means to an end.

So, when I began to heal, I had to question everything I thought I knew. *What did sex really mean? Could it be more than what I'd experienced?*

I had used my body like a bandage, something to temporarily dull the ache and prove, at least to myself, that I was still in control.

But I wasn't.

And honestly, I didn't even know how to ask for help. Not from God. Not from anyone.

How do you unlearn something when it's the only form of intimacy you've ever known?

I prayed for breakthrough, but I didn't know how to break free. Then something began to shift. Not all at once. Not with thunder or lightning. But gradually, quietly.

Sex stopped feeling good. What once gave me escape started leaving me empty. For the first time, I felt guilt. Real guilt. Not shame from others, but a conviction that came from deep within. A weight in my chest that whispered, *This isn't for you anymore.*

God began putting a burden on my heart: Let it go. Delete the numbers. Block the Instagram accounts. Turn off the music that glorifies lust. Stop going to places that lead you into temptation.

Still, I thought I had it all under control. I was new to faith, but I was confident. Maybe too confident. I thought I could handle myself better than God could.

Celibacy? That's easy. Thirty days. Ninety. A whole year. Check, check, check.

It felt like a challenge I could win through willpower alone. And to be fair, it wasn't hard at first. I wasn't seeing anyone. I was caught up in other battles, my DUI case, my father's mess. I didn't even have the energy to entertain anyone.

I told myself: *You're good. You're healing. You're becoming.*

I didn't see the point in going deeper, changing my playlists, cutting ties, deleting social media followers I had no business keeping. Nobody was checking for me anyway, so what's the harm?

Then one night, I went out. Just one night. Because I could "handle myself," right? That was the lie. If I were being honest...I wasn't full of Jesus. I was full of myself.

Still worldly in ways I didn't want to admit. Still leaning on my own understanding, thinking I had just enough Jesus to flirt with danger and walk away untouched.

That night, I ran into an old partner I hadn't seen in six months, someone who had moved to California. It felt casual. We caught up, laughed, and exchanged numbers. He just wanted to take me out to eat. *What's the harm?*

Then, I met someone new, a man from Jamaica, just visiting. He was charming, easy to talk to, made me laugh, bought me a drink. He asked about food spots, said he wanted somewhere chill to hang. *It's just food. Just conversation.*

But within a week, I had slept with both of them.

Drinks. Dinner. Laughter. And then... guilt. Not just guilt. Regret. Disappointment. Emptiness.

It happened so easily, it almost didn't register, until the stillness came. Until I had to sit with myself. And God. I knew I hadn't just crossed a line, I had sprinted past it. Everything God had been whispering to my heart...I ignored it for a moment of control I thought I still had.

The guy from Cali? He left. No follow-up. No check-in. Poof, gone like he'd only been passing through my life on his way to somewhere better.

The Jamaican guy? Dry texts. Missed calls. No energy. No effort. The kind of slow fade you can see coming, but still don't want to believe is happening.

And even though I didn't want to admit it, I felt something I wasn't prepared for: I actually wanted them to want me. I wanted more than the sweat and skin. I wanted to be seen, to be chosen, to be worth more than just a body in their bed.

Out of a strange mix of rejection and anger, I blocked both their numbers, not just to protect my peace, but to salvage whatever pride I had left.

But then came the other worry, the one that kept my stomach in knots. I couldn't remember if I'd used protection with the Jamaican guy. I'd heard about Plan B before, but never used it. This seemed like the time to try. I bought the box, read the instructions twice: *must be taken within 72 hours.*

I was at hour seventy. I swallowed the pill and prayed it would work. And just when I thought it couldn't sting any worse...

My period didn't come.

I waited a few days. Then a week. Told myself maybe my cycle was just off. But nothing. I called Bella.

"Hey, can you talk?"

"Yea, what's up, cuzzo? I'm just cleaning up, bout to start cooking dinner."

Tears were already falling down my face. She could hear it through the phone.

"You okay? What's wrong?"

"I fucked up... again. I went out last week. You know I haven't been out in a while. I've been doing so freaking good. No drinking, no sex. I've been doing good... and then it just happened so fast. Cuzzo, why did I do this?"

"Alright, just breathe. Let's not beat ourselves up. We can handle what happened. I'm here for you. I've seen a change in you lately, for real. And I know you've been carrying a lot. Did you drink too much? Is it the DUI case? Your dad?"

"I think I'm pregnant."

I heard her gasp. It sounded like she almost dropped her phone. "What the fuck? Wait, back it up, cuzzo. I need you to tell me what's going on."

"It hurts. I don't want this to be my story again. I can't do this. I'm supposed to be better. I'm supposed to be walking in the light. I've been going to church. Reading the Word. How did I let this happen to me?"

"Breathe. Listen to me. Tell me what happened, not how you feel."

"I went out, like I said. Just wanted a normal night. Grabbed something to eat. Then a drink. I thought I could handle one drink, right? But I can't. I'm not like you."

"Where'd you go?"

"Ybor."

Dead silence. She didn't need to say anything. I could already hear her thinking it.

"I saw Richie there..."

"Richie? Dang, didn't he move to Cali?"

"He did. But he was there. And then after I saw him, I kept walking and ran into this Jamaican dude. He complimented me and asked if he could buy me a drink. I figured... why not?"

"I mean, I could give you several reasons 'why not,' but go ahead."

"Ugh. Well, nothing happened that night. I went home. So I felt good about myself. Like, 'I got this.' Then I started talking to both of them. Went out to eat, had some drinks. That led to wanting to smoke, more conversation, and... you already know. I'm worse than before. How can I be following Jesus and doing this stupid shit? I'm a hypocrite, literally the definition of one."

"Cuzzo, calm down. This doesn't mean you're a bad person. You just made some bad choices."

"Yea, well, that's my *whole* life, bad choices stacked on bad choices. I'm too grown for this. For this drama. And I'm not even talking to either of them. Richie's back in Cali, and the other dude already pissed me off."

"Damn... that answers my next question. So... did you take a test?"

"Yes. I'm in the bathroom right now with it. I'm pregnant, cuzzo." The words felt unreal as they came out of my mouth.

I wasn't even sure who the father was. My memory blurred under the haze of alcohol. The timelines didn't add up. Fear wrapped itself around me like a second skin, tight, suffocating.

I did what I thought I had to do. So I chose to end the pregnancy.

"Cuzzo, thanks for coming with me. I never thought I'd be here again. I don't want to do this again."

We sat in her car outside the clinic while protestors stood on the sidewalk, shouting through their signs, waving their truth in our direction. I watched as a few women walked past them, eyes lowered, heads bowed, quiet, heavy, resigned.

"I'm here with you," she said. "This isn't an easy decision. You're not alone."

My hands trembled in my lap. "Can God forgive me this time? I don't even know if I've been forgiven for the last ones... but this one feels different. I'm such a fuck up. How can He love me? How can He choose me?"

"I'm sure He will," she said gently. "Don't beat yourself up. I love you. And I'm staying with you through this."

I stepped out of the car, numb. The chanting of the crowd faded behind me as I followed the others into the clinic, heads down, lips sealed, grief shared but unspoken. It was like stepping into a silent procession of sorrow. I walked not just into a building, but into a space I promised I'd never return to. A space where my pain had a name. A space I had once sworn off, and yet here I was again.

Inside, I kept asking myself: *Was I playing God? Was I trying to fix a mistake by making another one?*

All I'd ever been taught about pregnancy was laced with fear, fear of judgment, fear of poverty, fear of how another child would break me. I had been a mother since I was sixteen. Starting over again? I couldn't imagine it. I didn't want to be reckless, but I had been. I didn't want to end a life, but I couldn't see how to keep it. And that pain, the pain of that impossible tension, is one I wouldn't wish on anyone.

It's real. It's deep.

And it doesn't go away quietly. This time, though, something was different.

This time, I knew Jesus. This time, I had tasted His grace. I had begun to learn the shape of His love, the truth of His mercy. And yet, *even in knowing Him,* I still clung to the old lie: *It's my body. It's my choice.*

As if I belonged to myself.

The truth is, I didn't yet understand what surrender truly meant. Not fully. Not when it came to this. My belief system was still cracked, still bent under the weight of the world's logic and my own history of pain.

And so, I went through with it. Not proudly. Not defiantly. Just... broken. Still trying to outrun the parts of me I hadn't let Him heal.

Then, a few months later, while I was still reeling from the fallout of my choices, barely trying to gather myself again, it happened.

A DM.

It was from an old flame. Someone I had history with. Someone I should have ignored. But I didn't. This time, though, he was married.

I wasn't sure why he was reaching out to me, and a part of me, curious, hungry, broken, answered. I shouldn't have. I wasn't close to God in that season. I felt guilty about everything that had transpired and had convinced myself I didn't deserve forgiveness anyway. So I stayed in the dark, punishing myself with silence, shame, and distance.

He can't just forgive me. I don't deserve to be forgiven or chosen.

That's what I believed. I figured God must have gotten it wrong about me. That I wasn't who He thought I was. So when this man messaged me, I entertained it.

The conversation was casual at first, just checking in, "How've you been?" I did the same. But he didn't mention his marriage. We didn't follow each other on Instagram, so I couldn't check his page, but I remembered we had a mutual friend. I reached out and asked, and just like that, confirmation came. Yes, he was married. Pictures and all.

I told myself I wouldn't cross *that* line. That this was just a conversation. That I was stronger than temptation.

But eventually, what we entertain in the shadows evolves into something more.

He asked to see me. At first, I hesitated. I asked about his wife, and he dodged the question. Still, *he* persisted. And despite everything in me screaming *Don't,* I gave in. I was curious. I wanted to feel wanted again. I wanted something...*anything*...to fill the hole in my soul I had carved out with guilt and silence.

So I met up with him. And there I was... doing the very thing I swore I'd never do. The affair didn't last long. We only saw each other twice. But the damage? It was instant.

The guilt came first, a tight ache in my chest whispering: *You messed up.* Then came shame. And shame didn't just say I made a mistake. Shame told me *I was* a mistake.

What made it worse was that this wasn't just any man. I had known him for years. I had been infatuated with him for as long as I could remember. There was something about the way he looked at me, the way he spoke to me, that made me feel seen. Even if it was wrong. The temptation was easy to fall into because, deep down, I still didn't believe I was worthy of better.

And just like that, I was falling again. Back into the trap. Back into the lie that I was only good for what I could give. Back into the darkness I had once fought so hard to leave behind.

Sex had always come with consequences, but this time, they felt heavier than ever. That same month, everything came crashing down.

The emotional relapse was instant. The nightmares returned, flashes of old faces, decisions I couldn't undo. The voices in my head were relentless: *You're a hypocrite. You don't really follow Jesus. You're nothing but a liar, a failure, a fraud.*

All the worst parts of my past played on a loop inside my mind, like a torment I couldn't escape. So I withdrew. For months, I stayed to myself. No going out. No people. Just me, buried beneath my shame.

Eventually, I reached out to Amara and we linked up.

"Hey, how's it been going?" she asked, her eyes studying me. She could already tell something was off.

"It's been rough," I admitted. "I just don't know if I'm built to be good at this thing called life. I can't stop making wrong choices, and I keep hurting myself over and over again... and that ends up hurting others too. I thought church would help, but maybe I'm just too far gone for Jesus."

"Girl, nah," she said, her voice sharp with love. "Don't say that. Listen, there is nothing you can do that will make Him stop loving you. He *chose* you, B. You've got so much potential, with your writing, your poetry. You love helping people. You're a great mom. I've seen the change in you since you started going to church. But you gotta stop beating yourself up. You have to *start healing*, B. Like really healing. Let go of it all."

"Amara," I whispered, "you don't know what I've done. It's worse. A lot worse."

She softened. "No, I don't know. Do you wanna tell me? What's up?"

I looked down, my hands trembling. "I was in a spiral. I slept with someone who's married."

She blinked. "Dang."

"I did it more than once."

I put my head in my hands, tears slipping through my fingers.

She exhaled slowly. "Breathe, B. Okay... yeah. That's a tough one."

"You know who it was, too."

She didn't say anything, but she knew. I had told her he'd messaged me not long ago.

"Please don't say it," I begged. "Don't tell me what I already know. I should've known better."

"I'm not gonna lecture you," she said gently. "You know how I feel about him anyway. But what I *am* going to say is this: don't throw yourself a pity party. It happened. You're self-aware now, right? You didn't reach out to him. *He* messaged *you*. And you didn't sleep with yourself, he made that decision too."

I nodded, ashamed.

"You gotta pray about it, B. You gotta give it to God. You *cannot* keep carrying this alone."

"But God doesn't want me," I said. "Who *would* want me? I had an affair. An abortion. I've been sleeping with men who don't even care about me. I'm just a broken person."

She pulled me into a hug, tight and sure.

"That's where you're wrong," she whispered. "God doesn't see you as broken. He calls you *worthy*. I don't see you as broken either. I see a woman who needs to love *herself*, who needs to heal. You need to stop listening to that devil in your head. He's a liar. What you did was wrong, yes. But are you going to imprison yourself for it over and over again? How is that helping?"

We sat in silence for a long time. I wiped my face, trying to keep myself together.

"I don't know how to forgive myself," I said quietly.

She looked at me, soft but steady. "But God does, B."

I returned to celibacy, not out of my strength this time, but out of faith that God could and would restore me. I wasn't trying to prove anything. I just wanted to heal. To breathe. To stop letting everything around me swallow me whole.

And just as I started to find a little bit of silence...I ran into another old partner. A different one this time. But this encounter changed everything.

I didn't plan on having sex with him. That wasn't the goal. I just wanted to feel something close to fun again, something light, something that didn't feel like work. After everything I'd been through, I was desperate for a kind of relief that didn't come with shame attached to it.

So when we reconnected, it felt harmless. We went to brunch, laughed, and shared a few mimosas. It felt good to be seen without judgment. To have someone smile at me like I wasn't broken.

After brunch, we headed back to his place. I told myself I wasn't falling into the old cycle. I was just going to hang out, maybe catch up a little more. I'd be clear about my boundaries. I'd make sure he knew where I stood.

But before anything could happen, he sat down across from me, looked me dead in the eyes, and said, "You hurt me."

I froze.

He continued talking, really talking. "B, you used me," he said quietly, like he was trying to keep his voice from shaking. "You treated me like I was nothing more than a hookup." He dropped his gaze, holding his head in his hands for a moment before continuing. "I wasn't able to get you out of my mind since our last time together. It messed me up bad, B. Because of you, I couldn't trust any other woman. After having sex with you, I had this expectation that my next girl couldn't live up to. I would fantasize about you while I was with them. I wanted more. I thought we could be more. I thought we had a future. And you just left me cold. You hurt me."

I sat there, staring at him, my mouth open but empty of words. And the worst part was... I had nothing to say and wasn't ready to hear it. So I walked out.

But he was right. I had never given him a chance. I had been so consumed with protecting myself from pain, so wrapped up in my own numbness, that I had never considered how my walls might have been wounding someone else. My whole life, I'd believed I was the one being used. I had never thought *I* was capable of using someone.

That night, when I got home, I shut myself in my prayer closet. And I wept. Not polite tears, floodgate tears. A deep, shaking kind of crying that came from somewhere far below the surface. For the first time, I saw how detached I'd become. How focused I was on my own survival. How blind I was to the pain I might have been causing.

That realization broke something open in me.

I tried to reach out again, to talk it through, but this time he was busy. He didn't have time for me. Soon, his voice disappeared from my life. And for the first time, I was the one left standing on the other side of the emotional pain I had inflicted.

For years, I'd convinced myself that cutting men off was an act of mercy, protecting them from getting too close to someone who could ruin their life if they really knew me. It was also my way of protecting myself from the sting of them leaving first. But seeing myself through his eyes, I realized something I had never wanted to admit: the same knife I thought I was using to shield myself... could be cutting someone else just as deeply.

And I didn't like what I saw.

Chapter 29

My Name Is Shame

I t took time, but I finally understood something that changed everything for me: God had created sex to be beautiful. Not just an act, not just for reproduction, but for joy, for intimacy, for unity. And that beauty was meant to be cherished within the sacred bond of marriage.

I know how traditional that sounds, especially in a world where cohabitation is normal, where commitment often takes a backseat to convenience. Living together feels safer. It gives people an out. But marriage? That is something deeper. It is a covenant, a promise, a transformation into something greater than yourself.

I never imagined myself choosing celibacy, but here I am, years into this journey. I got deeper into God's word, and even into scientific research, I began to see how wrong my understanding had been.

Sex isn't just physical. It is deeply emotional. It is spiritual.

Our brains release chemicals like oxytocin during sex, bonding us, forging connections, and making us attached in ways we don't even realize. It's meant to create intimacy, to reduce stress, to bring unity. But for me, there had never been unity. There had only been distance.

I had engaged in what the world calls "casual sex," seeking pleasure without attachment, without emotional connection. Physical attraction was enough. Character didn't matter.

Before I fully surrendered to God, I didn't realize His hand was already at work in me. He was reshaping my desires in ways I didn't understand at first. The pleasure I once found in casual encounters began to fade. It wasn't an instant shift, and it wasn't just the result of prayer alone, though prayer was crucial.

I was still showing up at church every Sunday. I was still listening to gospel and Christian hip-hop. I was reading the Bible more than ever. But the real transformation went deeper than my habits. It was about my *beliefs*. What did I truly believe about myself? About men? About sex?

One Sunday, our church's executive pastor said something that struck me: *"The enemy attacks what you believe."*

And in that moment, I realized just how much of my life had been shaped by false beliefs. I had spent years carrying toxic thoughts about my own worth, about the role of men in my life, about what sex even meant. In my search for clarity, I came across Dr. Juli Slattery, a Christian psychologist who spoke on integrity and sexuality. She challenged me to see my sexuality as something to be *stewarded*, not something to be ashamed of, not something to be exploited, but something to *honor.*

She posed a question that stayed with me: *"What does it look like to give your sexuality to God?"*

At first, the question made me uncomfortable. It felt too big, too personal. I had never even considered what God thought about my sexuality. I had spent my whole life trying to separate the two.

But she was right. God created sex. He designed it with purpose. And yet, the world I grew up in had warped and twisted it, turning it into something vulgar and transactional.

For so long, I believed purity was all or nothing; you either had it or you didn't. But I was learning that purity wasn't just about *what I had done*, it was about *how I lived moving forward.*

That was the shift.

I started asking myself hard questions: ***Am I being a good steward of my sexuality? Am I allowing Jesus to heal me, or am I still burying myself in shame?***

These questions kept me up at night, forcing me to confront the lies I had believed for so long. So I continued writing.

I journaled about my triggers. I made a list of every man I had been with. I wrote down why I was drawn to them. I traced my patterns back to their roots. For the first time, I was being brutally honest with myself. It wasn't pretty, but it was necessary.

As I confronted my flaws, something unexpected happened; I didn't drown in shame. Instead, I found *compassion* for myself. For years, I had refused to give myself grace. I had judged myself more harshly than anyone else ever could. But now, I was starting to see myself the way *God* saw me.

I prayed for forgiveness, not just from God, but for myself. I wrote letters to the people I had hurt and the people who had hurt me. I never sent them. Instead, I took them to the ocean and burned them, watching the flames consume years of shame, regret, and pain.

That was when I truly *let go.*

Forgiveness isn't always a face-to-face conversation. Sometimes, it's a divine realization that God holds the power to transform hearts, including mine. I had to change my *beliefs*, but I also had to change my *patterns.*

I started evaluating everything that influenced me, the places I went, the music I listened to, the things I consumed, the relationships I entertained. Each one of those things had played a role in my addiction to pain. And if I was going to be celibate, I had to *make room* for something new.

It was one of the hardest things I had ever done, releasing the very things I had once clung to for validation. But that was the point. God needed me to be *empty* so I could finally be filled with *Him.*

I kept up with my journaling. I buried myself in Scripture, searching for verses that reminded me of my worth. Because when you remove toxic behaviors, you have to replace them with something else.

So instead of texting old flames, I read Proverbs 31:30 (ESV): *"Charm is deceitful, and beauty is vain, but a woman who fears the LORD is to be praised."*

Instead of craving validation from men, I reminded myself, *"You are altogether beautiful, my love; there is no flaw in you."* (Song of Songs 4:7) (ESV)

And then there were the verses that spoke directly to the deepest parts of me, the parts that still felt unworthy: *"Why, even the hairs of your head are all numbered. Fear not; you are of more value than many sparrows."* (Luke 12:7) (ESV)

"For you formed my inward parts; you knitted me together in my mother's womb. I praise you, for I am fearfully and wonderfully made. Wonderful are your works; my soul knows it very well." (Psalm 139:13–14) (ESV)

For the first time, I started to believe it. God had been calling me to healing for so long. And I was finally ready to answer.

Chapter 30

The Long Road to Understanding

G od's grace is unmerited favor. It is love that comes without conditions, without earning it. It is the hand reaching out when you are drowning, the voice calling you home when you are lost.

For me, encountering God's grace felt like being pulled from an ocean of shame, gasping for air, realizing I had been trying to breathe underwater for too long. I spent years believing I had to carry my brokenness alone, that I was beyond redemption. But grace whispered otherwise.

Grace did not erase my past...it *transformed* it.

It gave me hope where there had been despair. Strength where there had been weakness. Purpose where there had been emptiness.

Isaiah 43:18-19 (ESV) says, *"Remember not the former things, nor consider the things of old. Behold, I am doing a new thing; Now it springs forth, do you not perceive it? I will make a way in the wilderness and rivers in the desert."*

That question stayed with me: *"Do you not perceive it?"*

God *was* doing a new thing in me. But for so long, I had been too caught up in my past to notice.

Accepting grace meant learning to see myself the way God sees me, loved, forgiven, redeemed. It meant learning to steward my sexuality, not out of shame, but out of integrity. I no longer wanted to make choices based on brokenness. I wanted to honor both myself and the divine gift of sexuality with which I had been entrusted.

God's grace is the greatest gift I have ever received. It is the foundation of my faith, the source of my strength, and the reason I am no longer defined by my brokenness, but by the unending, relentless love of a God who *sees* me.

After years of carrying the heavy burden of shame, I finally found the strength to step out of the grave that had imprisoned me. The beliefs that once defined me, the lies I had accepted about my worth, about sex, about men, no longer had a place in my life. Shame had whispered to me for too long, convincing me that my past mistakes and occupations determined my value. But now, in its place, I nurtured something new, a garden of grace and empathy for myself.

Each flower and leaf whispered stories of redemption, every bud a testament to the beauty that can emerge from darkness. This garden, once barren and filled with self-loathing, now bloomed with the vibrant colors of forgiveness and renewal.

I had to accept a hard truth: *I am not my own.*

This realization went against everything the world had taught me. Society glorifies self-ownership, *my body, my choices, my life, my rules.* We are told to hustle, to pull ourselves up by our bootstraps, to define our worth on our own terms. But the revelation of *1 Corinthians 6:19-20* (ESV) shattered that illusion for me.

Paul writes: *"Or do you not know that your body is a temple of the Holy Spirit within you, whom you have from God? You are not your own, for you were bought with a price. So glorify God in your body."*

That verse struck me with the force of revelation. *You are not your own.*

It was a truth so simple yet so profound that it required me to recalibrate everything I thought I knew. For years, I had lived under the assumption that my body was mine to do with as I pleased. My choices were mine. My sexuality was mine. But in those words, I encountered something that challenged the very core of my beliefs.

I had never heard this before. I had never been told that I was created for something greater than just my desires or my survival. To embrace this truth meant unlearning deeply ingrained patterns, breaking away from the shifting sands of my past, and stepping onto a foundation of undeniable certainty.

To say, *"I am not my own,"* was not a loss of power; it was a step toward liberation. It was an invitation to live with purpose, to see my body not as something to be used, traded, or defined by the world, but as something sacred. Something already bought at a price. Something worthy of honor.

For most of my life, the mere mention of men stirred up a storm of emotions within me: anger, distrust, resentment. I carried what the world calls *daddy issues,* but it ran deeper than that. My wounds were layered, built from childhood pain, reinforced by betrayal, and fueled by my own choices.

The men in my life had taught me that I had to outsmart them to survive, that love was a game, that power was the only way to avoid being used. Some of my closest friendships had been with men, and I made it my mission to beat them at their own game. I kept my heart locked away, believing that control equaled safety. But as I walked deeper in my faith, I reached a moment where I had to surrender those old beliefs. I had to learn the truth about men, not through the lens of my past, not through the world's broken perspective, but through God's eyes.

God's perspective on men is different.

He sees them as He created them, *not as stereotypes, not as enemies, not as disappointments,* but as individuals made in His image, capable of strength and vulnerability, of leadership and humility. In God's design, men are not bound by toxic expectations of masculinity. They are called to love sacrificially, to lead with wisdom, to serve selflessly.

God's vision for men includes redemption, restoration, and the ability to transform. He does not see them solely for their flaws, but for who they are meant to be. And if God, in all His grace, can look at men with compassion, then who was I to see them through the eyes of bitterness?

Letting go of my toxic beliefs about men has been *a process*. I am not who I used to be, but I also know I haven't fully arrived. I am still learning, still growing, still unlearning the lies that shaped me for so long. But what I do know is this: *it is getting easier.*

With each step forward, I feel my heart opening, releasing its grip on resentment, making space for compassion, love, and understanding. It is freeing. It is healing.

And now, I am waiting. Waiting for God to bring my future husband into my life.

I used to think God's silence meant He wasn't listening. But now I understand: God doesn't always answer when we *want* Him to, but He is always on time.

Every day, I feel like I am getting closer. Closer to meeting the man I will build a life with. Closer to becoming the wife I am meant to be.

And in this season of waiting, I have realized something profound: *intimacy is more than physical.* It is more than attraction, more than lust, more than passion. True intimacy is connecting on a soul level. It is sharing your fears, your hopes, your dreams. It is being seen, fully and completely, and knowing you are safe in that love.

That is what I am holding out for. That is what I believe God has in store for me. I have finally come to a firm answer about what I want in my partner: *intimacy.* The kind of intimacy that God intended when He created marriage.

Chapter 31

The Beauty of Becoming

A s I worked through the process of forgiving my father, untangling years of lies and wounds that had shaped my view of love, identity, and trust, God's voice interrupted my prayers with a question that stopped me cold:

"What about you?"

At first, I didn't understand. I was already peeling back layer after layer of pain, facing the truth about my past, confronting my present. Wasn't that enough? Why was there still more?

It took time before I realized what He meant. I hadn't forgiven myself.

That truth hit hard. Forgiving myself meant facing the woman I used to be, the choices I made, the things I allowed, the moments I was too blind or too broken to do better. Yes, I was growing in faith. Yes, I was learning to embrace the woman I was becoming. But there were entire versions of me I wished had never existed: the scared little girl, the ashamed teenager, the woman who used her body to survive.

God wasn't asking me to erase them. He was asking me to forgive them. All of them. To see them the way He sees me, with compassion, grace, and love.

It was one of the hardest parts of my journey. The grief of what I had done, and what I hadn't done, was heavy. But I knew I had to stop punishing myself for what I didn't know then, and for the times I knew better and still chose wrong. I had to see myself as God does, not defined by mistakes, but redeemed in His truth.

One evening, while I was deep in this work of self-forgiveness, I decided to stop by my cousin Bella's. I thought it would be just another visit. Instead, it became a divine appointment.

As I was walking up, a familiar voice called out, "Ayo... wait a minute. Is that? Girl, is that you?"

It was Shy. I hadn't seen her in years, not since the trap house days after Benny got locked up, back when Knox and I were constantly at war and I was drowning myself in liquor, smoke, and chaos. Back then, we'd pass the time talking in between the drama. There was an unspoken understanding between us, two women trying to survive the mess around us.

Now, her eyes lit up like she'd just seen a ghost. "Oh my God... you look amazing. Like... glowing. You always been beautiful, but this? This is different."

I laughed softly. "It's been a journey."

She shook her head, still taking me in. "Last time I saw you... girl, you were in it deep. That trap house off Barry Road, that dude, what's-his-name? I remember praying you'd get out. The boys are good? Heard you had another one with Knox."

"Yeah," I said. "The boys are good."

Her hand went to her chest. "People talk, you know. But now? It's good things. 'She's in church now.' 'She's helping other women.' 'She's starting her own business.' Girl... you're not who you were. You're proof nobody's too far gone."

I stood there, caught between gratitude and disbelief, while Bella listened from the side. Shy kept going. "So many people never made it out of that life. You remember Lexi? The dancing took her soul. But you, whew. You don't even walk the same. You walk like a woman who knows who she is."

Her words sank deep.

"Well, when you let Jesus into your life, things change," I told her. "I don't deserve any of it. But He changed everything."

She smiled. "You deserve all the props. You're living proof you can glow up without selling out. Don't let anybody forget it."

Shy wasn't part of my inner circle. I hadn't shared my faith journey with her. But she spoke as if she could see every inch of it, a mirror reflecting the work God had done in me. I believe it was God using her to remind me: even when you think your transformation is quiet, the light still finds a way to shine through.

That encounter shook something loose in me.

I hadn't even realized how much I'd been wrestling, how much I'd been struggling to believe that God had truly changed me. Changed my name.

I'd said I believed it. I even prayed like I did. But deep down, I was still dragging the weight of who I used to be. Still wondering if people could really see the difference... and if I could, too. Then, in that unexpected moment with someone from my past, God handed me the kind of confirmation you can't argue with. It wasn't abstract. It wasn't quiet. It was visible. Tangible. Undeniable.

He had changed my name.

Not just the way others saw me, but the way I saw myself. Something clicked. I finally recognized it. And more than that... I finally believed it.

What I didn't realize then was that self-forgiveness, the real kind, the deep kind, isn't a one-and-done act. It's a daily tending. Like a garden, you pull up the weeds and somehow, they still try to creep back in. Even after forgiving myself for the big things, I still fall short. I still wrestle with thoughts I don't want, still question why I react in ways that don't line up with the woman I know I am. The residue of the old me still lingers. But now, instead of shaming myself for it, I speak to myself with gentleness. I remind myself that perfection isn't the requirement for being chosen. I don't have to get it all right to be loved. Even when I stumble, I'm still a daughter of the Most High.

I tell myself I am made to soar like an eagle, not scratch like a chicken in the dirt. And every day, I anchor in this truth: God still chooses me, just as I am.

Getting there wasn't easy. It started with taking responsibility, owning my part in the harm I caused, without letting myself sink into the pit of self-condemnation. That's a delicate balance. I had to separate my choices from my identity, to see that my mistakes weren't the sum total of who I was or who I could become.

The hardest part was letting myself actually feel. I'd lived numb for so long; numbness was my armor. It was easier to stay detached than to risk being vulnerable. But the truth was, even when I felt frozen inside, my emotions still ran wild on the outside. I was emotionally driven, not character driven, reacting out of pain instead of responding from a place of truth. Healing meant peeling back that armor and sitting in the rawness I had avoided: grief, regret, shame. It meant not running from it.

From there, I began to practice self-compassion. I learned to talk to myself the way I would to someone I loved. I stopped punishing myself for not knowing what I didn't know back then. And I stopped just going through it, I started growing through it.

I took the pain and sifted it for lessons. Turned it into wisdom. And then came the part that nearly broke me: letting go of resentment toward myself. I had carried it for years, whispering, *You should have known better. You should have done better.* But I learned that holding onto resentment doesn't change the past; it only keeps you living in it. Forgiveness became the gift I gave myself, the key that let me finally put the burden down.

Then came rebuilding trust with myself. That meant setting new boundaries, realigning my life with my values, and surrounding myself with words that told the truth about me, affirmations, scriptures, reminders that I am redeemed.

I also learned that you can't heal in isolation. I had to open my hands and let go of the relationships that no longer fit the woman I was becoming. That made space for the ones God was sending, sisters in Christ who could hold my story without judgment.

Now I know: self-forgiveness isn't a destination you arrive at. It's a road you keep walking, mile after mile. It takes time. It takes grace. And it takes patience. Every morning, I start again with the same simple reminder: *Be gentle with yourself.*

It's not just a quote to me. It's the way I live now.

Chapter 32

My Son Walked Into the Water

The womb is a sacred space. I didn't know that when I gave away my virginity. I didn't know that when I found myself pregnant as a teenager. I didn't know that when I endured the kind of assault that rearranges how you breathe. I didn't know when I kept feeding myself lies about what my body was worth.

What I did know, what I could feel but couldn't name, was that the body remembers. Every moment. Every wound. Every goodbye that came too soon.

God gave me more chances at motherhood than I thought I deserved. Between Amadeus and Justice, there were four pregnancies I didn't carry, one with Knox early in our relationship, the others with men from my past. Fear whispered I wasn't ready. Insecurity told me I wasn't worthy. Money screamed I couldn't afford it. My own twisted beliefs agreed with all of them. I said yes to those voices, and each time I did, a thin layer of grief settled deeper into me.

And then came Justice.

By the time he arrived, I'd lived a little more, stumbled a little harder. With Amadeus, I used to joke that we were growing up together. With Justice, I felt like I was finally arriving in motherhood. He's sunlight in motion, outgoing, expressive, the kind of child who treats strangers like old friends. Our connection was instant, like we'd been waiting our whole lives to meet. I carried the lessons from raising Amadeus into this second round, determined to do better.

But even with Justice, it wasn't until I found God that I truly stepped into motherhood the way He intended. That was the turning point, the moment my home, my heart, and my relationships began to heal.

It started with a simple introduction. My sister in Christ, Etta, sent me sermons by Sarah Jakes Roberts, "Sit Down," "Becoming a Different Person," and the one that cracked me wide open, "Girl, Get Up." Her voice was like a steady hand on my back, pushing me forward. She spoke of women who rise after falling, who dare to love again, live again, stand again, no matter the mess they've been through. I didn't just hear her words. I moved on them.

Somewhere in that season, my relationship with my mother began to shift. It didn't happen all at once. But slowly, the resentment I carried toward her, the endless comparisons, started to dissolve. I stopped seeing her as someone I had to outgrow and started seeing her as someone I was blessed to have.

Forgiveness crept in, soft and unassuming, like light spilling under a door. I had already forgiven my father. I had forgiven myself. Now I forgave her, too.

Drawing close to God revealed something I'd never experienced before, being known, completely and without condition. Psalm 139 says He reads my heart like an open book. My choices didn't shock Him. That truth lifted the weight I had been dragging for years. His love covered me like a blanket in winter, and what He gave me in that intimacy spilled over onto my family.

When Justice started school, I let my mother step in, handle homework, dinner, grocery runs, and sports schedules. I stopped trying to micromanage her way of loving my children. She cooked like no one else could, decorated like the holidays were a spiritual calling, and knew how to create rhythms that made my boys feel safe. She wasn't the same kind of mother I was, and that was okay. She was their grandmother. The only one they had.

For years, I told myself I needed space. I imagined her moving out, leaving me with the quiet I thought I wanted. But somewhere along the way, I realized she had never been in my way. She had been doing life with me, loving me, loving my children. Now, the thought of her leaving feels like ripping pages from the middle of a story.

Being home more changed me. I hadn't realized how much I was rushing through life until God slowed me down. In the stillness, home became something sacred, not something to escape. I noticed the sound of laughter ricocheting off the walls, the warmth of a shared meal, the comfort of my mother humming in the kitchen.

It was in that stillness that I began to see Amadeus differently. For years, I thought his quietness was just who he was. I compared his life to mine, and because I couldn't see a reflection of my own pain in his, I dismissed his. I didn't notice the heaviness. I didn't hear the silence for what it was. I didn't know my son carried suicidal thoughts. I was so busy surviving my own story that I didn't realize I was a chapter in his.

One afternoon, I sat beside him.

"Hey, baby, can I talk to you for a minute?""Yeah, what's up?""I need to tell you something... I'm sorry. For how I misunderstood you when you were younger."He was quiet for a moment. "It's okay, Mom. I know things were rough back then.""No, it's more than that. I didn't just miss signs, I dismissed them. I compared your pain to mine and made it feel like it didn't count. That wasn't fair."He looked down, voice low. "I didn't know how to say it either. But... yeah. It hurt. I had suicidal thoughts back then. I just didn't know how to tell you. You were just not emotionally available."

Tears rose before I could stop them. I pulled him close. "Promise me you'll never listen to those thoughts. Ever. I'm sorry, kid. Truly. I hope you can forgive me."

"Promise, Mom. I get it now, you were surviving. I see that. I do wish things could have been better between us during those dark days I was having. But I'm working on myself now, for once. Therapy...

therapy gave me the words. And now, talking about how I feel is easier. I can express myself without anyone comparing their life or experiences to mine."

Hearing him say that cut deep, but it also filled me with hope. "That makes me happy to hear. It's also a sad reality to face that, as your mother, I thought I was giving you all I had and protecting you. To know I caused some of your pain... that is a truth I have to accept, because it is your truth. I'm going to keep working on myself. I can't make up for what's been done, but I can make our future together count."

"Yeah... that would be nice, Mom. I'd like that."

"Maybe we should plan to have mother-son dates, you know? Do something together, make sure we're checking in with each other more often. I'll put in the effort, not just to listen to your feelings, but to really hear you. To learn how to communicate better with you. Cool?"

"Yeah, Momma. I believe we can. Love you."

"Love you too."

***

When Amadeus first started talking about moving out, I thought I was ready. I'd been telling him since high school, "Get ready to be an adult, boy. You're about to be eighteen and leaving the nest." I promised myself I wouldn't be one of those mothers who falls apart when her child steps into the world. In fact, I even got excited at the thought of moving Justice into his room, since he was getting older, so he could finally have his own space. Truthfully, our three-bedroom, two-bath apartment had started to feel too small for all of us. The dog was another layer; he was our family's emotional support animal, and the new management at the apartment complex was giving us more headaches than help about his expired papers.

But when the day came, I realized I'd only rehearsed the idea in my mind. The reality was a whole different ache. Beneath the pep talks and my "go-get-'em" cheerleading, my heart was already cracking. My firstborn was leaving. As we packed the last boxes into his car, I hugged him tight. That night, I cried like a child myself, wondering, *Did I do the right thing? Did he know enough about life? Did I push him out too soon with my words? Would we still see each other often? Would he forget about me now that he had his own apartment?*

For Amadeus, it wasn't just about independence. It was about feeling restricted. He'd started dating, and I wasn't comfortable with his girlfriend spending the night. He wanted the freedom to bring friends over, to stay up playing Xbox until 3 a.m. without the noise carrying through the walls between my room and my mother's. He wasn't in school anymore, and our schedules didn't align. When the lease renewal came up, the choice was clear: stay another year under my rules, or go. He chose to go. Similarly, he made his own choices when it came to church. While I started to attend church regularly and brought Justice with me, I would ask Amadeus if he wanted to come with us, and most times he decided not to.

It ached that Justice was growing up in the church, and Amadeus wasn't. Every Sunday, the contrast stared me in the face, Justice sitting beside me, hands lifted during worship, soaking in the Word, while Amadeus had never even set foot inside the sanctuary while he was a child. He saw his little brother going, and my attitude towards Amadeaus was, "I'm not going to force him." I wanted him to *want* to come for himself, not because he was being asked. But now, he wasn't living under my roof, and I couldn't even ask him anymore. It grieved me. I felt like I was reaching one child and leaving the other behind.

Justice's faith took root early, and it's been a constant, living thing ever since. From his first years in private school, he'd come home telling Bible stories and offering spontaneous prayers, like they were as natural as breathing. His faith isn't just something he's been taught; it's woven into the way he sees the world. He'll boldly declare, "I am a child of God," not for show, but as if reminding himself and me that his identity is anchored in something unshakable.

He carries that presence everywhere. If someone's sad, he'll gently say, "God is with you." When his older brother is going through something, Justice will look him in the eye and say, "You need to come to church." If a dream unsettles him, he'll ask, "Is this from God?" When he doesn't understand something, his first instinct is, "I need to pray." His music choices speak just as loudly, gospel hip hop blasting when we are in the car over whatever else the culture says he should listen to. And when "Everlasting God" by William Murphy plays, he sings every word like it's part of his own story.

Church has never been a fight with Justice. He loves it, loves the people, the worship, the sense that he belongs there. Watching him, I've seen the difference it makes when a child's heart is nurtured in faith. And yet, that joy carried its shadow, the quiet ache that his brother hadn't had the same start.

I prayed constantly. I laid my guilt and worry at God's feet, some days trusting more than others, that He would reach Amadeus in His own way. I clung to the hope that my walk with God could be the testimony my son needed. I didn't know how or when it would happen, but I believed. And I kept on believing.

Then, one Sunday, it happened.

The week before Justice's baptism, I invited him over. "Hey , Amadeus, I know it's been a while... but would you come to church this Sunday? Justice is getting baptized, and it would mean a lot to have you there."

He paused. Shrugged slightly. "Yeah... I'll come. For Justice."

On the day of the service, the sanctuary buzzed with quiet excitement. Justice sat on one side of me, Amadeus on the other. Baptisms had begun.

The pastor's voice rang out from the pulpit, "If there's anyone else who feels led, if God's stirring something in your heart, you don't have to wait. Come. We're ready for you."

Amadeus leaned toward me, eyes steady, voice low but sure, "Mom... God's calling me. I gotta go."

I blinked, stunned, "What? Right now?"

"Yeah. I don't care that I don't have clothes. I need to go."

My throat tightened, "Then go, baby. Go."

I watched him step into the aisle, shoulders squared, walking toward the front with no hesitation. The church welcomed him with open arms. My heart pounded as he joined the line of people waiting to be baptized.

Two sons. Two baptisms. One day, I will never forget.

After the service, I wrapped him in the towel the church gave him. My voice shook. "I prayed for you, you know. Even when you weren't sure about God... I kept believing He'd reach you in His own way. And look at you now."

Water dripped from his hair as he smiled faintly. "I don't know what just happened, Mom... but it felt real. Like something inside me woke up."

"It was real," I said. "God had His hand on you the whole time. And today, He made sure you knew it."

He grinned. "Guess I'm coming to church with you more often now, huh?"

I laughed through my tears. "Only if it's on your terms. Just keep showing up. God will do the rest."

Justice bounded over, still glowing from his own baptism. "Bro, what just happened?! You got in the water too??"

"I know, right?" Amadeus chuckled. "One minute I'm sitting next to Mom... next thing I know, I'm walking to the front like a crazy person."

"Dude!" Justice punched his arm. "You could've warned me! We could've done a handshake or something before going under!"

"Sorry," Amadeus said, still laughing. "It just hit me all at once. But hey, we're both soaked now. Guess that means I'm stuck with you."

Justice beamed. "Best surprise ever! Seriously, I thought it was just gonna be me today... but you? Man... you made it ten times better."

"Wouldn't have been right watching you do it alone," Amadeus said quietly.

"I'm so glad you didn't," Justice replied.

God gave me a second chance with him, and I wasn't about to waste it.

Now, Amadeus and I make it a point to spend intentional time together, just the two of us. Sometimes it's as simple as grabbing ice cream, catching a movie, walking on the beach, or finding a quiet park bench where we can talk and check in on life. Other times, God surprises us with opportunities that stretch far beyond our everyday routines. By His provision, we've stood on the white sands of the Bahamas, explored the mountains of Tennessee, felt the spray of ocean waves in Grand Turk, wandered through Puerto Rico, and soaked in the energy of New York City.

Over the years, I've shifted how I approach birthdays, holidays, and celebrations. Instead of piling up material gifts, I focus on experiences. It's not that my kids never get presents; there's still something magical about unwrapping a thoughtful gift, but I know from my own childhood that most things fade from memory. What stays are the moments: a spontaneous road trip, laughter in a new place, the way a sunset looks when you're far from home. That's what I want for my children, memories that live in their hearts long after the wrapping paper is gone.

I want them to see the world beyond their front door, to understand that life is wide and full of cultures, traditions, and perspectives different from their own. I want them to know the joy of hearing a language they don't speak, tasting food they've never tried, and realizing that home exists in more than one place. And now, years later, I can see the difference it's made. My kids will flip through old photos or bring up a trip out of nowhere, remembering details that I thought they'd forgotten. Those shared experiences have a way of leaving their fingerprints on a person's soul.

Traveling with my family was a dream long before it became my reality. As a little girl, I'd imagine boarding planes, stepping onto ships, seeing places that only existed in magazines, and having my family there with me. God didn't just grant that dream; He multiplied it.

On a modest 9-to-5 income, I've watched Him open doors I couldn't have imagined, doors that let me bring my mom, Justice, and Amadeus along for the adventure.

One of my favorite memories is celebrating my mom's 70th birthday in Puerto Rico, where we also visited Bella. The trip was a patchwork of sunshine, music, and three generations laughing together, memories stitched so deeply into us that they'll never come loose.

Another was the Christmas I surprised Amadeus with a cruise to Bimini and Grand Turk for his birthday. It was his first time on a ship, and I wanted it to be unforgettable: swimming with sharks, snorkeling with stingrays, and standing on the deck watching the endless ocean meet the sky.

But there's one trip that holds a different kind of weight, New York City. I'd dreamed of going since I was a teenager, but God, in His perfect timing, didn't send me there when I was young. He saved it for a season when I could truly savor it. I wanted my son by my side for that milestone, to celebrate my birthday, and walk those electric streets together. Bella joined us, adding her laughter and energy to the mix. We took in the skyline, wandered through neighborhoods I'd only ever seen on screen, and Amadeus even reconnected with a friend. It wasn't just about finally checking New York off my list; it was about God's reminder that sometimes He holds certain dreams back until they can mean the most.

Through it all, our conversations flow easily. Sometimes they're about nothing at all; sometimes they cut right to the heart. Amadeus has never once shamed me, even when I've given him reason to. He is my miracle, a young man untouched by the street life that swallowed so many around him. Calm, steady, and quietly wise. I thank God for him every single day.

Through motherhood, God has grown a garden of miracles in me. It taught me the preciousness of life, the sacredness of presence, and the kind of love that changes everything. It taught me sacrifice, patience, and the courage to keep showing up, even when it's hard.

Motherhood broke me and remade me. It's where God met me, in the turmoil, in the stillness, in the moments I thought I had nothing left. And it's where I learned that real love doesn't just survive, it restores.

Chapter 33

This Time, I Choose Life

The first time I realized there was a war inside me, I didn't have a name for it. Some mornings, I would wake up ready to live for God, praying, worshiping, feeling unstoppable. By nightfall, I'd be texting someone I shouldn't, pouring another drink, slipping back into the kind of thoughts I swore I'd buried.

Then one day, I opened my Bible and landed on Galatians 5:16 (ESV): *"But I say, walk by the Spirit, and you will not gratify the desires of the flesh."* I didn't know why it hit me the way it did, but I wrote it on a flashcard and taped it to the bare wall of my prayer closet. I couldn't explain it, but I knew it mattered, like God had just handed me a key and was waiting for me to figure out which door it opened.

The flesh and the Spirit are like two gardens planted in the same soil, my soul. The flesh grows weeds, fast, wild, stubborn. It craves comfort, pleasure, validation, anything to keep me from surrendering. The Spirit grows fruit, love, peace, and self-control, but only if I tend it daily. Every single day, I have to decide which one to water. Paul said it best in Romans 7:15 (ESV): *"For I do not understand my own actions. For I do not do what I want, but I do the very thing I hate."* That was me, torn between who I wanted to be and the habits I couldn't seem to let go.

When God decided it was time to teach me how to walk by the Spirit, He didn't send me a sermon. He sent me Etta. We'd worked together for years, but I had never thought to ask her about her faith until one Monday morning when I ducked into her lab at the clinic.

"Hey," I laughed, peeking in, "can I hide in here for a minute? I just need a little peace... maybe some wisdom."

She kept labeling tubes but smiled. "You know you're always welcome. What's on your heart?"

"I've been thinking about God a lot lately," I admitted. "How do you know you're really changing? Some days I feel strong, other days... not so much."

She turned toward me, leaning on the counter. "Oh girl, if you only knew where I came from..."

"What do you mean?"

"I used to be a mess. Chain-smoker. Drank almost every day. Couldn't keep a relationship, didn't even want to. I was angry, suicidal, and my mouth could make a sailor blush." She laughed like she couldn't believe it herself.

I stared at her. "No way. You? I never would have guessed."

"That's what grace does," she said. "God cleaned me up so good, even I barely recognize the old me. And if He did it for me, He'll do it for you too. Just don't quit. Keep walking, even if it's slow."

I started showing up in her workspace almost every day after that. She taught me how to fast, how to tell my flesh "no" so my Spirit could breathe. That was harder than I thought it would be. She explained tithing, not as a bill I owed, but as a way of giving back to God what was already His.

I watched how she moved, slow, steady, Spirit-led. She didn't rush. She didn't bend for the world's timeline. She quoted Proverbs 3:5-6 (ESV) so often it etched itself into me: *"Trust in the Lord with all your heart and do not lean on your own understanding. In all your ways acknowledge Him, and He will make straight your path."*

Even after God elevated her to a new position and eventually led her to an entirely new job, we stayed connected. I knew it was the fruit of seeds she had been planting for years.

Her example helped me see my own battles more clearly. Money used to be my shield, proof that no one could hurt me. But God showed me that I couldn't serve two masters. Letting go meant trusting Him with my finances, and that trust led to promotions, investments, stability, generosity without fear.

Alcohol was another battle. In 2023, I fasted from it for a year. It had been my comfort, my social glue, my way to soften the edges. Without it, my mind became sharper, my sleep deeper, my prayers clearer. I became more present in my own life.

Each time I surrendered something, money, alcohol, control, God pulled up another weed from my garden. I stopped finding my worth in what I could hold on to and started rooting it in who He said I was.

The weeds still try to creep in. They always will. But I've learned to spot them early, and I've learned that the Spirit grows strongest when I make space for Him to work. Galatians 5:16 isn't just a verse on a flashcard anymore. It's the way I live, one choice at a time, walking slowly but steadily toward the kind of garden that's worth tending.

Chapter 34

Addicted...

I once called pain my companion and dysfunction my normal. But God.

I believed I was too far gone to be saved. But God.

I didn't deserve what He did for me, but He considered me worthy.

Jesus says that whoever tries to save their own life will lose it, but whoever surrenders it will find it. In the Kingdom, healing can feel backwards. You must deny yourself and begin seeking what God desires for you.

I struggled with that.

I had finally learned to love and care for myself, yet God was asking me to surrender even that version of me. Why? Why give up the "better" me?

But God...

Over time, He showed me that surrender isn't rejection, it's renewal. To suffer is to be made new. To give up is to receive more. My strength would never come from what I could build alone, but from what I could lay down in His hands.

Even now, the temptation to believe I'm "strong enough" creeps in. Pride. Ego. The illusion that I could ever outgrow my need for Him. But the truth is, I need Him more than ever. In success. In growth. In every breath. He is the source, the reason, and the sustainer of all good in me.

At 37, I finally went back to school to pursue the nursing degree I'd been running from for years. I'd worked in healthcare for nearly a decade, but every time I tried to step outside of it, God closed the door. Now I understand why it was never just about medicine. It was about ministry. Nursing is my calling to serve with compassion, healing, and care, just as He has cared for me.

This year, I finished my prerequisites. Balancing school, work, and life is a daily puzzle, but finishing this book feels like my way forward. I trust the seeds planted here will open the doors I'm meant to walk through next.

My relationships look different now, too.

Amara and I are going on twenty-four years of friendship, closer than ever. Though distance keeps us from seeing each other as often as we once did, we make it a priority to meet in person every other month, often at the beach, on a trip, or somewhere in between, because our friendship thrives in shared moments. We speak weekly about the big things and all the little things in between. Over the years, we've weathered storms that would have sunk most friendships: heartbreaks,

losses, financial strain, moves, and the unraveling of other relationships. Through it all, she has been my steady place, my encourager, my
family.

Without sisters of my own, she has become one, my best friend, my
sister from another mother, but the same heavenly Father. She's never
judged me in a way that tore me down, only built me up. Our children
have grown up side by side, our bond deepening with time. Even in
seasons of deep grief, she's shown a strength and faith that inspires
me daily. She's also my second half, the one who, when people hear
we're together, they already know we're laughing, making memories,
and squeezing joy out of life to the fullest. We meet no strangers.
We're impulsive in the best ways, witty, chill, ride-or-dies, completely
in sync.

Bella lives in Puerto Rico now, but distance hasn't weakened our
bond; it's simply given me a reason to visit more often. She's my favorite cousin, my mirror in so many ways. When I count my blessings,
I count her twice. Bella is a steady anchor, a voice of reason when I
start to doubt myself. When I need to make sure I'm not crazy, she's
the one I call. We think alike, advise each other honestly, and love each
other fiercely. She's been an important part of my transformation, and
our connection is one of those rare, unshakable bonds that time and
distance can't touch.

Milani and I don't hang out anymore; life took us in different directions in our early twenties. She was the first among us to follow Jesus
wholeheartedly, and her transformation was remarkable. Though we
now mostly connect through social media and email, we continue to
cheer each other on from afar. I am in awe of what God has done in her
life, her son's life, and her family. She has become a successful engineer,

balancing her career with single parenthood and living out her faith with grace and strength. Loria and I still check in, and she's thriving with her cleaning business. And I've gained new sisters along the way, women I may not have known in the turmoil of my past, but who now stand with me in the calm of my present.

As for my father, we no longer speak. That boundary wasn't born from bitterness; it came from healing. Some doors are meant to stay closed. Still, I pray for him: for his well-being, for forgiveness to take root, and for reconciliation if it's God's will before our time runs out.

Knox and I are no longer romantic partners. Co-parenting isn't always perfect, but we make the effort for Justice's sake. Mateo is no longer in our lives; Amadeus hasn't seen him since he was a toddler.

Friday nights are different now.

Once, they meant trap houses, smoke in the air, and drowning myself in anything that could numb me. Now they mean juvenile detention centers, opening my Bible instead of another bottle, speaking life where I once only knew death.

Through Urban Youth Justice and Steadfast Ministries, I meet young women whose stories feel like reflections of my own, only this time, I get to be the voice I once needed. God uses my past to reach them, and in their eyes, I see both the girl I was and the woman I'm becoming.

I've reclaimed my first love. Writing. This book is just the beginning. Two major projects are already in the works: *A Stripper's Guide to an Alternative Life* and *Unprotected Pleasure*. I've also released a free e-book, *Rewriting Your Truth: Letting Go of Toxic Beliefs for a Renewed Life*. My words are my ministry to heal, empower, and reveal God's redemptive power.

I serve in my church's kids ministry, where remembering a child's name or offering a smile plants seeds that could change their future. I write for the Chosen Pieces blog, pouring out what God has poured into me. I serve with Love Our City, showing up for people who may be hesitant or guarded, but who still need to be seen. Justice and I even volunteer at the Humane Society together. His love for animals has become something special we share.

At home, there is peace. Real peace.

Justice is thriving in private school, his smile a little brighter every time he brings home a new accomplishment. The scholarship that made it possible still feels like a miracle I get to witness every morning when I drop him off. Our home feels... whole. Emotionally. Spiritually. Relationally. The kind of healthy I used to think only existed for other people. My children are growing in the kind of environment I once only dreamed about.

And my mother, she's no longer just "my mother." Somewhere along the way, she became my best friend. I stopped seeing her as someone I didn't need and started recognizing her as someone I do. Now, she's the first person I call before making a hard decision, the one I run my feelings by before I speak them out loud to anyone else. She's my sounding board, my co-writer, my travel partner, my late-night movie buddy, my co-conspirator in planning the future. We shop together, binge TV series together, and lose hours in creative projects that make us both laugh.

She's in her seventies now, and I'm more attuned to her health than I've ever been. I notice the subtle changes, how she rests more, moves a little slower, but I also see how vibrant she still is. Being able to be present for her in this season, after everything we've been through, feels like its own redemption story.

I think back to that girl on Barry Road, the one who was "just passing time" and didn't realize time was passing her by. I think of the Friday nights that ended in tears, the mornings that began in shame, and how far God has carried me from there to here.

God didn't just restore what was lost. He gave me abundance.

So don't judge the beginning of this story. Don't get stuck in where I was. Look at where God has brought me. Let my life remind you: no one is too far gone. Grace reaches deep. Redemption is real. And sometimes, the words you once said, *"I would never"*, become *"I did."*

As I close this chapter, I want to leave you with this: our belief systems matter. Our experiences can shape what we believe about God, or our belief about God can shape how we experience life. God is more real than our reality, more constant than our emotions. Don't let what you see in front of you contradict what God has already concluded about you. Yes, there is an adversary whose mission is to kill, steal, and destroy. And if you've read my story, you know how close I came to being completely lost. But grace intercepted me. Mercy chased me down. God rewrote my ending before I even knew how to begin.

So, if you take anything from my life, let it be this: no matter how far you've gone, no matter how deep the pit, you are never beyond the reach of redemption. I am living proof that God still rescues, still restores, and still makes all things new.

Now my mission is clear: to rob hell by helping women break free from toxic beliefs, shame, and cycles that keep them stuck. To lead them into healing, identity, and self-awareness rooted in God's truth.

This is just the beginning.

May my journey be a living testimony of His love, truth, and mercy.

May it remind you that you, too, can rise from the ashes and bloom in God's garden of grace.

> *For the LORD comforts Zion; he will comfort all her*
> *waste places; and makes her wilderness like Eden, her*
> *desert like the garden of the LORD; joy and gladness*
> *will be found in her, thanksgiving, and the voice of song.*
> **Isaiah 51:3 (ESV)**

I am no longer addicted to pain. I am addicted to Jesus.

THE END

Resources:

W hen I first started going to church, I didn't always feel comfortable talking to people and sharing my thoughts and questions. And during the week when I wasn't in church, I needed to feel more connected, but wasn't sure how. I had all sorts of questions: *What music can I listen to that I could vibe to and also feel the closeness of God? Who else has gone through what I've gone through that I could listen to? Who could give me direction, insight, and inspiration in spoken or book form?*

If you are wondering the same things I did, here are some resources I put together for you that helped me in my walk in faith with God.

Music

Christian Hip Hop artists (CHH)

1kPhew

Andy Rebirth

Anike aka Wande

ASAP Preach

Caleb Gordon

CiCi Childlike

Bryann T

BRANDY GRILLO

DEE-1
Erica Mason
KB
Kieran The Light
Lecrae
Miles Minnick
Porscha Love
Sevin/HogMob
Young Bro
Zauntee
Gospel Artists
Bethel Music
Brandon Lake
Crowder
Franchesca
Jonathan McReyonalds
Kirk Franklin
Koryn Hawthorne
Maranda Curtis
Naomi Raine
Tasha Cobbs
Victor Thomas
William Murphy
Yvonne Armour-Sigars
Contemporary Worship Music
Elevation Worship
Hillsong
Maverick City

Reggae

Christafari

Books

A Stripper's Guide to an Alternative Life and *Unprotected Pleasure* (coming soon) - Brandy Grillo

Rewriting Your Truth: Letting Go of Toxic Beliefs for a Renewed Life - Brandy Grillo (e-book only - can be found on my website)

Enemies of the Heart - Andy Stanley

Garden Within - Dr. Anita Phillips

More Than Pretty - Erica Campbell

Gentle and Lowly - Dane Ortlund

Limitless Life - Derwin L. Gray

Relational Intelligence - Dr. Dharius Daniels

Empty Out the Negative - Joel Osteen

Soundtracks - John Acuff

Living Beyond Your Feelings - Joyce Meyer

Fervent - Priscilla Shirer

Woman Evolve - Sarah Jakes Roberts

Crash the Chatterbox - Steve Furtnick

Frames - Tommy" Urban D" Kylloen

Podcasts

WordzThatSpeak - my own

Southside Rabbi

The Pour Out – Christian version of news

The Skillful Podcast - Not Christian-based, but a therapy-based podcast.

Truth over Tribe

Healing Queenz

Gods promises:

God promises to strengthen you - Ephesians 3:14-16

God promises to give you rest - Matthew 11:28-30

God promises to take care of all your needs - Philippians 4:19

God promises to answer your prayers - Matthew 7:7

God promises to work everything out for your good according to His will - Romans 8:28

God promises to protect you - Psalm 91:2

God promises freedom from sin - 1 John 1:9

God promises that nothing can separate you from Him - Romans 8:38-39

God promises everlasting life - John 3:16

Daily prayer:

Enlighten what is dark in me.

Strengthen what is weak in me.

Bind who bruised me.

Mend what is broken in me.

Heal what is sick in me.

Revive whatever peace and love have died in me.

About The Author

Brandy is the founder of WordzThatSpeak, a platform that shares blogs, poetry, prayer journals, and creative products designed to help women transform pain into resilience and brokenness into power.

She has worked in healthcare for over a decade and is now pursuing her nursing degree, blending her professional journey with her passion for ministry and writing. Her story is deeply rooted in faith.

Brandy is an active member of Crossover Church and serves with Urban Youth Justice, mentoring young women in juvenile detention centers. She has seen firsthand how God can take what the enemy meant for destruction and turn it into purpose, using her own life as proof that no one is too far gone to be redeemed.

Beyond her work and ministry, Brandy is a proud mother who finds joy in traveling with her family, serving her community, and creating safe spaces where women can heal and grow.